Welcome to the iPhone App Directory Vol 3

Your guide to the best applications for iPhone & iPod touch

Over 250 applications reviewed and rated by the makers of

iCreate

Imagine Publishing Ltd
Richmond House
33 Richmond Hill
Bournemouth
Dorset BH2 6EZ
☎ +44 (0) 1202 586200
Website: www.imagine-publishing.co.uk
Thank you for supporting Imagine
Publishing – an independent specialist
magazine publisher where quality,
innovation and excellence are paramount.

Editor in Chief
Dave Harfield

Group Art Editor
Lora Barnes

Compiled by
Andy Betts

Design & layout by
Charlie Aspery, Lora Barnes, Dani Dixon,
Anastasia Paukste, Kate Logsdon

Proofed by
Daniel Peel, Amy Squibb,
Jon White

Head of Design
Ross Andrews

Printed by
William Gibbons, 26 Planetary Road,
Willenhall, West Midlands, WV13 3XT

iPhone App Directory Vol 3
© 2009 Imagine Publishing Ltd

978-1-906078-45-4

IMAGINE PUBLISHING

www.iphonekungfu.com

Welcome app fans…

As you will no doubt be aware from Apple's ubiquitous adverts, no matter what task you want to perform with your iPhone, "There's an app for that!" It's not just a spurious marketing slogan either, it's true. The sheer range and breadth of iPhone and iPod touch apps available never ceases to amaze, highlighting just how the device has captured the imagination of users and developers like nothing else. There are now over 85,000 apps in the App Store, and the Store has handled over 2 billion downloads. It is a true phenomenon, and one that shows no sign of slowing down any time soon. Apps range from tiny utilities performing single functions, right through to massive titles from famous publishers – check out the Navigation section, for example, for the first full turn-by-turn sat nav apps from the likes of TomTom and Navigon, or the Games section for some truly impressive action worthy of the best videogame consoles. Volume 3 of the iPhone App Directory is sectioned out in exactly the same way as the App Store itself. With 20 different categories it could not be easier to find the titles you are looking for, while our rating system ensures you will be able to instantly discover the best of the bunch. But don't stop there – half the fun of the App Store is in making new discoveries and opening your iPhone up to a whole new world of functionality. From the banal to the brilliant, and sometimes both at the same time, if there's something you want to use your iPhone for, it's likely that someone else has had the same thought and has made an app specifically for that purpose. This book will help guide you through the best of them.

iPhone App Direc

Your guide to the best apps for the iPhone and iPod touch

www.iphonekungfu.com

contents

tory Vol 3

www.iphonekungfu.com

Inside this book
The hottest downloads from the iTunes App Store categories...

6 Books
Keep your own library of classics with you on your iPhone

12 Business
Get ahead in the office with help from these great business tools

20 Education
Get help with your studies, or just brush up on your trivia

28 Entertainment
Fill those spare hours with a wealth of entertainment apps

38 Finance
Keep track of your money wherever you are

44 Games
From puzzles to arcade classics, a whole world of gaming is here

62 Health & Fitness
Get that body in shape with these essential fitness tools

70 Lifestyle
An eclectic collection of apps for your everyday life

80 Medical
Master self-diagnosis with these powerful medical programs

84 Music
Don't just listen to music, make it too with your iPhone

94 Navigation
The first range of turn-by-turn navigation apps tested in full

102 News
Follow the news with apps from across the political landscape

112 Photography
Turn your iPhone into the ultimate digital darkroom

122 Productivity
Make a fortune or just get more done with these tools

128 Reference
Turn your iPhone into a fountain of all knowledge

136 Social Networking
Access Twitter, Facebook and co while out on the road

146 Sports
Follow the ups and downs of your favourite team

154 Travel
Travelling the world? Then these apps will be your guide

162 Utilities
A miscellany of apps for pretty much any occasion

170 Weather
Don't get caught in the rain with this collection of applications

176 A-Z index of apps
A massive 280 apps painstakingly listed for your convenience

178 App setup guide
Quick and easy guide to running apps on your iPhone

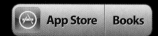
Books

The ability to be able to take a library of hefty tomes with you wherever you go has a number of benefits. Fairy tales, classics and recipe books, they're all here…

Price: £1.79/$2.99 **Developer:** Ubiklabs

A Charles Dickens Collection

Six classic novels from the master of prose

 Charles John Huffam Dickens was born on 7 February 1812 in Portsmouth. Shortly thereafter, his family relocated to Chatham and Dickens later described how these were the happiest and most idyllic years of his childhood. However, his contentment was short-lived and the family moved to London in 1822. Although they were middle class, Dickens' father's financial management skills were weak and constant overspending led to debt and a subsequent period of internment at Her Majesty's pleasure. Charles was the oldest of the Dickens children and his father's imprisonment led to him being taken out of school at the age of 12 in order to work in a local warehouse. Although he later recanted how this led to periods of unhappiness, it was clear that the experience was to have a marked impact on his novel writing.

In 1833, Dickens began penning short stories for contemporary periodicals and magazines. He was without doubt the most popular English novelist of the Victorian era and an active social reformist both in his personal endeavours and within the themes of his literary work. He was a fierce critic of the poverty and social

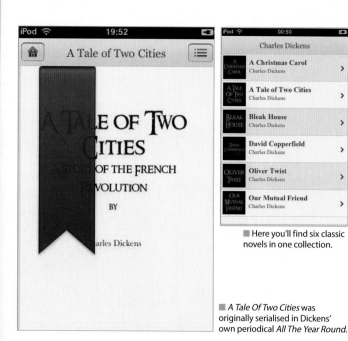

■ Here you'll find six classic novels in one collection.

■ *A Tale Of Two Cities* was originally serialised in Dickens' own periodical *All The Year Round*.

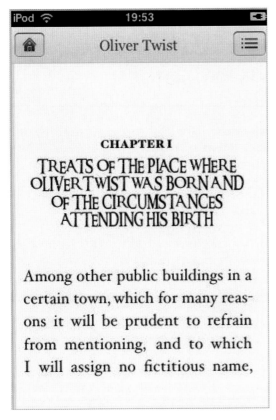

The novels are well presented and easy to navigate too.

Navigating the chapters is a breeze.

An authentic book jacket is included with the app.

Price: £1.19/$1.99 **Developer:** Your Mobile Apps Inc

The Sea-Wolf

Chronicle the voyages of Wolf Larson

Renowned American author Jack London (1876-1916) may have only lived only a short life but he still managed to pen a number of adventure stories, of which *Call Of The Wild* remains the most famous. London's early experiences of poverty led him to become heavily influenced by socialist theories and his beliefs were openly advocated and reflected in books that often criticised social abuse.

The Sea-Wolf is a classic and London's stated intention in writing this gripping 1904 novel was to place a man and a woman (both intellectual and affluent) into the challenging environment of a seal hunting boat and watch them battle to survive. In doing so, London created a captivating literary character called Wolf Larson, the ruthless and tyrannical captain of the 'Ghost'. As a bonus, the story can be enjoyed as either an exciting sea adventure or as a discourse on late 19th Century society.

Ratings

Longevity	Fun factor	Practicality	Value
★★★★☆	★★☆☆☆	★★★★☆	★★★☆☆

Overall Rating ★★★★☆

---

stratification of Victorian society and his second novel, *Oliver Twist* (published in 1839), shocked readers with its images of poverty and crime and was eventually responsible for the clearing of the actual London slum that formed the basis of the tale.

Dickens' mastery of prose, intricate plots, depictions of the hardships of the working class and a rare ability to continually create interesting and believable characters has ensured that his novels remain popular even in the 21st Century. Beginning with *The Pickwick Papers* in 1836, Dickens penned a number of novels and this superb collection of tales will take pride of place on any iPhone or iPod touch. Easy to navigate and read, the app includes classics such as *A Christmas Carol*, *A Tale Of Two Cities*, *Bleak House*, *David Copperfield* and *Oliver Twist*. Whether you are new to Dickens' literary work or a seasoned reader of English literature, you will find each novel a real pleasure to read.

Ratings

Longevity	Fun factor	Practicality	Value
★★★★★	★★☆☆☆	★★★☆☆	★★★★☆

Overall Rating ★★★★☆

■ The app has large, easy to read text that scrolls smoothly as you read.

■ This is one of English literature's darkest narratives.

Price: Free Developer: BeamItDown Software

Wuthering Heights

A gripping tale of thwarted desire

Emily Brontë's only novel, *Wuthering Heights* was first published in 1847 under the pseudonym Ellis Bell. Posthumously edited and renamed by Emily's sister Charlotte, the story is now widely considered a classic of English literature. The narrative certainly remains one of literature's darkest romantic fictions. Set amid the stormy Yorkshire moorlands, the tale centres on the all-encompassing relationship between the characters Heathcliff and Cathy and describes how unresolved passion eventually destroys their love.

One of the real benefits of this classic book is the approach to reading that it has adopted. The majority of reader apps display text on individual pages. However, the publisher's iFlow Reader uses a different approach and auto-scrolling enables you to sit back, relax and read. The scrolling speed is controlled by tilting your iPhone or iPod touch and you can even customise the text size and colour, which is great for enhancing readability.

Ratings

Longevity	Fun factor	Practicality	Value
★★★★★	★★★	★★★★	★★★★★

Overall Rating ★★★★

Price: £1.79/$2.99 Developer: Ubiklabs

H. G. Wells Collection

Watch out, the Martians are coming!

Herbert George Wells (1866-1946), known by his pen name of HG Wells, was an English author, futurist, essayist, historian, socialist and teacher. Most well-known for his work in the popular science fiction genre, HG Wells is often credited, alongside Hugo Gernsback and Jules Verne as being one of the fathers of science fiction.

This collection of classic novels includes *The Time Machine*, *The Invisible Man*, *The Wheels Of Chance* and our favourite, *The War Of The Worlds*. Who can't recall the invasion of Earth by aliens from Mars and tripods attacking with heat rays? *War Of The Worlds* quickly became one of the first internationally read of the modern science-fiction stories. In fact, 40 years after its publication, Orson Welles' radio broadcast of the novel in 1938 caused widespread panic in New York. This story and seven other HG Wells classics will keep you entertained on many a dark night.

Fairy Tales by Hans Christian Andersen

Entertain the kids with this collection of fairy tales

■ This is an extensive collection of fairy tales that will keep the kids amused for hours.

■ You can customise the reader to suit your personal preferences.

iPod 🔋	23:11	🔋

H. G. Wells

The Wheels Of Chance >
H. G. Wells

The Time Machine >
H. G. Wells

The Island Of Doctor Mor... >
H. G. Wells

The Invisible Man >
H. G. Wells

The War Of The Worlds >
H. G. Wells

The First Men In The Moon >
H. G. Wells

When The Sleeper Wakes

iPod 🔋	23:11	🔋

🏠 The Time Machine ☰

III

'I told some of you last Thursday of the principles of the Time Machine, and showed you the actual thing itself, incomplete in the workshop. There it is now, a little travel-worn, truly; and one of the ivory bars is cracked, and a brass rail bent; but the rest of it's sound

■ This book app includes *The Time Machine* and *The Invisible Man*.

■ Eight classics in one volume from the father of science fiction.

Ratings

Longevity	Fun factor	Practicality	Value
★★★★☆	★★★☆☆	★★★★★	★★★★☆

Overall Rating ★★★★☆

Price: Free **Developer:** BeamItDown Software

Hans Christian Andersen (1805-1875) was a Danish poet and author most renowned for writing good old fashioned fairy tales. His poetry and tales have been translated into more than 150 languages and as well as inspiring a number of ballets, films and plays, they have delighted children around the world. During 1835, Andersen published the first part of what was to become the immortal *Fairy Tales*. Stories were added over the next 12 months and the first complete volume was published in 1836. Rather surprisingly, sales were initially poor. However, the extensive collection of tales eventually became a bestseller and there are few who have not heard of stories like *The Snow Queen*, *The Ugly Duckling*, *The Princess And The Pea* and *The Emperor's New Clothes*. The good news is that you can now revisit these and 128 other fairy tales on your iPhone or iPod touch.

Ratings

Longevity	Fun factor	Practicality	Value
★★★★★	★★★★★	★★★☆☆	★★★★★

Overall Rating ★★★★★

Recording Video (iPhone 3GS)

It's one of the biggest perks—if not *the* biggest perk—of the iPhone 3GS: It can record video as well as still photos. And not just crummy, jerky, microscopic cellphone videos, either; it's smooth (30 frames per second), sharp, colorful video that does surprisingly well in low light.

Using video is almost exactly like taking stills.

Pop into the Camera mode. Then tap the 📷 / switch so that the 🎥 is selected. You can hold the iPhone either vertically or horizontally; it doesn't care if your video is tall and thin or wide and squat.

This glorious feature doesn't work in every program, alas. Fortunately, it works in some of the programs where you do the most typing: Mail, Messages (text messages), the Safari browser, Contacts, and Notes.

■ Explore your smartphone's hidden features courtesy of a range of hints and tips.

■ Step-by-step instructions help you get more from your iPhone.

Price: £2.99/$4.99 **Developer:** O'Reilly Media Inc

iPhone: The Missing Manual (3rd Edition)

Unlock the full potential of your iPhone

Anyone reading this volume of the **iPhone Apps Directory** will no doubt be aware that the iPhone is an outstanding device. With its solid design and impressive 480 x 320 pixel screen, the iPhone is not only great to look at, but also a real pleasure to use. Without doubt, the 3GS has certainly raised the bar for multifunction convergent devices and the smartphone is extraordinarily easy to use for such a feature-packed piece of kit. Beneath the bonnet lies a very powerful engine with a number of hidden features and functions. *iPhone: The Missing Manual* is designed to help you get more from your device. Penned by the *New York Times'* technical expert, the manual gives you a guided tour of your iPhone. Hints and tips enable you to boost productivity and step-by-step instructions help you to perform a range of tasks, including how to take better snapshots and how to troubleshoot common problems.

Ratings

Longevity	Fun factor	Practicality	Value
★★★☆☆	★★☆☆☆	★★★★☆	★★★☆☆

Overall Rating ★★★☆☆

Price: £0.59/$0.99 **Developer:** BeamItDown Software

Children's Classics

16 popular books in one rather handy collection

Whether you are a parent with young children or an adult who is young at heart, we are sure that you will enjoy this collection of some of the most popular children's classics ever written. The 16 books include classics such as *Aesop's Fables*, *The Secret Garden*, *Pinocchio*, Daniel Defoe's *Robinson Crusoe*, Rudyard Kipling's *The Jungle Book* and Anna Sewell's *Black Beauty*. Fans of Jack London will appreciate *The Call Of The Wild* and *White Fang* and science-fiction aficionados will enjoy reading the classic Jules Verne novel *Journey To The Centre Of The Earth*. The reading experience is first class courtesy of an app that scrolls text much like a teleprompter. The precise scrolling speed is controlled by subtle screen tilts and with practice, this becomes intuitive and natural. All in all, this is one of the best collections of classics available for the iPhone and iPod touch.

Ratings

Longevity	Fun factor	Practicality	Value
★★★★★	★★★★★	★★★☆☆	★★★★☆

Overall Rating ★★★★★

A Little Princess

Once on a dark winter's day, when the yellow fog hung so thick and heavy in the streets of London that the lamps were lighted and the shop windows blazed with gas as they do at night, an odd-looking little girl sat in a cab with her father and

Anne of Green Gables

There are plenty of people in Avonlea and out of it, who can attend closely to their neighbor's business by dint of neglecting their own; but Mrs. Rachel Lynde was one of those capable creatures who can manage their own concerns and those of

■ The auto-scrolling feature ensures a great reading experience.

■ With this you get sixteen classic books in one great value app.

Price: Free Developer: Attogear

Bill Gates QuickQuotes

A selection of quotes from the most renowned entrepreneur of the PC revolution

Love him or loathe him, Bill Gates is one of the most well-known of the entrepreneurs in the field of personal computing. The Microsoft co-founder is consistently ranked as one of the world's wealthiest people and during his career he has held the position of chief software architect and CEO. And what better way to try and get inside his magnificent mind than to browse a collection of quotes that he has used over the years. You can bookmark your favourites and email quotes to friends and family, and other features include the generation of a random quote by shaking your iPhone and a user-configurable font.

Easy Recipes – Food & Drink

■ View great quality, full screen images of each recipe.

■ A very polished app with an interface that promotes easy navigation of the database.

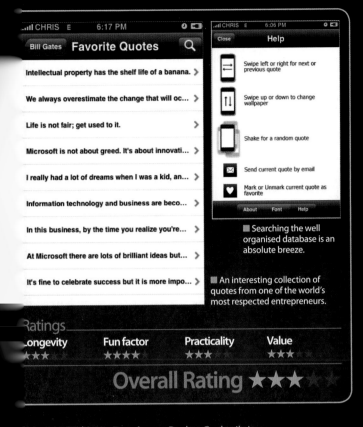

Bill Gates **Favorite Quotes**

Intellectual property has the shelf life of a banana. >

We always overestimate the change that will oc... >

Life is not fair; get used to it. >

Microsoft is not about greed. It's about innovati... >

I really had a lot of dreams when I was a kid, an... >

Information technology and business are beco... >

In this business, by the time you realize you're... >

At Microsoft there are lots of brilliant ideas but... >

It's fine to celebrate success but it is more impo... >

Help

Swipe left or right for next or previous quote

Swipe up or down to change wallpaper

Shake for a random quote

Send current quote by email

Mark or Unmark current quote as favorite

About   Font   Help

■ Searching the well organised database is an absolute breeze.

■ An interesting collection of quotes from one of the world's most respected entrepreneurs.

Ratings

Longevity	Fun factor	Practicality	Value
★★★	★★★★	★★★	★★★

Overall Rating ★★★

Price: £0.59/$0.99 **Developer:** Pocket Cocktails Inc

The ultimate portable recipe book for iPhone owners

Cooking has grown in popularity over the last decade or so and this has led to a dramatic increase in 'celebrity chef' television programmes. In turn, this has inspired a proliferation of accompanying and often very expensive recipe books. *Easy Recipes – Food & Drink* is one of the best recipe books available for the iPhone and iPod touch and it is the only app to sport great quality full-screen pictures of each recipe item. Step-by-step detailed instructions are provided for each recipe and as a bonus, the inclusion of a dedicated ingredients list for each meal ensures that shopping is painless. Enjoy one-touch access to a menu of starters, sides, chicken, seafood or dessert dishes, or search the entire food and drink database by category using handy thumbnail images that help you decide on the perfect meal for your loved one, friends or family.

Ratings

Longevity	Fun factor	Practicality	Value
★★★★	★★★★	★★★	★★★★

Overall Rating ★★★★

Price: £0.59/$0.99 **Developer:** DMBC

Holy Bible King James Version

The Old and New Testaments in the palm of your hand

This authorised King James Version of the Holy Bible is an English translation of the Great Book. Around 54 of the best scholars and linguists of their day were nominated to carry out the task of translation in 1604. The finished tome was published by the Church of England in 1611. This Bible was the first authorised version issued by the Church of England during the reign of Henry VIII. The app is easy to navigate and sports a number of handy features. For example, you can choose to view the Old and New Testaments in portrait or landscape mode, bookmark pages, write notes or search the entire text using keywords. You can even record audio notes, or (if you have iPhone 3.0 software installed), copy your favourite scriptures and paste them into a text or email message.

Ratings

Longevity	Fun factor	Practicality	Value
★★★★★	★★	★★★★	★★★★

Overall Rating ★★★★

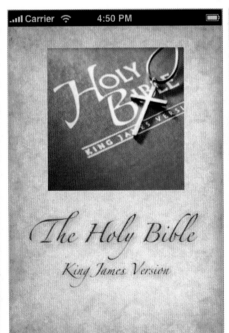

16 ¶ For God so loved the world, that he gave his only begotten Son, that whosoever believeth in him should not perish, but have everlasting life.

■ You can choose to read in either portrait or landscape view.

■ The app is easy to navigate and sports great cover art too.

Business

The iPhone is fast becoming an important business tool and in this section you will find all the apps you need to stay productive while mobile

Price: £5.99/$9.99 **Developer:** Spb Software

Spb Wallet

A secure information manager guaranteed to keep confidential data safe and secure

The increased incidence of identity theft means that keeping sensitive information secure is more important than ever. The only safe way to keep confidential information secure on an iPhone or iPod touch is to invest in a dedicated secure information manager. There are only a handful of such tools that use a truly secure, but user-friendly interface and Spb Wallet is without doubt one of the best. A relative newcomer to the digital wallet arena, Spb Wallet works on the principle of storing user-created cards in a virtual wallet. The key to the success of a secure information manager lies in the level of encryption that it offers the end user and thanks to the fact that it employs strong 256-bit AES algorithms, Spb Wallet certainly scores highly in this area. File encryption is via a key generated with your wallet

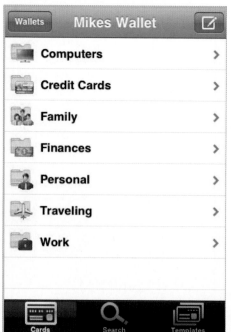

■ Convenient search options enable you to access confidential information quickly and easily.

■ The ability to organise cards into handy categories is a useful feature.

More than 60
predefined card
templates are
included and the
online gallery
gives you access
to 7,000 more.

password and security features include different password strength levels, a password hint function and automatic wallet locking. The app also includes a password generator that is useful for creating strong passwords.

eWallet was the first secure information manager to put information from a card into a user interface that resembles the actual card and the old adage 'if it ain't broke don't fix it' seems pertinent as the developers of Spb Wallet have used the same concept. The app sports a number of handy features, the most notable of which is an intuitive and polished interface. Highly customisable, more than 60 predefined card templates are provided and these can be used to store passport information, bank account and credit card details, access and PIN numbers, login details and passwords. Can't find a card that meets your needs? No problem. Browse the online template gallery and you can choose from over 7,000 cool-looking cards. On a final note, if synchronisation with a desktop PC is important, then you will be pleased to learn that you can opt to download the desktop companion from www.spbsoftwarehouse.com for a reasonable price. Once configured, this enables you to sync data with your iPhone via Bonjour using Wi-Fi.

Ratings

Longevity	Fun factor	Practicality	Value
★★★★★	★★☆☆☆	★★★★★	★★★★★

Overall Rating ★★★★★

Price: £0.59/$0.99   Developer: DAVA Consulting

Recorder Pro

Create and manage voice memos on the go

Without doubt, the ability to be able to record voice notes enhances the functionality of any iPhone or iPod touch and Recorder Pro does a good job of letting you quickly, easily and conveniently record voice notes, reminders, dictations, meetings or interviews. Sporting a practical interface, the app has a range of features that make it suitable for personal, educational or business use. Each recording is assigned a tag with the date, time and duration. In addition, the user can assign a name for the file, an icon (handy for grouping recordings into categories) and priority status (low, medium or high). Recordings can be sorted according to the aforementioned attributes and this ensures that managing a library of voice files is a breeze. On a final note, you will no doubt be pleased to learn that this handy app lets you sync voice files with a PC or Mac via a Wi-Fi connection.

Ratings

Longevity	Fun factor	Practicality	Value
★★★★☆	★★☆☆☆	★★★★☆	★★★★☆

Overall Rating ★★★★

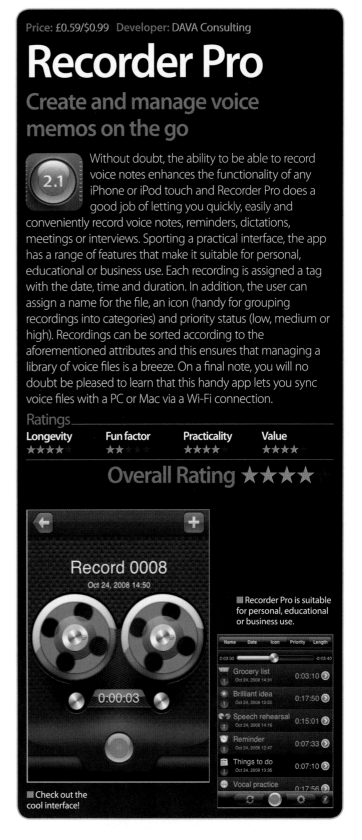

Recorder Pro is suitable for personal, educational or business use.

Check out the cool interface!

Price: £0.59/$0.99   Developer: Yuyao Mobile Software Inc

PDF Reader Pro

Access and manage PDF files while mobile

PDF (Portable Document Format) is well established as the industry standard when it comes to document exchange and the PDF format (also known as Adobe Acrobat) is widely used by individuals, businesses and government agencies around the world to communicate documents, manuals, visions and ideas. PDF Reader Pro will no doubt become an essential tool for those who need to access and manage a library of PDF files while away from the desktop and features include accurate rendering and the ability to be able to upload or sync files with a PC via Wi-Fi. As a bonus, the app promotes effective document management courtesy of commands that let you cut, copy, paste, delete or rename files. All in all, PDF Reader Pro is a functional app but be aware that although the high-resolution setting is great, rendering is slow. If you need to open a large file, try the low-resolution setting.

Ratings

Longevity	Fun factor	Practicality	Value
★★★☆☆	★☆☆☆☆	★★★★☆	★★★★☆

Overall Rating ★★★★☆

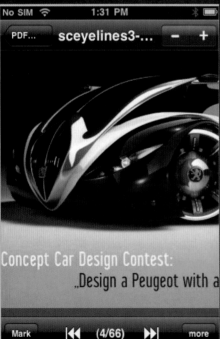

■ Managing a library of PDF files is a breeze.

■ The app allows accurate rendering of all Adobe Acrobat documents.

Price: Free   Developer: Polar Bear Farm Ltd

Convert Lite (PBF)

Convert units quickly and easily at the touch of a button

We all know that an iPhone makes organising a busy schedule a breeze. However, the ability to be able to enhance productivity by way of installing third-party apps means that a growing number of people are using their device to be more productive while away from the desktop. Convert Lite is a simple but functional app, and one that may well prove very useful to a number of people. Its primary function is to allow the mobile user to perform a whole range of unit conversions. Because it is free, the app offers only a limited range of categories, but for many, this may well be all that is required. In short, you can convert weight, length and area measurements from metric to imperial and vice versa. Sporting an intuitive interface, the unit converter is a pleasure to use and if more functionality is required at any time, simply upgrade to the full version for just £2.39.

Ratings

Longevity	Fun factor	Practicality	Value
★★★☆☆	★☆☆☆☆	★★★★★	★★★★★

Overall Rating ★★★☆☆

■ Unit conversions are organised into categories.

■ The interface makes unit conversion calculations easy.

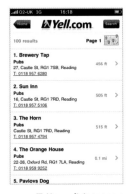

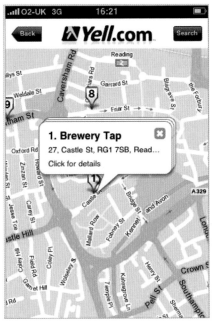

■ Use a digit to tap a telephone number or opt to add the address to your Contacts database.

■ Integrated maps let you view nearby business premises and service providers.

Price: Free **Developer:** Yell.com

Yell.com

Tap into the power of the UK's local search engine

Yell.com is described as the UK's local search engine for business listings and the mobile version of the service lets you use your iPhone to search for local businesses and service providers listed in Yell's comprehensive UK Yellow Pages. For example, you can use the app to locate businesses such as cafes, restaurants, pubs, taxis, shops or even nearby ATM machines. As a bonus, the app uses your iPhone's GPS to automatically display your current geographical location and an integrated map lets you view the nearby business that you are looking for. Key features include an intuitive interface, the ability to be able to call a business with a single tap and the option to be able to save an organisation's contact details to your iPhone's Contacts database. You can also request step-by-step instructions that will guide you from your current location to the business that you are searching for. How's that for efficiency?

Ratings

Longevity	Fun factor	Practicality	Value
★★★★★	★★☆☆☆	★★★★☆	★★★★★

Overall Rating ★★★★★

■ Manage multiple PCs while mobile.

■ The app uses the latest embedded thin-client application development technology.

Price: £11.99/$29.99 **Developer:** Wyse Technology Inc

Wyse PocketCloud

Experience the freedom of mobile computing

Wyse PocketCloud is fast becoming one of the most popular business apps in the App Store. In short, it lets you view and manage your PC's virtual Windows desktop from anywhere using your iPhone. So how does it work? In simple terms, by employing a secure and highly optimised Remote Desktop Protocol (RDP) and VMware View 3.1 client. The app uses the latest embedded thin-client application development technology and the protocol specifications are licensed by Microsoft and VMware. Despite it being expensive, Wyse PocketCloud does offer clear benefits and you'll be pleased to learn that the app supports enterprise-grade security with FIPS for RDP and SSL for VMware View. Please note that this is a business app and although Windows XP Media Center Edition and Vista Ultimate, Enterprise and Business are supported, it is not compatible with home editions of Windows XP and Vista.

Ratings

Longevity	Fun factor	Practicality	Value
★★★★☆	★★★★☆	★★★☆☆	★★☆☆☆

Overall Rating ★★★★☆

Price: £1.79/$2.99   Developer: Symply Soft

Milog – Mileage Log Tracker

Keep track of vehicle costs while you're on the road

Expense managers are without doubt important and indispensable tools and keeping an accurate record o expenses incurred while travelling is essential if you are planning to reclaim costs at a later date. If you use a car for business, Milog will take the guesswork out of claiming travelling expenses and help to ensure that you are properly reimbursed for any fuel costs incurred. This handy application lets you keep track of mileage courtesy of start/stop odometers and/or distance travelled. Features include additional support for recording parking charges, tolls and other fees incurred while travelling and the ability to be able to assign a category (such as Business or Personal) to each trip. Metric (km) and imperial (miles) measurements are supported and the currency symbol displayed is based upon the configuration of your iPhone. As a bonus, the database is fully searchable using criteria such as date or vehicle.

Managing travel expenses is easy courtesy of the intuitive interface.

Ratings

Longevity	Fun factor	Practicality	Value
★★★★	★	★★★★★	★★★★★

Overall Rating ★★★★★

Price: £1.79/$2.99   Developer: Enfour Inc

SpellChecker (Email & SMS)

A top third-party spell checker

The more you use your iPhone to compose texts and emails, the more you're left wondering whether your spelling and grammar is correct. Unfortunately, the iPhone doesn't sport a built-in spell checker, so you have to rely on one of the dedicated third-party solutions available for download from the App Store. Each is designed to ensure that words spelt incorrectly are questioned and alternative spellings offered. SpellChecker is a first-class app and the next best thing to a built-in spell checker. Not only does it check each word for accuracy as you type, but it also identifies capitalisation, grammar and punctuation errors and offers alternative suggestions. You can import 'Contacts' words into the user dictionary and multilingual support is included as standard. For example, you can choose to use US or British English as well as French, German, Spanish, Italian or Dutch dictionaries.

The app includes support for grammar errors and capitalisation.

Take the guesswork out of spelling.

Ratings

Longevity	Fun factor	Practicality	Value
★★★★★	★	★★★★★	★★★

Overall Rating ★★★★

iDiary

Price: £3.99/$6.99 **Developer:** Triple Creeks Studio

No more need for your yearly diary update

Do people still keep good old-fashioned diaries? Our guess is that the growth of social networking means that many now keep an online diary with entries that are shared with friends. That said, judging by the sales of digital diary apps for mobile platforms, some people still opt to use an electronic diary to record thoughts and journal entries. If you want a diary for your iPhone or iPod touch, look no further than iDiary. This useful app is handy for recording ideas, events, plans and daily encounters and in short, it is best described as a password-protected notebook. Boot up the app for the first time and you are asked to enter a password. You will quickly learn that iDiary is very easy to navigate courtesy of its intuitive interface that allows you to edit, view, organise or preview diary entries. As a bonus, Blowfish encryption ensures that your journal is kept safe from prying eyes.

■ Double tap on a day to bring up a notepad.

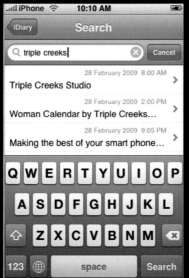
■ Record and manage ideas, events, plans and daily encounters.

Ratings

Longevity	Fun factor	Practicality	Value
★★★	★★★★	★★★	★★

Overall Rating ★★★

Task PRO (ToDo and GTD)

Price: £1.79/$2.99 **Developer:** Alijsoft

Make sure you keep on top of things with this handy app

Do you keep an organised and up-to-date list of daily tasks? It is not easy on an iPhone as a dedicated tasks app is notably absent from the OS. Task PRO lets you record, list and manage all your daily tasks quickly and easily. Convenient and flexible, the app is unlike simple list managers as it lets you organise a whole range of tasks, from a simple shopping list or to-do list to a fairly complex work project. Features include sub-tasking, with each task able to have a number of sub-tasks. This opens the door to infinite possibilities regarding task management. You also get full-screen landscape mode editing for faster and more accurate typing and the ability to be able to sort or group tasks by due date, alphabetically or manually to suit your personal preferences. And like all powerful task managers, you can search tasks (either the current list or the entire database) by keyword, which is very useful for those with a lot on.

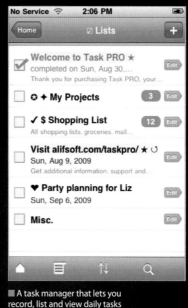
■ A task manager that lets you record, list and view daily tasks and to-do items.

■ Each task can have a number of sub-tasks.

Ratings

Longevity	Fun factor	Practicality	Value
★★★★	★★	★★★★	★★★

Overall Rating ★★★★

JobFinder

Price: Free **Developer:** Organise Ltd

Search the 'situations vacant' pages for your ideal job

■ A handy feature is the ability to bookmark and store favourite jobs.

■ Search for jobs using keywords or by location.

We all know only too well that we are experiencing a global recession at present and the credit crunch has certainly had a major impact on both the British and American economies. Careers are at risk and jobs are not as easy to come by as they have been in more recent times. In these troubled times, it is vitally important to get your job application completed and sent in as early as possible and what better way to be able to do this than to be aware of new vacancies even when you are away from your desk. JobFinder is a free app and an absolute 'must-have' for anyone who's out of work, in the market for a change of career or for those who simply want to see what's out there. Its primary task is to let you quickly and easily search for employment opportunities in the UK or US, in any industry, from an iPhone. Features are myriad and include the ability to select temporary and/or permanent posts.

Ratings

Longevity	Fun factor	Practicality	Value
★★★☆☆	★★☆☆☆	★★★★☆	★★★★★

Overall Rating ★★★★☆

Calc VAT – UK VAT Calculator

Price: £0.59/$0.99
Developer: Aaron Wardle

No more complex VAT calculations!

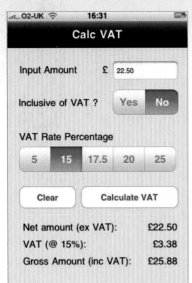

■ Change the VAT percentage rate and the amount will automatically be adjusted.

■ Calc VAT does VAT calculations much faster than a traditional calculator.

Value added tax (VAT) is a consumption tax levied on a product or service. Unlike personal consumers, businesses and organisations can recover VAT on materials and services that they buy to make further supplies or services directly or indirectly sold to end users. Businesses also need to add VAT to product prices. Calc VAT is an easy to use UK VAT calculator that has been designed with one task in mind: to make such VAT calculations much faster than a traditional calculator. Simply enter the amount you wish to calculate in the Input Amount field and indicate whether you want to find the inclusive VAT or add VAT to the amount. Calc VAT will then show you a breakdown of the amount and changing the VAT rate will automatically adjust the result. By default, the rate is set to 15% (the current VAT rate). However, this can be changed as and when required.

Ratings

Longevity	Fun factor	Practicality	Value
★★★★☆	★☆☆☆☆	★★★☆☆	★★★★☆

Overall Rating ★★★☆☆

iCandy
iPhone App Store

iPhone App Store

The endless possibilities offered by the iPhone App Store takes Apple's mobile to a whole new level. Limited only by the imagination of developers, this is a groundbreaking feature

Education

The key to education is to make learning fun and here we have a selection of apps that will appeal to everyone from toddlers to adults

---

Price: £1.79/$2.99 **Developer:** Vito Technology Inc

Star Walk

Impress your friends with your knowledge of the stars

Take a look above you on a dark and clear night and you will be treated to a truly awesome sight. It is difficult not to appreciate the vastness and beauty of the tiny bit of the universe that you have right above you. However, although the celestial bodies appear to be fixed and unchanging, the night sky is dynamic and continually revolving. Gaze for long enough and you will note that the sky's appearance changes right before your very eyes.

If you have ever looked up and wondered what some of the constellations or bright stars are called, then Star Walk is for you. Aimed at anyone with an interest in astronomy, Star Walk lets you discover the stars, planets and constellations in the night sky in a fun and educational way. The app has a range of useful features and is without doubt one of the most realistic stargazing guides currently available for the iPhone. Once installed, you can observe the night sky in real-time from anywhere in the world, and it couldn't be easier.

■ The app is easy to use and everything's simple to understand.

■ Star Map is one of the most realistic stargazing guides available for the iPhone.

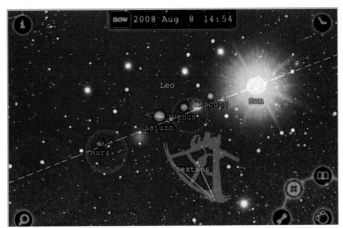

■ Impress friends by being able to identify constellations in the night sky above you.

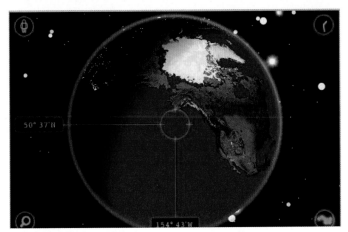

■ View the night sky in real-time from any location in the world.

If you have an iPhone 3GS, simply tilt your phone and the Star Spotter function will be activated and a live representation of what you see in the sky above you will appear. Move and the sky will follow. Touch the display and the feature will deactivate. Click the clock icon and the date and time will show. Now slide your finger over the hours and watch the sky move accordingly. Change the year, month or time and you will see how the stars, planets and other celestial bodies were aligned at any given time in history.

Other features include a number of configuration options, the ability to be able to track the phases of the moon and Wikipedia links to a number of well-known celestial bodies. Whether you want to know the names of a few stars or to impress friends and family with an in-depth knowledge of the night sky, this reasonably priced app will provide you with all the astronomical information you will need.

Ratings

Longevity	Fun factor	Practicality	Value
★★★★★	★★★★★	★★★★☆	★★★★☆

Overall Rating ★★★★★

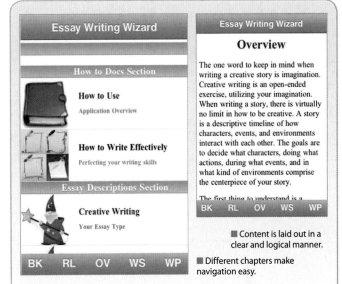

■ Content is laid out in a clear and logical manner.

■ Different chapters make navigation easy.

Price: £2.99/$4.99   **Developer:** Niles Technology Group Inc

Creative Writing PRO

Why not enhance your creative writing skills?

They say that there is a book in every one of us, but getting a story down on paper is never easy. Whether you are about to embark on your first novel or trying to pass your latest English assignment, the ability to be able to write creatively is an important skill to master. For example, good quality dialogue advances a story and fleshes out characters, while providing a break from straight description.

Though it takes time to develop an ear for dialogue, knowing some simple rules and avoiding obvious pitfalls makes a huge difference. Writing better dialogue isn't difficult if you are prepared to learn and Creative Writing PRO is just the tool you need to help enhance your writing skills. Essentially a step-by-step writing planner for students of creative writing, the app presents content in a carefully laid out and logical order, therefore making it easy to learn.

Ratings

Longevity	Fun factor	Practicality	Value
★★★★☆	★★★☆☆	★★★★☆	★★★☆☆

Overall Rating ★★★★☆

Price: Free **Developer:** Antek Szadaj

Mathematical Formulas

A library of complex mathematical formulas in the palm of your hand

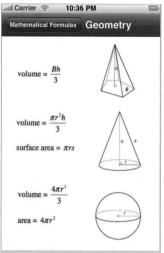

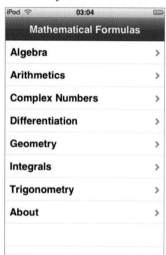

■ Handy diagrams help you select the appropriate formula.

Students of mathematics will be well aware of the sheer number of mathematical formulae that need to be recalled when making algebraic, geometric or arithmetical calculations. If you are one of the many who forget important formulae, then Mathematical Formulas is the perfect app. We all know how difficult it is to remember even a simple – let alone complex – formula and having a library of formulae in one handy place has obvious benefits. The app includes all the features needed to quickly recall a formula, simplifying even quadratic equations. Formulae are arranged into categories such as Differentiation, Trigonometry, Geometry and Algebra and this makes the app easy to navigate. Diagrams are also included and these help the student perform a range of calculations, such as accurately determining the volume of a sphere to calculating the surface area of a cone.

Ratings_____

Longevity	Fun factor	Practicality	Value
★★★☆☆	★☆☆☆☆	★★★★☆	★★★★★

Overall Rating ★★★★★

Price: £0.59/$0.99 **Developer:** A. R. Ermes

Secrets Of iPhone

Get that little bit more out of your trusty iPhone

The first thing that strikes those new to the iPhone is the fact that the device is extraordinarily easy to use. However, beneath the bonnet lies a very powerful engine with a huge number of hidden features and functions. Secrets For iPhone is a continually evolving guide designed to help you boost productivity. Well presented, the app includes a number of helpful hints and tips. For example, you will learn how to take better snapshots, improve battery life, get quicker directions in Maps, quickly search for apps, enhance your typing skills and how to ensure that data remains secure.

Some critics may argue that the majority of the hints and tips can be found online, but the real benefit of this app is that you don't need to waste time searching for and collecting the information. It is all stored in the palm of your hand and accessible at any time.

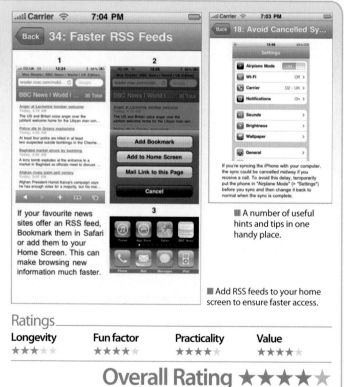

■ A number of useful hints and tips in one handy place.

■ Add RSS feeds to your home screen to ensure faster access.

Ratings_____

Longevity	Fun factor	Practicality	Value
★★★☆☆	★★★★☆	★★★★☆	★★★★☆

Overall Rating ★★★★☆

Compare And Contrast PRO

Price: £2.99/$4.99   **Developer:** Niles Technology Group Inc

Comparative essay writing made easy

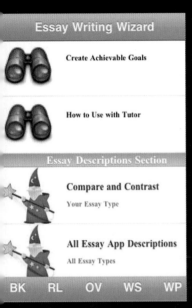

ESL ESSAY WRITING

The focus of a comparative essay is to analyse the effects, outcomes or conceptual differences and similarities between two or more viewpoints. It is not good enough to only point out how two things may be the same or different. In order to be credible and therefore get good marks, it is important to compare and contrast viewpoints in reference to similar and, if possible, identical situations. This useful essay writing wizard will help you to write a convincing comparative essay by teaching you the concepts of critical thinking and logical reasoning. In addition, it instructs you how to review and revise your work in order to achieve maximum clarity and meaning. If you are having difficulty thinking clearly and developing your ideas and arguments, this app will help guide you through the process of comparative essay writing using an easy to follow step-by-step wizard.

■ Learn how to write a comparative essay using a clear step-by-step guide.

Ratings

Longevity	Fun factor	Practicality	Value
★★★★☆	★★☆☆☆	★★★★☆	★★☆☆☆

Overall Rating ★★★★☆

Flags Fun – World

Price: £0.59/$0.99   **Developer:** Lima Sky

Learn the flags of the world

Vexillology is the study of flags and the word is a synthesis of the Latin word vexillum and the suffix -logy, meaning 'study of'. The vexillum was a particular type of flag that was used by Roman legions and its name is a diminutive form of the word vela meaning sail, and therefore literally means 'little sail'. There are countless online sites dedicated to vexillology, so the pastime is obviously popular. If you want a fun and educational game that will help you learn the flags of the world, then look no further than Flags Fun – World.

   Essentially two addictive games in one app, the program ensures that learning and memorising the flags of the world is a fun rather than arduous task. You probably know what the national flag of Canada looks like, but if you want to be able to identify the flags of either Laos or Myanmar, this app is for you.

■ Two educational games that make learning fun.

■ How many of the flags of the world could you recognise?

Ratings

Longevity	Fun factor	Practicality	Value
★★★☆☆	★★★★☆	★★☆☆☆	★★★★☆

Overall Rating ★★★☆☆

Price: £0.59/$0.99   Developer: Duck Duck Moose

Wheels On The Bus

A great way to keep the kids entertained

The dRiveR oN The BUS Says

MoVe oN BACk!

■ Listen to the driver!

It doesn't matter how old you are as there is an educational app for everyone. If you have young children, then encouraging cognitive, language and motor skill development is important and there are a number of fun ways to get them excited in the App Store, while at the same time fostering the learning and honing of new skills. Sporting great graphics, Wheels On The Bus is without doubt an enjoyable way for toddlers to keep entertained and occupied while in the car or at home when you are trying to catch up on your favourite soap.

As an educational tool for the kids, it's hard to beat as great artwork, music, sound effects and an interactive approach to learning are all supported. Board the bus, spin the wheels, open and close the doors, make a dog bark and a whole lot more besides. What could be more fun?

Ratings

Longevity	Fun factor	Practicality	Value
★★☆☆☆	★★★★★	★★★☆☆	★★★★☆

Overall Rating ★★★★☆

Price: £0.59/$0.99   Developer: iTot Apps

Promote learning with these multi-sensory flashcards

Toddler Flashcards

■ Did you know that a puppy is called le chiot in France?

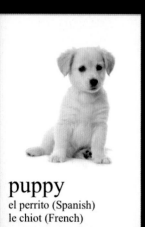

puppy
el perrito (Spanish)
le chiot (French)

Easy
- 🐜 Animals
- 🍎 Food
- 🏀 Things
- 🔀 Mix It Up

Advanced
- ❤️ Shapes
- 〰️ Colors
- A Alphabet
- 5 Numbers

■ Choose to display flashcards randomly or by category.

When you introduce your toddler to basic learning, you set in motion the wheels of further language development as well as a range of other important early learning activities. Toddler Flashcards thrives on its simplicity and it has been specifically designed to introduce young children to basic words using flashcards in a fun, exciting and toddler-appropriate way. Just like traditional flashcards, the app has cards that teach toddlers the names of animals, foods or objects using fun and interactive methods. Also included are cards that teach the alphabet and numbers. You can choose to display cards using the 'easy category' (foods, animals or things) or the 'advanced category' (alphabet, numbers, shapes or colours). Alternatively, add variety by using the 'mix it up' feature to shuffle the cards. On a final note, multi-language support means that you can teach each word in English, French or Spanish.

Ratings

Longevity	Fun factor	Practicality	Value
★★☆☆☆	★★★★★	★★★☆☆	★★★★☆

Overall Rating ★★★★☆

World Countries

Price: £0.59/$0.99   Developer: ADS Software Group Inc

A pocket reference book for 260 of the world's countries

■ World Countries is a fact book that contains a wealth of useful trivia.

■ View facts, figures and statistics for 260 countries around the world.

Essentially a fact book of the world's countries, this educational app makes learning trivia a whole lot of fun. The book contains a wealth of information, including basic content from Wikipedia, an index of countries with flags and capital cities, and flashcards that can be viewed in landscape mode. If you get tired of browsing the plethora of facts and statistics, try your hand at the quiz as this uses an interactive and fun approach to learning. Alternatively, you can choose to play a memory game that makes learning the flags of the world a breeze.

World Countries is an impressive app and the only reason that we didn't give it full marks is because of the poor quality of the low resolution atlas images. However, the developers are planning to address this by introducing much improved maps in an update to be released shortly.

Ratings

Longevity	Fun factor	Practicality	Value
★★★★	★★★★★	★★★★	★★★★

Overall Rating ★★★★

Price: Free   Developer: Christopher Fennell

And one for the budding chemists

The Chemical Touch: Lite Edition

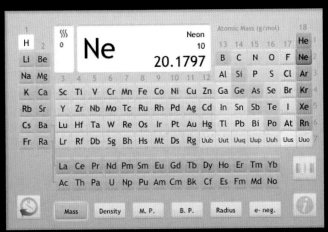

■ View an element's atomic number or boiling point at-a-glance

The Education genre of the App Store caters for students of all the sciences and this includes budding young chemists. The Chemical Touch: Lite Edition is a free and easy-to-use periodic table of the elements that is compatible with the iPhone and iPod touch. In short, the app is a simplified version of the table that enables you to view properties such as density, mass and atomic number, or the melting and boiling point of an element quickly and easily.

If you need more information about an element, use a digit to press the internet button and the Wikipedia page for that element will open. The latest version of the app includes enhanced graphics and configuration options that allow you to recolour the table by mass or atomic number, density or boiling point. All in all, an absolute must for anyone who happens to be studying chemistry.

Ratings

Longevity	Fun factor	Practicality	Value
★★★★	★★	★★★★★	★★★★★

Overall Rating ★★★★

Price: £0.59/$0.99 Developer: Abel Learning Ltd

The Hazard Perception Test

The perfect way to start preparing for your Theory Test

The Driving Standards Agency (DSA) recommends that candidates carefully study the Highway Code prior to sitting their Theory Test. However, regardless of driving experience, candidates are also advised to make full use of available study material in order to prepare for the multiple choice and hazard perception elements of the test. What better way to do this than to use The Hazard Perception Test as an opportunity to practice on your iPhone or iPod touch. The app ships with eight different video clips, each of which has at least one hazard somewhere. As a bonus, there are more clips available should you require them in the future.

A word of advice; there are times when you think a hazard will arise and it won't. Watch carefully as a potential hazard will surely develop and it is up to you to identify it before it turns into a dangerous situation.

Ratings

Longevity	Fun factor	Practicality	Value
★★★☆☆	★★★☆☆	★★★★☆	★★★☆☆

Overall Rating ★★★★☆

■ How many potential hazards can you spot?

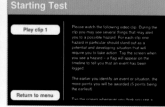

■ Different tests ensure that learning a new language is fun.

■ All you need to get started with learning French.

Price: Free Developer: 24/7 Tutor

FREE French Tutor

Have fun learning a new language

There are a number of reasons for wanting to learn a different language. For example, you may want to work in another country or have a desire to discover your roots. Intellectual curiosity, romance and travel are other factors. There is a wide range of materials and tools available to help with your language studies and the most important thing to remember is that learning should be fun. If you have ever thought about learning French, then we have just the app for you. FREE French Tutor is… yes, you guessed it, free, and it goes beyond the simple talking phrasebook or flashcard method of teaching. The learner is provided with a set of interactive and engaging study tools that really do make learning French a fun experience. For example, the introduction of a quiz, tests and puzzles teaches you to remember key words and phrases from a selection of topics.

Ratings

Longevity	Fun factor	Practicality	Value
★★★☆☆	★★★★☆	★★★★★	★★★★★

Overall Rating ★★★★★

Price: £0.59/$0.99 **Developer:** Frogameleon Ltd

Flash Tables (Times Tables)

Like going back to school all over again…

■ The gesture-based interface ensures that learning math is never dull.

 Practising mental arithmetic is a great way to help keep the old grey matter in good working order and Flash Tables offers children a great way to learn basic arithmetic. In short, the app offers the user interactive multiplication 'times tables' flashcards with the added convenience of always being to hand. This means that you can now keep the kids occupied on long journeys, as long as you can bear to temporarily relinquish your iPhone or iPod touch while they learn. The app provides a full set of activities that assist the child in mastering the principles of basic multiplication and the gesture-based interface ensures that learning math is always fun. Another handy feature is the option to sit timed or untimed tests after having learned each table as this certainly promotes greater speed and accuracy. Go on, try it – mastering your multiplication tables has never been easier!

Ratings

Longevity	Fun factor	Practicality	Value
★★☆☆☆	★★★★☆	★★★★☆	★★★☆☆

Overall Rating ★★★★★

Price: £1.19/$1.99 **Developer:** Pearson Education

Adobe Photoshop CS4: Learn By Video

Learn to create images with instant impact

■ Learn how to professionally edit your images.

 Adobe Photoshop CS4 is the industry standard when it comes to digital imaging solutions and the latest version of this software boasts a wide range of enhancements that deliver first-class editing freedom, an intuitive user experience and increased productivity for creative professionals, serious amateur photographers or web designers. It is clear that CS4 is an essential tool for creating images with instant impact, but its power and complexity can create problems for novice users. This is where Adobe Photoshop CS4: Learn By Video will help. You get two hours of high-quality video tutorials that guide you through the software's many features. The most essential topics are covered in detail and regular tests are used to track your learning progress. Notable features include the ability to be able to bookmark areas that you need to review further and the option to follow the latest Adobe press news on Twitter.

Ratings

Longevity	Fun factor	Practicality	Value
★★★☆☆	★★☆☆☆	★★★★☆	★★★★☆

Overall Rating ★★★★★

Entertainment

A wealth of intriguing apps to keep you entertained, from face-stretching antics to challenging quiz games

Price: £0.59/$0.99/Free   Developer: Robot Wheelie LLC

FaceGoo

Take a photo, then stretch it into distorted shapes using only the tips of your fingers

The artists who retouch photographs of models and celebs to make them appear skinnier are often called digital wizards. They're not really, as they probably use this ingenious pocket-sized app called FaceGoo. Simply load it up, import a photo (preferably of yourself looking rather pear-shaped), or take a photo from within the app if you're using an iPhone, and then use your finger to push and stretch the image to your heart's desire. It really is as simple as dabbing on the screen – within minutes you'll have transformed yourself into

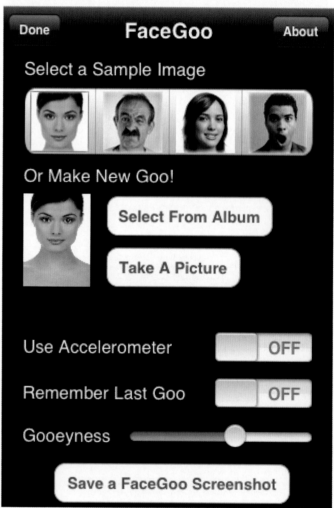

■ Loading your own photo is a simple process

a skinny, distorted clone. It's also incredibly fun, as the results are often unexpected and bizarre.

One impressive feature is the app's multi-touch abilities. You can use up to four fingers to simultaneously transform the image in real-time. It's particularly handy for squeezing or expanding both sides of an image at the same time. You can of course save the results to your photo album for easy sharing. It's perfect for anyone who wants to tease their friends with a distorted image of themselves. Or those who are trying the online dating scene and want to appear slimmer than they actually are (please note we do not endorse this action!)

Tricking potential dates aside, there's one other feature that we would like to mention. By pressing the play button in the lower corner of the screen you can enable a wobbling version of the image that always retains its original shape. As before you can use your finger to distort the photo, but once you lift your finger off the screen the image will wobble back into shape. You can also use the iPhone's accelerometer to shake the device and create a convincing wobble.

If we still haven't persuaded you that this app is a keeper, then head over to the App Store where there's a free copy titled FaceGoo Lite. It doesn't allow you to import or take photos, but it does give you the opportunity to try out every unique feature of this app. For its price, this is a fun title that should give you lasting enjoyment, and plenty of giggles.

Ratings

Longevity	Fun factor	Practicality	Value
★★★★☆	★★★★☆	★★★★☆	★★★★☆

Overall Rating ★★★★☆

■ The default image, perfect for practising.

■ In seconds you'll have warped the poor woman's face.

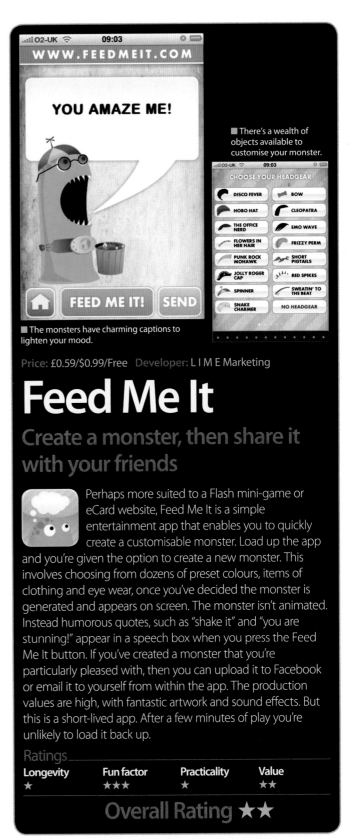

■ There's a wealth of objects available to customise your monster.

■ The monsters have charming captions to lighten your mood.

Price: £0.59/$0.99/Free   Developer: L I M E Marketing

Feed Me It

Create a monster, then share it with your friends

Perhaps more suited to a Flash mini-game or eCard website, Feed Me It is a simple entertainment app that enables you to quickly create a customisable monster. Load up the app and you're given the option to create a new monster. This involves choosing from dozens of preset colours, items of clothing and eye wear, once you've decided the monster is generated and appears on screen. The monster isn't animated. Instead humorous quotes, such as "shake it" and "you are stunning!" appear in a speech box when you press the Feed Me It button. If you've created a monster that you're particularly pleased with, then you can upload it to Facebook or email it to yourself from within the app. The production values are high, with fantastic artwork and sound effects. But this is a short-lived app. After a few minutes of play you're unlikely to load it back up.

Ratings

Longevity	Fun factor	Practicality	Value
★	★★★	★	★★

Overall Rating ★★

Price: Free Developer: Trippert, Inc

What's Your IQ?

A set of questions that have nothing to do with your IQ

Calling this an IQ test is a bit of a misnomer. It's actually a series of ten fairly challenging questions, each chosen at random, with a random score awarded at the end. That last line might surprise you. But yes, the score is completely random. We purposely chose ten incorrect answers, and then played again making sure to answer correctly, both attempts gave us an IQ score of 116 and 120 respectively. Even more bizarrely, is that often the correct answer isn't one of the options available to you. For example one question asks you to take 60, divide it by two, then subtract 20. The answer certainly isn't 30, which is the lowest figure available to choose from. What worries us is that some users will take the final score as an accurate IQ number. The fact that the score is randomly generated and the questions are completely irrelevant may lead some to the wrong conclusion. Despite the fact it's free, this is an app to avoid.

Ratings

Longevity	Fun factor	Practicality	Value
★☆☆☆	★★☆☆☆	★☆☆☆☆	★★★★★

Overall Rating ★★☆☆☆

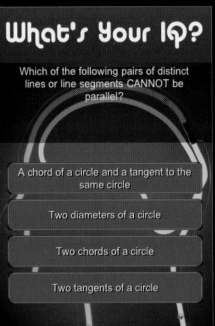

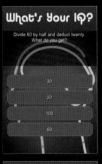

■ Our random tappings gave us an IQ of 140. Impressive.

Price: £0.59/$0.99 Developer: SKHM, LLC

iSpy Cameras

Play James Bond with this neat little app

Imagine if you had a window onto the entire world. That in a second you could pull up a live feed from the other side of the planet – or even in your hometown – to see what's going on. That's exactly what this app enables you to do. Open it up, and a random assortment of 12 webcams and CCTV cameras appears on your iPhone screen. Tap on one of them and it zooms right in to fill the screen. In total, the app can load up 120 cameras in one go, although a useful search window allows you to find a specific location from thousands of other cams. There's one other clever feature included with iSpy Cameras as well. It's also possible to control many of the cameras. Simply swipe the screen with your finger and the camera will move in that direction, allowing you to see what's going on elsewhere in the camera's vicinity. Often you'll have to queue to take over the controls, but it's totally fascinating and worth the wait.

Price: £0.59/$0.99 Developer: Marco Cavazzana

Skull Toy

Revel in a world of interactive spinning cartoon skulls

Skulls. Some people just can't get enough of the things, while others would rather not think about those macabre laughing bones that reside within their very faces. If you happen to be in the former group, then you're going to love the Skull Toy app. Load it up, and dozens upon dozens of cartoon skulls begin to slide and bounce across your iPhone's screen. Press and hold your finger on the screen and a stream of skulls flows outwards. You can invert the colour of the skulls by tapping three times on the iPhone's screen, and it's also possible to somehow summon a hidden pink skull – although don't ask us how as we haven't managed to figure it out ourselves yet!

This is a fun app for playing around with, although it's usefulness is admittedly limited. After some practice you'll be creating interesting collages of multicoloured skulls. Take a screenshot (by pressing the home and sleep button together) and set it as your home screen for extra skull-themed antics.

■ When first loaded you'll see a random selection of cameras.

Ratings

Longevity	Fun factor	Practicality	Value
★★★★	★★★★★	★★★	★★★★

Overall Rating ★★★★★

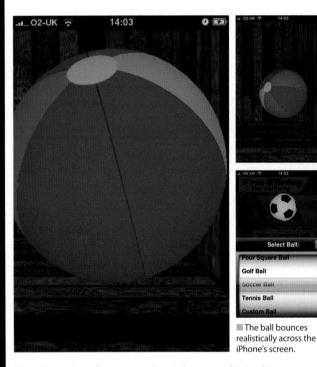

■ The ball bounces realistically across the iPhone's screen.

Price: Free   **Developer:** Jonathan Johnson and Brian Pratt

Awesome Ball

A great example of the accelerometer in use

A fun title that uses the accelerometer to good effect, Awesome Ball is a free and simple showcase of the hardware utilised within both the iPhone and iPod touch. Load the app and you'll see a 3D basketball rolling around within the confines of a wooden box. Tilt your device to roll the ball around, give it a shake to bounce the ball, and swipe on the screen with your finger to move the ball in any given direction.

But that's not all you can do with this clever interactive toy. Double tap on the iPhone's screen to bring up a hidden options screen. From here you can change the ball type and the background texture, with this latter option also allowing you to take photos using the iPhone's built-in camera. Chances are this won't stay installed on your device for too long, but as a free app it's a great way to show off the unique features of the iPhone and iPod touch.

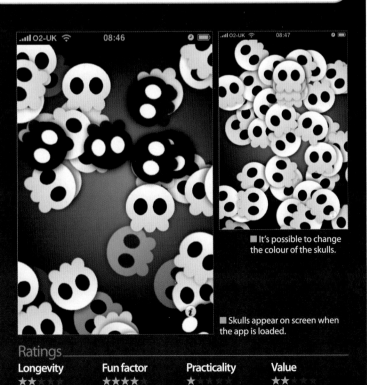

■ It's possible to change the colour of the skulls.

■ Skulls appear on screen when the app is loaded.

Ratings

Longevity	Fun factor	Practicality	Value
★★	★★★★	★	★★

Overall Rating ★★★

Ratings

Longevity	Fun factor	Practicality	Value
★★	★★★	★	★★★★★

Overall Rating ★★★★

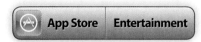

Price: Free **Developer:** BSkyB

Sky+

Never miss a programme or movie using this handy app

The ultimate convenience app for Sky+ users, this title enables you to programme your Sky+ box to record a television show or movie from your iPhone. The interface will be familiar to all Sky TV users, with a blue themed background and yellow highlights for selected TV programmes. It's easy to navigate, too, as it has the same genres of programming that are found on your television, such as documentaries, sports, news and movies. There are a few requirements for using the app. You'll need to set up a free Sky Remote Record account beforehand, programmes must be set to record 30 minutes before they begin, and if you haven't guessed already by the app's name – you'll need to be a Sky+ subscriber. We'd like to see a couple of improvements to enhance user experience – landscape support and speed improvements – but considering this is a free app, it's a nice bonus for Sky+ users on the go.

Ratings

Longevity	Fun factor	Practicality	Value
★★★★☆	★☆☆☆☆	★★★★★	★★★★★

Overall Rating ★★★★☆

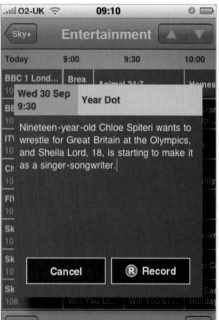

■ Programmes are listed just as they are on a real Sky+ box.

Price: £0.59/$0.99 **Developer:** Soonio Productions

Donkey

The most challenging and unique puzzler on the App Store

There aren't many apps that intentionally try to drive you up the wall, but here's one, and it's called Donkey. It's a puzzle game with plenty of infuriating puzzles. Get an answer incorrect and the app plays the sound of a donkey's hee-haw, before throwing you back to the beginning of the game. But what's most puzzling is that Donkey is actually fun to play and incredibly addictive. The mocking sound effects and repetitive actions soon fade away and are replaced with sheer determination as you attempt to complete the game with a respectable high score. The questions range from tapping coloured balloons in the order of a rainbow, to simple maths puzzles. There are a few trick questions along the way, and often the arrangement of objects moves while you're playing. It all adds up to create what's possibly the most challenging puzzle game in the App Store. One that's well worth a look.

Price: £0.59/$0.99 **Developer:** Thanatist Software

iKITT

Bring a touch of Knight Rider to your car's dashboard

The recent attempt at relaunching *Knight Rider* for a modern audience came and went without success. Nevertheless the charm and retro appeal of the original series continues without abate. On first appearance iKITT simply looks like a cheap cash-in. When the app is loaded up you're presented with a soundboard of choice quotes from KITT (Knight Industries Three Thousand) – the talking car from the David Hasselhoff-starring series. Tap on a button to listen to a quote, and double tap on the centre of the screen to zoom in. But dig a little bit deeper and you'll find a surprising addition to the app. By tilting your iPhone sideways, a dashboard appears on screen. It uses the built-in GPS to detect the speed at which you're travelling, and displays it on screen in km/h. As a result you can sit your iPhone on your car's dashboard (safely strapped down of course), and pretend to have your very own built-in KITT.

Press the number with the largest value.

113   17

59

23   99.99

29
DONKEY'D: 9

You (CUTE LITTLE) DONKEY!!!
TRY AGAIN!

■ The puzzles begin easy enough, but soon get tricky.

■ Get an answer wrong and the donkey appears to mock you.

Ratings

Longevity	Fun factor	Practicality	Value
★★	★★★★	★	★★

Overall Rating ★★

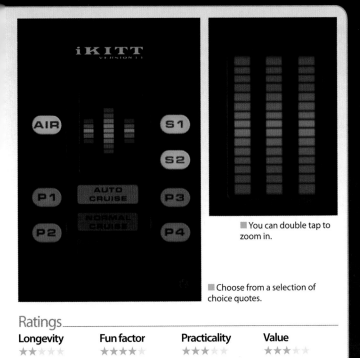

iKITT
VERSION 1

AIR   S1

             S2

P1   AUTO CRUISE   P3

P2   P4

■ You can double tap to zoom in.

■ Choose from a selection of choice quotes.

Ratings

Longevity	Fun factor	Practicality	Value
★★	★★★★	★★★	★★★

Overall Rating ★

Price: Free   **Developer:** iHandySoft Inc.

Coin Flip Free

Leave your fate in the hands of this coin-flipping app

 Have you ever needed to flip a coin when there wasn't one to hand? To give an example: perhaps you've just been mugged of all your change, and can't decide whether to chase down the assailant or not. Well, if you've managed to get lucky and the robber has left you with your iPhone, you could whip it out and load up this sometimes-useful app. Its sole purpose is to enable you to flip a coin without needing a coin to do so. The app uses a random algorithm to decide if the coin should land heads or tails up and gives you a choice of coins from various currencies – US dollars, pound sterling, the euro and more. Using the app is simple enough, either flick your finger upwards over the screen or use a flick of the wrist while holding your iPhone. The graphics are sharp and well rendered, although we should also mention there are obtrusive adverts for alternative versions of the app with more coins to choose from.

Ratings

Longevity	Fun factor	Practicality	Value
★	★★★	★★★★	★★★★★

Overall Rating ★★★★

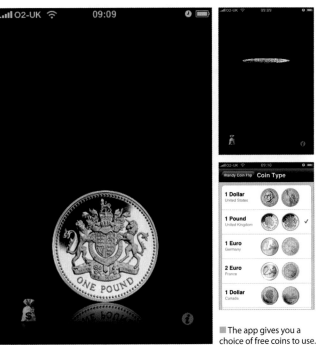

■ The app gives you a choice of free coins to use.

Price: £1.19/$1.99/Free   Developer: id Software, Inc

Wolfenstein 3D Classic

The original shooter that spawned a genre appears on the App Store

Surely this should be listed in the games section of the App Store? That was our first thought when we originally spotted *Wolfenstein* within the entertainment section. Not that we're complaining, as it gives us some respite from soundboards and interactive toys and instead lets us blow up Nazis and also features a cartoon Hitler. This is easily the best port of *Wolfenstein 3D* to date. The graphics are upgraded, with higher-res textures filtered through the iPhone or iPod touch's GPU, and its controls are wonderfully intuitive, too. This is actually the first classic id Software game to be released for the iPhone and touch, but the company has promised to release its back catalogue of titles within the App Store over the next couple of years, with *Doom Classic* coming next. Never played *Wolfenstein 3D* before? Then make sure to check out the free demo that includes the first three levels of the game.

Ratings

Longevity	Fun factor	Practicality	Value
★★★★☆	★★★★☆	★★☆☆☆	★★★★★

Overall Rating ★★★★☆

■ The graphics have been given a facelift.

■ The quality of the comics is far higher than in print.

■ There are 20 comics available to download for free.

Price: £0.59 (UK only)   Developer: Tapisodes Ltd

Alex

A long-running comic strip is brought to life

Alex is a comic strip that features in the *Daily Telegraph*, with its right-wing politics having entertained readers since it was first published back in 1987. This app brings 20 comic strips to your iPhone or iPod touch in the form of short animated episodes. The controls are easy to pick up. You tap the right side of the screen to go forward a panel and the left side to go back. Tapping the bottom will display how many panels remain, plus an exit button to return you to the main menu. In-between panels the characters briefly come to life, and the camera zooms and pans around the scene. As a result this is part-cartoon, part-comic book. The app comes with two episodes built in, with the ability to download more for free at the tap of a button. In all, this is a successful and charming attempt at bringing a classic comic strip to an interactive audience and if you're a fan it's worth checking out.

Ratings

Longevity	Fun factor	Practicality	Value
★★★	★★★★★	★★★★	★★★

Overall Rating ★★★★

Price: £1.79/$2.99/Free **Developer:** Hobbyist Software

VLC Remote

Control the world's most versatile media player from your sofa

If you haven't heard of VLC Player, it's a free versatile media player that will allow you to play anything you throw at it. Xvids, HD movies, Windows Media Player files, QuickTime movies – if we were to go through them all the list of compatible file types would fill this review. This app works in a similar way to Apple's Remote app, but as well as giving you control over audio levels and the timeline, it also enables you to browse through your computer for files and switch to full screen. It's a breeze to set up, requiring only a small setup file to be installed on the host machine. Once done VLC Remote will automatically scan for available computers and connect you with only the tap of a finger. Not sure about buying this app? You'll find a free ad-supported version that allows you to test-drive the app, allowing you to control VLC Player but not select files on external drives.

Ratings

Longevity	Fun factor	Practicality	Value
★★★★★	★★★☆☆	★★★★★	★★★★☆

Overall Rating ★★★★☆

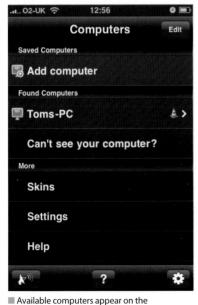

■ Available computers appear on the home screen.

■ There are more skins available to download for free.

■ The tool wheel is an intuitive way to access the app's features.

■ You can save your paintings to the Photo Library.

Price: £1.79/$2.99/Free **Developer:** Autodesk Inc

SketchBook Mobile

A powerful painting tool that fits in your pocket

SketchBook Pro was always designed with graphics tablets and tablet PCs in mind, so it's only natural that a mobile version has made its way to the App Store. Using the same paint engine as the desktop version, this is the most powerful painting tool you'll find for the iPhone and iPod touch and at a great price, too. SketchBook Mobile enables you to paint with realistic brushes, pencils and airbrushes using only your fingertip. It also supports up to six separate layers, an intuitive zoom feature using multi-touch and also offers a full-screen painting environment. To access the tools, simply press the small icon at the bottom of the screen and a wheel will appear in the centre of the screen. Then simply tap on your tool of choice to select it. The app needs some optimisation to make it perfect, as brushstrokes are currently drawn with a slight lag. But for the asking price, this is a brilliant art tool to enable you to paint on the go.

Ratings

Longevity	Fun factor	Practicality	Value
★★★★★	★★★★☆	★★★★☆	★★★★★

Overall Rating ★★★★☆

Stick It Action

Price: £0.59/$0.99   Developer: Stick It Productions LLC

An entire animation suite in the palm of your hand

■ Create your own animated band.

Stick It Action is one incredibly ambitious app, aimed at only those with some serious spare time to fill. It enables you to create your very own stick-figure-animated productions on your iPhone or iPod touch. The first step is to choose a background – there are seven available for you to select from. Once you've chosen the background a menu at the bottom of the screen allows you to drop in stick figures, props, weapons, sound effects and special effects. The app works one frame at a time, so this is a laborious process of moving the figures limb by limb, then hitting a camera icon to capture the frame. You can move figures, props and effects by simply tapping on your chosen object and then dragging it with your finger. To move the stick figures' limbs, double tap on a figure and the camera zooms in to reveal the moveable joints. It's simple to learn, fun to use, but very tricky to master.

Ratings

Longevity	Fun factor	Practicality	Value
★★★☆☆	★★★☆☆	★★★☆☆	★★★☆☆

Overall Rating ★★★☆☆

Price: £0.59/$0.99   Developer: Joymaster Inc

Pharaoh's Quest

A jewel-matching game that requires more polishing

This is an alternative to *Bejeweled*, the classic game of matching three of the same blocks or more. The rules are simple: you tap on a jewel, hold your finger down, and slide it horizontally or vertically to match it with corresponding jewels. Once you have matched three or more the jewels explode allowing more jewels to fall down. It's an addictive game, with dozens of versions available for most consoles and mobile phones. Unfortunately, this version feels like a cheap clone. The graphics are rough, the animation jerky, and the built-in music is awful. Perhaps the developer realised this, as the game gives you the option to silence the music every time the app is loaded. *Pharaoh's Quest* does at least attempt to keep things interesting by introducing gadgets while you play. These include bombs that explode when matched and cross fires that clear an entire line, but the lack of polish inevitably drags things down.

■ The boards take a wide variety of shapes.

■ You'll be clearing lines in no time.

Ratings

Longevity	Fun factor	Practicality	Value
★☆☆☆☆	★★★☆☆	★☆☆☆☆	★★★☆☆

Overall Rating ★★☆☆☆

A virtual pet fish with entertaining tricks

Pocket Fish

Price: £0.59/$0.99   **Developer:** Controlled Chaos LLC

Part digital pet, part aquarium simulator, Pocket Fish is an entertaining app for keeping children busy for a short period of time. When the app is loaded up, a 3D fish plops into an underwater environment. You can attract the fish by tapping on the screen, and you can get the fish to do tricks by tapping on bubbles that appear at random. The bubbles contain small icons that hint at the trick, such as a music note that tasks the fish with playing a virtual guitar. The app also includes a number of extras, including a choice of eight virtual fish, a tank or plastic bag environment, the ability to choose the time of day, and a choice of various camera angles. The tricks are varied and mildly entertaining, and the fish have their own charming designs. Our only concern is the loading times on older iPhone and iPod touch models – usually around 17 seconds to change the tank or time of day – which can be slightly frustrating.

■ The fish models have a life of their own.

■ Tap on a bubble to get your fish to perform a trick.

Ratings

Longevity	Fun factor	Practicality	Value
★★☆☆☆	★★★☆☆	★☆☆☆☆	★★★★☆

Overall Rating ★★★★☆

AirCoaster 3D

Price: £0.59/$0.99   **Developer:** Ziconic

A rollercoaster simulator for your iPhone

This is a great app for thrill seekers who are happiest when corkscrewing through the air at 80mph. It enables you to not only generate a random rollercoaster track and then ride it, but also create and tweak your very own track. The random generator is simple to use. You have five sliders that control the maximum height and length of the track and the number of loop-the-loops, spirals and corkscrews. Once you've chosen the parameters, tap on the ride button and away you go. It's possible to ride in a regular train carriage, a hanging cage carriage, or view the track from a floating camera. Designing your own track is actually rather tricky and takes some practice. The interface is similar to many 3D modelling packages, and enables you to tweak every twist and turn of the track. With practice and time you could potentially design the rollercoaster track of your dreams.

Ratings

Longevity	Fun factor	Controls	Value
★★★★☆	★★★★☆	★★★★☆	★★★★☆

Overall Rating ★★★★☆

■ You'll soon be whizzing around your own tracks.

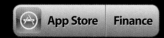

App Store | Finance

Finance

With an iPhone in your pocket there's almost no need to carry a wallet. From keeping a visual record of your receipts, to monitoring the stock exchange in real-time – the App Store has absolutely everything you need!

Price: £0.59/$0.99/Free   Developer: SnapTap

BillTracker

Manage all of your bills with one easy-to-use app

Unfortunately, paying bills is something we all have to do, perhaps with the exception of children, anyone living at home, and the very fortunate who have somehow managed to sneak through the system. If you're like us then it's likely you have a pile of bills stacked dangerously on the side of a table or chair, each patiently waiting to be paid by Direct Debit or over the phone.

This charming app helps you to stay on top of those bills. It boasts a simple interface and some very handy features. When first loaded you're presented with a bare looking screen, with a button in the centre for adding a new bill. Tap the button and a window slides up that enables you to add a surprising amount of detail. These include an account number, website address, phone number (once added

■ You can alter the default currency from within the settings window.

■ Upcoming bills are listed in order of importance.

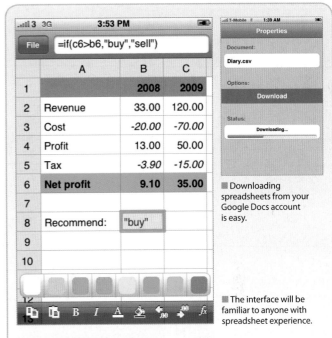

■ The calendar features customised scribbles to mark each bill.

■ Downloading spreadsheets from your Google Docs account is easy.

■ The interface will be familiar to anyone with spreadsheet experience.

you can call the number from within the app), payment amount and date of payment. Need to create a recurring bill? You'll also find an option to repeat it daily, weekly, monthly or yearly. Tap Save and the bill is added to your account.

Once you've added all your bills you can check on them easily by tapping on the calendar button at the bottom of the screen. This section cleverly mimics the default calendar app, but with one exception – all bills are shown using a hand-drawn circular mark on the relevant date.

The accounts page displays a history of every bill ever paid, plus all upcoming bills. The app saves an indefinite amount of bills, so it's possible to keep your entire history of bill paying antics – handy for those in business or with multiple households.

Finally, the settings page holds some clever features. Worried about your privacy? There's an option to set a four-digit passcode. Once enabled you'll be prompted to enter the code every time the app is opened.

For its price this is easily the best bill-tracking app to be found within the App Store. It's a polished title, packed with useful features and is a doddle to use.

Ratings

Longevity	Fun factor	Practicality	Value
★★★★★	★★☆☆☆	★★★★★	★★★★☆

Overall Rating ★★★★☆

Price: £1.79/$2.99 **Developer:** SavySoda

iSpreadsheet
Create and edit spreadsheets from your iPhone

Spreadsheets are a blessing for anyone in business who relies on detailed and up-to-date information. Both the iPhone and iPod touch enable you to view spreadsheets, but not create or edit them. Until now.

When this app is first opened you're given the option of creating a new folder or a blank spreadsheet. Editing spreadsheets is just the same as on your desktop PC, but with the menu tools accessible from the bottom of the screen. It's possible to execute complex arithmetic formulas, format cells, resize columns, fill colours and more – all with your fingertip. Have a Google Docs account? If so you can log into it from within the app to manage and save your worksheets.

Working with the tools is rather fiddly, and it takes some practice, but for anyone who needs to edit spreadsheets on the go, this could be just what you're looking for.

Ratings

Longevity	Fun factor	Practicality	Value
★★★★☆	★☆☆☆☆	★★★★☆	★★★★☆

Overall Rating ★★★☆☆

App Store | Finance

Price: Free **Developer:** Capital Accumulation Services Ltd

shareprice.co.uk

Real-time share prices on your iPhone or iPod touch

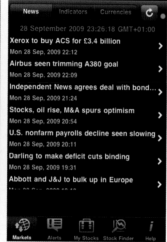

■ Brilliant, Apple's stocks are up!

There are a number of stock-watching apps available for the iPod touch and iPhone, but this has one unique feature to set it apart from the others – real-time streaming price data from the London Stock Exchange. For US iPhone owners, there's an option to enable a 15 minute delayed US stocks watch too.

That's not the only clever feature to be included with this app; you can also receive real-time alerts via Apple's Push Notification Service. These let you know of any significant price movements, enabling you to buy and sell at the most opportune time. Unfortunately, iPod touch owners cannot take advantage of this clever feature. There's one other large caveat to the Push Notification system – you're required to register via the Shareprice website and tick an agreement box to receive news and updates. Many are likely to be turned off by this requirement.

Ratings

Longevity	Fun factor	Practicality	Value
★★★★☆	★★★☆☆	★★★★★	★★★★★

Overall Rating ★★★★☆

Price: £0.59/$0.99 **Developer:** Graham Haley

Meter Readings

Stay on top of your electricity bills with this intuitive app

Accurate electricity bills are still a distant dream for most. Until automated electronic meters are fitted into every home, regular checks of the meter and phone calls to the electricity company are set to continue. This handy app intends to alleviate some of the hassle often associated with tracking your meter readings. It enables you to add readings, check the usage in between readings, and keep an eye on costs. You will find a wealth of minor features that all add up to one impressive package, including the ability to configure three separate tariffs for each meter, graph usage for reading periods, and support for an unlimited number of meters too.

It's a breeze to use, with an intuitive interface that uses Apple's standard buttons and scroll bars. If you've recently had trouble with a utility supplier, or want to keep track of your usage levels, then this is app comes highly recommended.

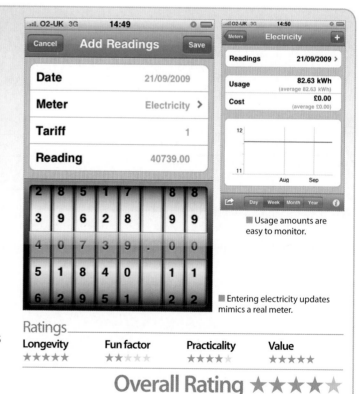

■ Usage amounts are easy to monitor.

■ Entering electricity updates mimics a real meter.

Ratings

Longevity	Fun factor	Practicality	Value
★★★★★	★★☆☆☆	★★★★☆	★★★★★

Overall Rating ★★★★☆

AceBudget

Price: £0.59/$1.99 / Free   Developer: SVT Software

A budget expenses app with a wealth of features

■ The home screen displays your total budgets.

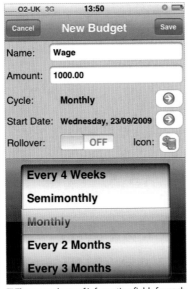

■ There are plenty of information fields for each budget type.

Staying on top of every single expense can be a tiring chore. After all, writing down or memorising each and every expense isn't always practical. Thankfully AceBudget is here to help.

It's a powerful application for tracking your daily expenses. When first loaded you're presented with the budgets page. From here you can tap the plus icon to add new budget, such as your wage, bills, food and travel costs. To add an expense to the budget, simply tap the plus icon, followed by the expense details. You can choose whether to cycle the expense, as well as an icon to help you immediately recognise the expense from the main menu. A reports section automatically generates expense reports for each month too. It enables you to compare expense vs income, and see spending by budget. For its price you'll be hard pressed to find a better alternative.

Ratings

Longevity	Fun factor	Practicality	Value
★★★★☆	★★☆☆☆	★★★★☆	★★★★☆

Overall Rating ★★★★☆

iBank

Price: £2.99/$4.99   Developer: IGG Software, LLC

Stay on top of your spending with this mobile app

An easy way to track your transactions and account balance, this is a mobile version of the Mac desktop program iBank. It's one of the simplest financial apps that we've come across. A large plus icon at the bottom of the screen enables you to add ingoings and outgoings, which then appear on a graph in the centre of the screen. It's possible to set up multiple accounts, each representing a different transaction such as savings, cash and assets.

There are a couple of other interesting features to this app. For added security you can set a passcode lock from within in the settings window. Once enabled you'll have to enter the code every time the app is launched. And if you have a copy of iBank 3.5 installed on your Mac, then it's possible to sync both the desktop and mobile versions together via Wi-Fi or MobileMe. This app gives a great way to keep a track of juggling your finances.

■ The new amount window has extra large number keys for easy entry.

■ The home screen, with available cash and bar chart.

Ratings

Longevity	Fun factor	Practicality	Value
★★★★★	★★☆☆☆	★★★★☆	★★★☆☆

Overall Rating ★★★★☆

Price: £1.19/$1.99 Developer: Graham Haley

Account Tracker

Get to grips with your financial accounts with this app

■ Your cash flows can be seen in a bar chart – ours isn't looking too good!

On first appearance this is a bare-bones accounts management app, but dig a little deeper and you'll discover some useful features within.

The home screen displays your total financial accounts. Adding new accounts is easy, simply tap the plus icon, give it a name and it appears on the home screen. Tap on the new account to add any income or outgoings, set the date of the cost, repeat it, add it to a category, and add further notes.

Back on the home screen, you'll notice a small pie chart icon in the bottom-left corner. Tap on this to see your financial reports as a cash flow chart. You can swipe this screen to see seven day income and spending reports.

The features mentioned above make this one useful app to have, especially for anyone looking for a cheap way to control their financial accounts.

Ratings

Longevity	Fun factor	Practicality	Value
★★★☆☆	★★☆☆☆	★★★☆☆	★★★☆☆

Overall Rating ★★★☆☆

Price: £2.99/$4.99 Developer: Mitek Systems

Mobile Receipt

A essential app for anyone who records their receipts

Maintaining a record of your receipts can often be a painstaking task, especially if your job involves expenses. This is a fantastically clever app that's here to make your life much easier.

It's packed with clever features that you won't find in any other receipt app. For example, when taking a photo of your receipt, the app will automatically scale and crop out the background so that only the receipt is saved. It does this via a patent-pending technique that works perfectly – even in low-light conditions.

Another clever feature is the ability to email each receipt as an expense report to yourself, directly from within the app. The reports arrive as PDF attachments, and if you're offline when sending the receipt then the reports are sent as soon as you go back online.

This is an essential purchase for any user with receipts to keep track of and is one of the iPhone's better finance apps.

■ It's even possible to email expense reports to yourself.

■ The receipts are automatically cropped and scaled.

Ratings

Longevity	Fun factor	Practicality	Value
★★★★★	★★★☆☆	★★★★★	★★★☆☆

Overall Rating ★★★★☆

Money Diary

Price: £2.99/$4.99   Developer: Aesthology Inc

A feature-packed money management organiser

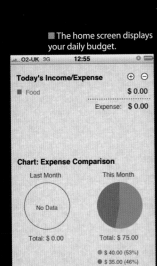

■ The home screen displays your daily budget.

■ The tab system in action – it works a treat.

We've looked at many income and expenses apps within this bookazine, so what makes this one different from the others? Most apparent is the unique interface, built from the ground up and focused around using tabs to enter information. It gives this app a feel of its own, and works brilliantly. The tabs, although simple in appearance, slide up from the bottom of windows whenever you need to enter any details. After a few minutes of using them you'll be wondering how you managed without it.

Each section of the app is easy to navigate, with your cash flow pictured as a graph on the home screen. In seconds you can work out if your spending is getting out of control. Some of the other features included are a passcode lock, the ability to export reports as CSV files, and an easy to use backup system. It all adds up to one feature-packed app.

Ratings

Longevity	Fun factor	Practicality	Value
★★★☆☆	★★☆☆☆	★★★★★	★★★★☆

Overall Rating ★★★★☆

CNNMoney.com

Price: Free   Developer: CNN

The latest financial news at the tap of a button

CNN has an extensive finance section on its website and this app is a portable version with up-to-the-minute news, a personalised stocks window and a video section. It's intuitive to use, with the three main sections easily accessible via buttons at the bottom of the screen.

The news screen includes a miniature market index with the latest news displayed below. The stocks page updates quickly, and automatically displays stocks from Apple, Microsoft, Google, and a handful of other technology based companies. Adding more stocks is a simple one-button affair. The videos section displays the latest 12 videos from the CNN Finance website and each plays full screen, similar to Apple's default YouTube app.

We only have two complaints with this app; it's sometimes slow to load, even over Wi-Fi, and the buttons are too small. However, for the latest financial news, this is one highly recommended app.

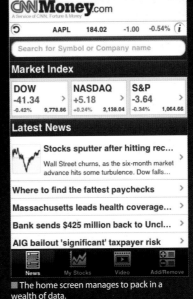

■ The home screen manages to pack in a wealth of data.

■ The videos window lets you catch up on the latest financial news.

Ratings

Longevity	Fun factor	Practicality	Value
★★★☆☆	★★☆☆☆	★★★☆☆	★★★★★

Overall Rating ★★★☆☆

Games

With the iPhone now proving that it is up there with the top handheld gaming consoles, we take a look at some of the latest and greatest games that you can download for your device. Enjoy…

Price: £2.99/$5.99   Developer: Kojima Productions

Metal Gear Solid Touch

Solid Snake in the palm of your hand

Kojima's first iPhone game caused plenty of controversy when it was first announced, mainly because Xbox fanboys thought it was a new game for Microsoft's 360. Their loss is our gain, however, for *Metal Gear Solid Touch* proves to be an interesting take on the lightgun-styled games that are constantly popping up on Apple's machine. Even if it's not quite as sophisticated as we were hoping from the director of Konami's insanely popular franchise.

Loosely based on events from *Metal Gear Solid 4*, you basically have to shoot down a set amount of enemy soldiers before you can move on to the next stage. The difference here is that rather than simply tap on enemies to kill them you have to guide a reticule over them, meaning that the same degree of skill that can be found in normal lightgun games is present.

Pinch the screen and you can switch between weapons, tap the screen to shoot and taking your finger off will allow Snake to hide behind cover and eventually recover life. It's an extremely fluid system that's further enhanced by some truly impressive visuals and plenty of familiar music and sound effects from the *Metal Gear Solid* world.

Indeed, *Metal Gear Solid Touch*'s visuals still look cutting edge on the iPhone's razor-sharp screen, despite the fact that the game is now over seven months old. Animation is limited but very

■ The soldiers that you'll face later in the game require several hits to kill so you'll find yourselves tapping the screen wildly.

■ The *Metal Gear* series has excelled on the consoles, and its appearance on the iPhone is certainly a welcome one. The cut-scenes look fantastic.

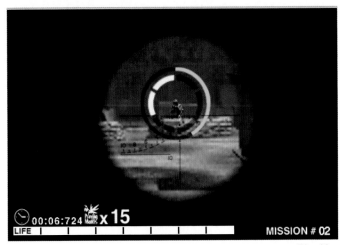

■ Pinching the screen will allow you to swap between weapons, meaning you'll be able to snipe out-of-range opponents.

effective, backgrounds are beautifully drawn, while effects like smoke and dust cling to the screen giving Kojima's game a really immersive feel.

Yes, you could argue that it's not going to take long to blast through the game and the gameplay itself can be incredibly simplistic at times, but that's a fault of this style of game rather than any issues on Kojima Productions' part.

It's certainly not the *Metal Gear Solid* we were expecting, but this is a perfectly enjoyable take on an age-old genre and Kojima and the rest of his team should be commended for coming up with such an enjoyable and easy-to-use interface. Fans of Snake will not be disappointed.

Ratings

Longevity	Fun factor	Practicality	Value
★★★	★★★★	★★★★★	★★★

Overall Rating ★★★★☆

■ It's possible to block and counter your opponent's moves.

■ Surprisingly the virtual D-pad works perfectly using touch controls.

Price: £3.99/$6.99 Developer: Gameloft

Blades Of Fury

A polished and feature-packed beat-'em-up

Gameloft must have some voodoo hidden up its sleeves. Against all odds it's managed to craft what's possibly the best control scheme for a beat-'em-up on the iPhone. The game offers the choice of a virtual joystick or D-pad for movement, with buttons on the right-hand side of the screen to control your attacks and defences. Using these it's easily possible to build up special attacks and combos. There are ten characters to choose from, each with their own set of weapons and moves. The game offers story, arcade, survival and practice modes, plus a multiplayer mode allowing two players to battle over Wi-Fi or Bluetooth. As you may have noticed from the screenshots on this page, the graphics are polished and sublime, and thankfully everything runs at a steady frame rate. Put simply, this is the greatest fighting game to be found in the App Store.

Ratings

Longevity	Fun factor	Practicality	Value
★★★★	★★★★★	★★★★	★★★★★

Overall Rating ★★★★★

Duke Nukem 3D

Price: £1.79/$2.99 **Developer:** MachineWorks Northwest LLC

It's time to kick ass and chew bubble gum

■ Can you guess what the two control sticks are meant to represent?

A perfect port of the original *Duke Nukem* PC game – one-liners and humour fully intact – this is a classic example of when control methods don't quite live up to expectations.

The game offers the choice of analogue or digital on-screen controls, the analogue controls bordering the screen as buttons and the digital method appearing as two control sticks – one for movement and one for aiming. Problems arise when trying to slide the control sticks. The game has trouble registering the movement of your fingers across the screen, resulting in frustrating taps to get Duke to move. We should note, however, that a patch is promised that will improve controls and the inconsistent frame rate.

Even with the problems listed above, it's hard not to be charmed by this shooter. With all three original episodes of the game, plus the four difficulty levels, there's a wealth of gameplay here.

Ratings

Longevity	Fun factor	Practicality	Value
★★★★☆	★★★☆☆	★★☆☆☆	★★★★★

Overall Rating ★★★★☆

Price: £4.99/$4.99 **Developer:** *Digital Legends*

Kroll

Advanced arcade action on the iPhone

There was much to do when the first 3D scrolling game came to the iPhone. Digital Legends Entertainment (the game's maker) claims the graphics to be the most advanced of any game on a mobile device so far and while it certainly looks good the beat-'em-up gameplay leaves a little to be desired. Much like the coin-operated games of the Eighties and Nineties, the basic controls of *Kroll* are left and right movement with two levels of attack. End-of-level bosses make things a little different with strategic taps needed to avoid being crushed, although the user's control over the actual combat at this stage is somewhat limited.

All in all, *Kroll* will be a great time-waster for those who used to spend countless amounts at the arcade, but it may not keep dedicated gamers hooked for very long. This game will no doubt pave the way for a host of brilliant scrolling games on the iPhone, unfortunately, *Kroll* just isn't the finished article.

■ The graphics in this game are excellent and gameplay is very good, but by no means perfect.

Ratings

Longevity	Fun factor	Practicality	Value
★★★☆☆	★★★☆☆	★★☆☆☆	★★★★☆

Overall Rating ★★★★☆

$135,450

■ Shoot hats first before moving on to varmints.

+$100 X 9

$86,800

Wild West Guns

Price: £0.59/$0.99
Developer: Gameloft

Are you a quick draw? You'll need to be…

Everything about this style of game says that it should get very boring incredibly quickly. You simply have to tap the screen to shoot an object. Gameloft has done itself proud, though, by using the Wild West theme very well and creating some incredibly cool moving levels that keep you on your toes, waiting for your foes to reveal themselves so you can blast them to smithereens. You start off slowly, shooting badges and sombreros, but it is not very long at all before you are chasing trains and shooting Native Americans off of horses. On top of that, Gameloft also throws in a few extras for you to sharp-shoot while you're busy battling the baddies. If you ever enjoyed *Time Crisis*, then you will certainly get a kick out of this. It's fast paced, a lot of fun and a great exercise in hand-to-eye co-ordination and reactions. Not to mention that you get to shoot at some varmints, too.

Ratings

Longevity	Fun factor	Practicality	Value
★★★★☆	★★★★★	★★☆☆☆	★★★★☆

Overall Rating ★★★★☆

Price: Free   **Developer:** Discovery Interactive Technology

So addictive that you'll put your life on hold

Cannon Challenge

Round 3 of 15
Score 9500
Shot 8 of 15

63 ELEVATION   FIRE!   73 VELOCITY

■ This app may look simple but that just makes it even better.

Cannon Challenge is one of those games that you just don't want to put down until you've completed every single last level and even then there's a good chance you'll want to pick it up all over again once you've finished it. The premise is really rather simple: blow everything up. You have controls on your tank for both trajectory and velocity, which you must alter to hit each of the targets in the level. You have 15 shells per level and there are 15 levels to negotiate in total. On top of that, you also have to alter the way you fire each shot to avoid hitting cliffs and rocks and various other obstacles that stand in your way. As you reach the later levels on *Cannon Challenge* you will need to have ever greater levels of accuracy and timing to proceed, and ramping up the difficulty even further, there are even moving targets towards the end! This game is stunningly simple and devastatingly brilliant. Download it. Download it now!

Ratings

Longevity	Fun factor	Practicality	Value
★★★★☆	★★★★☆	★★☆☆☆	★★★★★

Overall Rating ★★★★☆

Price: £0.59/$0.99 **Developer:** EDG Entertainment

Parachute Panic

Whatever you do, be sure not to panic

From the moment you view *Parachute Panic*'s hand-drawn stickman visuals and listen to its laid-back theme tune being hummed, you'll know you're holding something special in your hands.

Parachutists randomly leap from overhead planes and you must use gusts of wind – created by swiping your finger in any direction – to guide them to the boats at the bottom of the screen. Tapping a parachutist will open his 'chute and it's possible to leave the opening to the last minute in order to increase your score.

To make things more difficult a variety of different hazards ranging from thunderclouds to hungry sharks will do their best to get in your way. Needless to say, as the levels progress you'll find your reactions tested to the limit as the suicidal stickmen keep leaping to their doom. Smart, funny and clever, *Parachute Panic*'s 59p asking price makes it another essential download.

Ratings

Longevity	Fun factor	Practicality	Value
★★★★☆	★★★★☆	★★★★☆	★★★★★

Overall Rating ★★★★☆

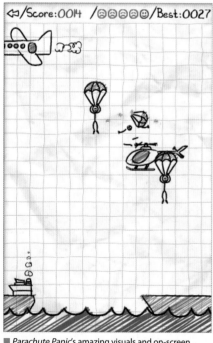

■ *Parachute Panic*'s amazing visuals and on-screen humour adds immensely to its charm.

Price: £0.59/$0.99 **Developer:** Click Gamer

Tankz

A simplistic game but very enjoyable nonetheless

At first glance, this game looks like it's been simplified too much and that the developers could have made a bit more of an effort in the design stakes. Once you start playing the game, however, these feelings will all dissipate as you absorb yourself in the task at hand; negotiating a battlefield in your tank, picking up tokens and destroying all of your enemies. Controls are rather simple and intuitive. You can use the accelerometer to move the barrel of your cannon left and right, and then a direction pad to move your tank forwards, backwards, left and right. You then also have a rapid-fire gun and a store of missiles at your disposal. In each level you have to negotiate a number of enemy tanks and towers, while picking up tokens at the same time. We enjoyed this game a lot and found it to be a lot of fun; it's great value for money and a nice addition to your iPhone games collection.

Ratings

Longevity	Fun factor	Practicality	Value
★★★★☆	★★★★☆	★★☆☆☆	★★★★☆

Overall Rating ★★★☆☆

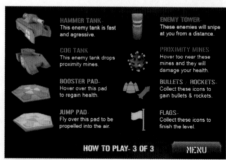

■ The action is fast and furious.

Price: £1.79/$2.99 **Developer:** Digital Chocolate

Crazy Penguin Catapult 2

Flying penguins and angry polar bears. What's not to like?

In real life, penguins and polar bears live at opposite ends of the Earth, but a little piece of trivia like that won't stop Digital Chocolate.

This sequel doesn't add much to the original, bar a few extra power-ups and new levels, but don't let that put you off, as flinging penguins at shaggy bears has never been so much fun.

Split into two stages, you'll first have to load up your penguins by launching them from your catapult at the correct time. After that it's time to use your penguins to dive-bomb the opposing polar bears; hit enough and you'll move on to the next stage.

Despite its simple touch controls, cartoon visuals and zany concept, there's a surprising amount of strategy involved here and despite a plethora of power-ups it's going to take a fair while to complete all the available stages. You'll be doing so with a huge smile on your face, though.

Ratings

Longevity	Fun factor	Practicality	Value
★★★☆☆	★★★★☆	★★★★★	★★★☆☆

Overall Rating ★★★☆☆

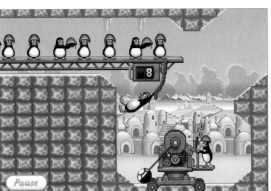

■ *Crazy Penguin*'s humour is abundant from the very beginning.

Price: Free **Developer:** IDP

Space Deadbeef

In space no one can here you swear

If there's one genre that suffers most on the iPhone it's the shoot-'em-up. While huge leaps and bounds have been made, titles like *Space Deadbeef* are a throwback to earlier days, when virtual sticks hadn't even been considered by developers.

Rather than use accelerometer controls like many other games, IDP came up with the idea of controlling your ship with simple up and down swipes. It's a clever enough idea, until you realise that tapping on an enemy ship to destroy it moves your ship as well and it's all too easy to fly into incoming bullets.

Some praise this risk-versus-reward gameplay, but the truth of the matter is that it is simply far too fiddly due to the response of the touch screen. As a result *Space Deadbeef* often becomes an exercise in frustration, which is a great shame. Still it's free at least, so give it a try. You may just like it.

Ratings

Longevity	Fun factor	Practicality	Value
★★☆☆☆	★★☆☆☆	★★★☆☆	★★★☆☆

Overall Rating ★★☆☆☆

■ Bosses are plentiful and soak up an insane amount of bullets.

■ It's a constant battle avoiding bullets as you lock on to enemies.

Price: £1.19/$1.99 **Developer:** Kiss The Machine

Reversi

The classic strategy game in its smallest form

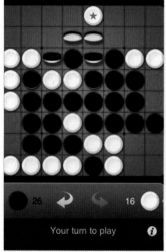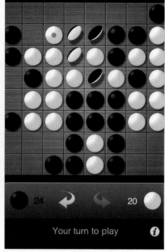

■ Anyone wanting quick satisfaction may want to give *Reversi* a miss.

Oddly enough, the best aspect of Kiss The Machine's *Reversi* is that it sticks to the basics. Bringing the classic game to the iPhone, it has all the standard features anyone would expect: multiplayer, a very well-rounded difficulty curve and a hints mechanic, teaching beginners how they should proceed. If you've ever been intrigued about Reversi and fancy wasting a few minutes on the train, then this is your best bet, especially when you take a look at some of the alternatives (that may or may not contain 'interesting' images of women).

It needs to be said that, even with the tips for those not familiar with the basics, this version is clearly for those who take their Reversi quite seriously. If, of course, this applies to you, then the cheapish price point and ease of use will appeal. Anyone else may want to wait until it drops to around 59 pence.

Ratings

Longevity	Fun factor	Practicality	Value
★★★☆☆	★★☆☆☆	★★★☆☆	★★☆☆☆

Overall Rating ★★★★☆

Price: £1.19/$1.99 **Developer:** Chillingo

Cyber Chess

Bringing a touch of class and nobility to the iPhone

 Chess is one of those games that we all love to play now and then – and we love it even more when we're good at it! So, does *Cyber Chess* have a wide enough appeal to interest those who are just learning the ways of this ancient game, as well as those who think they're the bee's knees? Emphatically, yes. Not only do you get a computer to play against with simple level settings for beginners right through to advanced, but you can even take the game online and play against rated players, which is possibly the game's best feature.

On top of that, you can have a live chat with them to plead for mercy, or chuckle as you destroy their defences. *Cyber Chess* is also refreshingly well priced for the content it holds, so if you don't already play chess then this is a great time for you to start out. If you do, there's more than enough here to provide you with a real challenge.

■ The different game modes let you play against the computer or against other iPhone owners.

Ratings

Longevity	Fun factor	Practicality	Value
★★★★★	★★★★☆	★★★★☆	★★★★★

Overall Rating ★★★★★

Domino

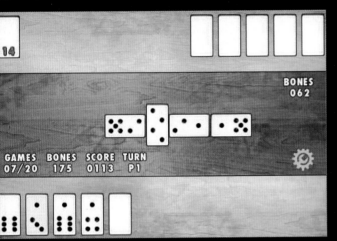

■ As ever, there's a multitude of different boards on offer. They're all okay…

■ Although there are enough single-player options to keep things interesting, multiplayer is far more compelling.

Price: £0.59/$0.99   Developer: Soneso

As old as time itself, dominoes makes its comeback on the iPhone

 It's only fair to say dominoes aren't as popular as they once were. Losing esteem over the last couple of decades, a select group of people would say the art has been lost. With all that said, Soneso's app is a moderately amusing, and cheap, attempt. Offering up four different versions and a much appreciated tutorial system to teach those not up with the format, it even boasts a form of online play through a worldwide scoring system.

Naturally, considering the nature of the game, having a touch screen at your disposal makes *Domino* ridiculously easy to use. Whether or not you'll be able to get some serious legs out of it depends on your love of the game, but at 59p you'd be hard-pushed to feel ripped off, even if you played it for a week. *Domino* certainly isn't groundbreaking but takes the age-old idea and makes it, somewhat, relevant again.

Ratings

Longevity	Fun factor	Practicality	Value
★★☆☆☆	★★☆☆☆	★★★☆☆	★★★☆☆

Overall Rating ★★★☆☆

Price: £0.59/$0.99   Developer: Liberty For One

The real reason PCs came into existence in the first place

Minesweeper Classic

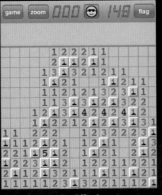

■ Cranking up the difficulty presents a challenge worthy of the greatest Minesweeper players.

■ Nothing is more frustrating than almost clearing the screen, and then hitting one of the bombs.

 Let's face it: iPhone apps, on the whole, are relatively cheap. With that said, we still believe it's hard to justify spending any money on *Minesweeper Classic*. A staple of any computer from the last 15 years, you simply tap a square to attempt to clear it. Any number that appears is an indicator of how many bombs are waiting in the adjacent squares. Find one of these and that happy little dude at the top of the screen starts to cry and it's game over. As ever having the touch screen makes playing it easier than ever, but *Minesweeper* has never been known for its longevity – it's usually what you do when you've become a little bored of *Solitaire*.

To Liberty For One's credit there's an impressive amount of options for an idea so simple, and the expert difficulty levels will test even the most skilled player. Again though, the premise, as it always has, gets very tedious, very fast.

Ratings

Longevity	Fun factor	Practicality	Value
★★☆☆☆	★★★☆☆	★★★☆☆	★★★☆☆

Overall Rating ★★☆☆☆

Price: £2.39/$3.99 **Developer:** Polarbit

Raging Thunder

Accelerometer steering is all the rage in this fun racer

There are now a whole host of racing games on the iPhone that use the device's built-in accelerometer to help you steer, and they seem to be getting better and better. *Raging Thunder* is by far the most graphically superior we've played so far. As well as being extremely fast and action-packed, it allows for online play, meaning you can pit your driving skills against other virtual petrol-heads from all around the world.

The best aspects of the game are high-speed banked corners and the ability to wreck other cars. The worst is the lack of a course map. If you're into racing games then this is a definite must-have app. If you're lucky you may even get it at a sale price, as Polarbit is known to discount games every now and then. There's definitely an evolution going on with regards to racing games, and Polarbit is edging its way to the top of the pile with this extremely well-made game.

Ratings

Longevity	Fun factor	Practicality	Value
★★★★☆	★★★★★	★★☆☆☆	★★★★★

Overall Rating ★★★★★

■ Cool banked corners add an extra element to this game. The action is frenetic and the graphics are great.

■ One of the best aspects of the game is the ability to smash into opponents' cars to wreck them.

Price: £0.59/$0.99 **Developer:** Gameloft

Asphalt 4: Elite Racing

■ The nitros are fun, giving you a massive speed boost as you race it out against CPU opponents through the streets of well-known cities.

Price: Free **Developer:** Storm8

Racing Live

MMO comes to the iPhone (well, sort of)

This game is a racing management simulation with a twist, as it's also an MMO. This means that when you use it, you are playing against millions (2.2 million according to iTunes) of other people. You take control of a basic car and have to work your way through standard races and drag races, accumulating cash and buying more and more powerful cars. You also gain experience points as you go, which determines whether or not you can beat your opponents. The interface is well made and looks slick, while the challenges are pretty cool. However, there's a distinct lack of action when it comes to the actual races. A result just instantly pops up, which falls a bit flat on its face really. Having said that, sitting through ready-made animations would probably have also grated on the patience. All in all, this is a cool game that's available for nothing, and announces itself as an interesting entrant into the world of MMO gaming.

Feeling the need for speed? This street racer may be for you

Asphalt 4 falls into the street racing category as you get to race Ferraris, Aston Martins, Bugattis and other super-fast sports cars through 12 cities including New York, Paris, Shanghai and Dubai.

The intro and menu interface are extremely slick and very well made, but we can't help feeling a little disappointed with the gameplay. It might be that we have very high standards now, but this game just didn't do it for us. We were impressed with the different control options, though. You can choose to use the accelerometer for steering, a wheel that appears on the screen or you can use a tap of the finger on the left or right of the car. The graphics are good, but gameplay overall is pretty standard. The nitro boosts make life interesting, as does being chased by the police, which gives it a *Fast And The Furious* feel. However, there are a number of better racing games out there. We're sure that with some updates, this game will improve.

Ratings

Longevity	Fun factor	Practicality	Value
★★★☆☆	★★★☆☆	★★☆☆☆	★★★☆☆

Overall Rating ★★★☆☆

■ Choose a rival crew to race against.

■ You can get your hands on some supercars, once you've earned some serious cash in the game.

Ratings

Longevity	Fun factor	Practicality	Value
★★★★☆	★★★★★	★★☆☆☆	★★★★★

Overall Rating ★★★★☆

■ Race the road ragged with this super high-speed game…

Price: £0.59/$0.99 **Developer:** Atod AB

Fastlane Street Racing

Weave through the traffic on winding city routes

There are so many racing games available for the iPhone that it's difficult to choose between most of them. What *Fastlane* has in its locker is a very cool look and feel and some great gameplay.

From the outset this looks slick and polished. Once you've negotiated through the menus and selected the game mode (from five options) and car of your choice (from ten), you have to finish each course in a high enough position to unlock the next one. It's a typical arcade-style structure.

Driving is a matter of using the accelerator button on the right or the brake on the left and then using a tilting action to steer left and right. Graphically, the game impresses and the courses are a mixture of race circuits and winding city routes. Currently available at a bargain price, this is definitely one of the best racing games on the iPhone, setting the benchmark even higher for apps to come.

Ratings

Longevity	Fun factor	Practicality	Value
★★★★☆	★★★★☆	★★☆☆☆	★★★★★

Overall Rating ★★★★☆

Price: £1.19/$1.99 Developer: LimeLife

Fashion Mogul

Business games are just so last year, darling...

Games like *Lemonade Tycoon* have shown that the iPhone, while perhaps under-equipped when it comes to doing full business simulators, is more than capable of running something on a smaller scale. *Fashion Mogul* aims to fall somewhere between your own lemonade stand and the transcontinental railroads and theme park empires of the desktop *Tycoon* games, and it's quite successful in this aim.

Starting with a small boutique, you aim to build your company across the increasingly competitive fashion centres – London, Milan, New York etc – all the way to the ultimate destination of the world's style capital: Paris. Like the industry on which it's based, however, it's only skin-deep, as the game's not really any different to most of its competitors. There's very little here that you wouldn't find in any other business game. *Fashion Mogul* is still decent at what it does, though, and fashionistas will no doubt enjoy the theme. Just don't expect anything special.

Ratings

Longevity	Fun factor	Practicality	Value
★★★★☆	★★★☆☆	★★★★☆	★★★☆☆

Overall Rating ★★★☆☆

■ The bright graphics suit the game's theme well and look quite appealing.

■ There's not all that much to differentiate between the various cities.

Price: £0.59/$0.99 Developer: Firemint

Flight Control

One of the standout games of the year

You can tell when an app has got everyone's attention, because all of a sudden a ton of suspiciously similar apps appear on the App Store to try and take a cut of its profits. That's exactly what happened with *Flight Control*, and although the developer was probably a little annoyed at the copycats, Firemint should just be flattered instead.

In *Flight Control*, you take charge of an airstrip and have to land the planes that come your way by dragging a line between them onto the runway. As more and more planes arrive on the screen, you have to make more elaborate flight paths for the planes to fly on in order to avoid any crashes. The more planes that you land, the higher your score. This game is brilliantly simple, addictive, frustrating and rewarding. There is a multiplayer option, but it's not as good as the single-player mode, so stick to that.

Pencil Doodle

Draw and sketch away, but beware if you create a stick man!

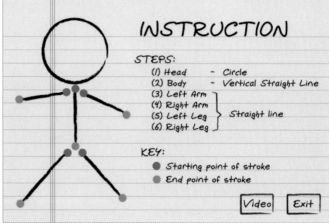

■ Create a little scenario that will benefit from the animated character and will keep you occupied for one, maybe two minutes.

■ The Info screen shows exactly how to create a stick man that will then come to life.

RAFT LANDED: 00011   HI SCORE: 00089

■ Pushing tin on the iPhone can soon get pretty stressful.

Ratings

Longevity	Fun factor	Practicality	Value
★★★★★	★★★★★	★★★☆☆	★★★★★

Overall Rating ★★★★★

Price: £0.59/$0.99 **Developer:** Cross-Discipline Technology

There are some applications and games that defy all logic. Welcome to the very strange concept of *Pencil Doodle*. Start the app and there's a yellow notepad, two pencils and an eraser. Okay, so you can draw stuff and erase it. All well and good. Where it enters David Lynch territory is if you draw a stick figure that the app recognises. Suddenly from a half-assed sketchbook, the stick man gets a face added and starts moving around, waving arms and legs. No, really, he does, though you may feel that you've had one too many when you see it work. The key is to draw a figure with specific end points, which the info page shows, otherwise Mr Sticky will just sit there. Get it right – and it isn't hard – and he comes to life. He even moans if you prod him and you can grab him by the head and move him. Obviously there's a world of missed opportunity here, like providing props to play with, being able to erase a leg and make him hop, or both legs and make him crawl. That would be funny. As it is, this is clever but ultimately pointless.

Ratings

Longevity	Fun factor	Practicality	Value
★★☆☆☆	★★☆☆☆	★★★☆☆	★★☆☆☆

Overall Rating ★★☆☆☆

Price: £0.59/$0.99 **Developer:** Kalio Ltda

TriDefense

Defend the tower to the last man. Then send for the women and kids

While the concept of tower defence games can seem like an exercise in lazy gameplay – it is, after all, like playing half of *Command & Conquer* – if it's done well, it's a viable genre for handheld gaming. The good news is that despite only being a pre-release at the moment (v0.9), *TriDefense* is done very well. There are two skill levels and three types of defensive weaponry that can be employed to fend off escalating attacks on the base, or tower. The trick is to place them most effectively at the start, so they destroy enough of the opposition to enable you to buy more units for increasingly heavy attacks. There's also terraforming, which adds a neat tactical twist. *TriDefense* successfully marries C&C-style graphics with impressive sound effects and challenging gameplay. Control is familiar pinch and pull for zooming, and tapping for unit placement. Buy it now with one main level and there's a free upgrade when v1.0 is released.

Ratings

Longevity	Fun factor	Practicality	Value
★★★★☆	★★★★☆	★★★★☆	★★★★★

Overall Rating ★★★★☆

Mission 01: Operations Base

Your mission is to secure a foothold for our forces to establish a forward operations base. Intelligence reports a massive enemy counter-offensive moving to your position from the North. Also keep an eye on the shores. You have been given full weapon systems authorization for this mission. Good luck!

Mission Objectives:

- Protect the Forward Operations

EXPERT   ROOKIE

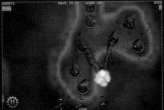

■ The missions are nicely presented at the start of a level and if you find it too tough, it can be played on Rookie level as well.

■ You can dig holes and add land to try to divert the attackers into long routes round and through concentrated fire positions.

Price: £0.59/$0.99 **Developer:** Chillingo

iPingpong 3D

Table tennis has never been so cool...

When it comes to porting sports from real life to computer games, table tennis doesn't have the world-renowned stars to make giant franchises in the same way as Tiger Woods has done with golf. That said, this classic indoor sport has made it successfully onto the iPhone, thanks to the team at Chillingo.

iPingpong is a lot of fun and infuriatingly addictive. You move your bat using a finger, and can, with practice, do everything from super-powerful smashes to devastatingly tricky swerve shots. In Tournament mode you can fight your way up the rankings to become king of pong. For 59p this game is a must for anyone with a competitive sporting streak.

Ratings

Longevity	Fun factor	Practicality	Value
★★★★★	★★★★★	★★★☆☆	★★★★★

Overall Rating ★★★★★

Price: £2.39/$3.99 **Developer:** Stephane Portha

Ace Tennis Online

Serve, tilt and volley

 Ah, tennis. The game of kings. And now you can play it on your iPhone. We weren't really expecting a great deal from this game as tennis simulations are pretty hit and miss on consoles, but as it turns out, the controls are intuitive and it's a lot of fun. Use your thumbs to move your player left and right, and then dictate the movement of your shot using the accelerometer. Left and right tilts do as you would expect, and forward and back tilts can throw lobs and drop shots into the equation too. Graphically *Ace Tennis Online* isn't as advanced as many other games we've played, but what it lacks in polish it makes up for in decent gameplay and manages to put the accelerometer to good use. You can also compete with players all over the world, and it only takes a few seconds to find an online opponent to test your skills against.

Ratings

Longevity	Fun factor	Practicality	Value
★★★☆☆	★★★★☆	★★★☆☆	★★★★☆

Overall Rating ★★★★☆

■ The graphics aren't massively advanced, but that's not important when you're prowling the baseline...

Price: £0.59/$0.99 **Developer:** Freeverse

Flick Fishing

Enjoy the tranquillity of fishing without leaving your house

The fact that Freeverse even considered creating a fishing game for the iPhone is a real testament to the versatility of the device. In this well-made game you use the accelerometer to cast a line into the sea or a lake and then, when you get a bite, you reel your fish in. Not only can you play for a bit of fun, you can also enter tournaments and fish in the toughest of conditions. The controls are very simple, making this a great game to pick up any time. You run your finger around a virtual spool to reel in your fish and can cast as many times as you want to get the ultimate spot on the water. You can even change bait to try to coax the fish onto your hook. For just 59p, *Flick Fishing* represents fantastic value coupled with incredible playability. A really fun app, especially for those with fond memories of *Sega Bass Fishing* on the Dreamcast.

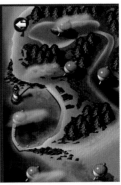

Ratings _____

Longevity	Fun factor	Practicality	Value
★★★★☆	★★★★☆	★★☆☆☆	★★★★☆

Overall Rating ★★★★☆

Price: £2.99/$4.99 **Developer:** Big Head Games Ltd

International Snooker

Can you make a 147 break?

As much as we like playing pool, it's just not quite as sophisticated as snooker, so we were very pleased to download *International Snooker* and get working on a 147 break. The game is well built, has good graphics and is extremely enjoyable; the only drawback we've seen is that there is an occasional lag on the processing of ball movements, which can be quite annoying when lining up a crucial shot. Apart from that, the creator has thought of everything. You get an easy-to-read directional guide for cueing shots, you can adjust the power and spin easily, as well as your viewing angle. This is perhaps not a game to dip in and out of, but one that to which you can easily lose a good few hours as you try to win the championship.

■ It takes a huge amount of patience and skill to hit that elusive 147 break. Give it a go.

Ratings _____

Longevity	Fun factor	Practicality	Value
★★★★☆	★★★★★	★★★☆☆	★★★★☆

Overall Rating ★★★★☆

Price: £2.99/$4.99 Developer: Chillingo

Orions: Legends Of Wizards

A strange but effective take on role-play and Top Trumps

This game is quite a departure from many games available on the App Store. It's a strategy title where you use cards with different properties to defeat the cards used by your opponent. Each set of cards has different powers and values, and as you drag them into play they can be used to take points from the cards your enemy lays down. The ultimate aim of the game is to defeat everyone in your path and conquer different realms. It's not for everyone and can be tough to learn, but if you want to be the ultimate warrior in the realm then this is the game for you.

■ A great-looking game with cool graphics.

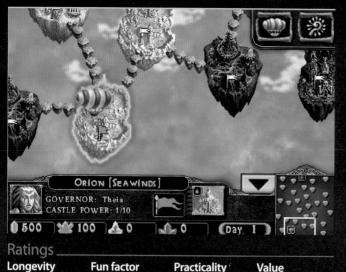

Ratings

Longevity	Fun factor	Practicality	Value
★★★★☆	★★★★☆	★★☆☆☆	★★★☆☆

Overall Rating ★★★☆☆

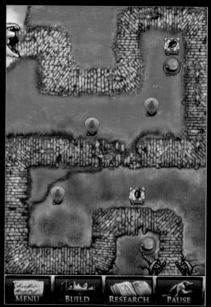

Price: Free Developer: Tapjoy.com

Tap Defense

Classic tower defence comes to iPhone free of charge

This is one of the best free games on the App Store without a shadow of doubt. Well made, expansive and incredibly engaging, this is another game in the siege genre and sees you battling all manner of fantasy beasts. Using the familiar top-down view, you have to put up defences along the path that the enemy treads. There are several game modes and environment options, and the range of weapons you can use to defeat your foes is extremely cool indeed. As you would expect, the levels start off easy and then quickly become more frantic. Unusually, we really enjoyed the sounds in this game. The music was fitting and the sound effects equally so. We highly recommend this application and encourage all developers of free apps to follow in its footsteps and develop to a high standard. A brilliant game that you'll really enjoy attempting to complete.

Ratings

Longevity	Fun factor	Practicality	Value
★★★★★	★★★★★	★★★☆☆	★★★★★

Overall Rating ★★★★★

■ Yet another sumptuously designed iPhone application.

Price: £0.59/$0.99 Developer: Chillingo

Knights Onrush

Flex your fingers and protect your castle

The siege genre – in which you must protect a base and then use a host of weapons to stop oncoming foes – has flourished on iPhone. In *Knights Onrush*, you live in the realm of the knights and have a castle to protect. You have a two-dimensional view, your enemies run at your castle and you have to pick them off using a flick of the finger. You can fire them into the air, hang them from a post for a medieval dragon to eat, or place them in a pit of lava. As you progress through the levels, you have the option to buy more advanced defences and weapons. The graphics have a cool cartoon look and the sound effects are a lot of fun. The levels start off easy, but you'll soon be frantically flicking knights all over the place and cursing their sheer numbers. This game is a lot of fun and really makes you want to beat it. A great-quality app.

Ratings

Longevity	Fun factor	Practicality	Value
★★★☆☆	★★★★★	★★★☆☆	★★★★★

Overall Rating ★★★★☆

Price: £0.59/$0.99 Developer: John E Hartzog

Stick Wars

The siege comes in stick format

Another game in the siege genre, *Stick Wars* has you doing battle with an oncoming army of stick men. At first they wield sticks and swords, but as levels progress they ride in on horses and then try and use drills to break your defences. As you successfully defend your perimeter wall through each level, you gain points and can strengthen your defences with extra wall protection. We love the fact that you can get a prison, create archers and even make bombs. The main area of defence remains your own quick fingers, though, as you have to flick your opponents out of the way as they charge. In the first few levels this is a very simple, and as levels progress your fingers become more frantic. *Stick Wars* is very enjoyable game that can quickly become addictive. It's not as graphically superior as some of its rivals on the App Store, but that doesn't make it any less engaging.

Ratings

Longevity	Fun factor	Practicality	Value
★★★★☆	★★★★☆	★★☆☆☆	★★★★☆

Overall Rating ★★★★☆

■ Be warned: there is a fair bit of gore involved.

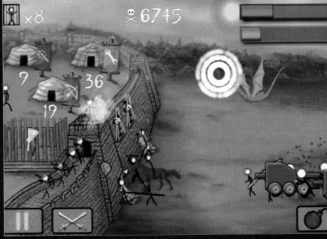

■ Getting rid of the hoard is flicking simple.

Gangstar: West Coast Hustle

■ Combat and shooting biatches is easy thanks to *Gangstar's* solid lock-on controls.

■ Vehicles are accelerometer based and require a hell of a lot of time to get used to.

Price: £3.99/$6.99 **Developer:** Gameloft

Gameloft achieves the impossible dream: GTA on the iPhone

We're seeing it but we still can't quite believe it. Gameloft has created an amazing *GTA* clone for the iPhone. Forget the top-down efforts that already exist as this is the real 3D deal. Technically incredible and with a huge open game world, *Gangstar* is an utterly superb title that shows just how much untapped potential the iPhone still has.

Plot-wise, it's as generic as they come, but still entertains as you steer a low-level crim named PThug to notoriety. Missions are varied and range from simple deliveries to extravagant hits, while the colourful characters you interact with are just as memorable as those from *GTA*. Even combat is extremely good thanks to a great lock-on system that makes scraps and gunfights a breeze.

Only a lack of side quests and the tricky accelerometer-assisted driving sections let down what is otherwise a stunning achievement. More please Gameloft.

Ratings

Longevity	Fun factor	Practicality	Value
★★★★☆	★★★★★	★★★★☆	★★★☆☆

Overall Rating ★★★★★

Assassin's Creed: Altair's Chronicles

■ Considering the price, six hours of gameplay is a fantastic bang for your buck.

■ Fighting is enjoyable throughout and has far more depth than it has any right to.

Price: £2.99/$4.99 **Developer:** Gameloft

The path of the assassin stretches to the iPhone

There are sceptics out there who claim the iPhone isn't capable of being a handheld gaming device; *Assassin's Creed* is the perfect evidence against such cynicism. Based on the Nintendo DS version, this is easily one of the best 'traditional' games to appear on Apple's gadget. Following a similar template to the original, it sees Altair hunting down an artefact known as 'the chalice' in the hope of bringing The Crusades to an end. Controlling our protagonist with the ever more common on-screen stick and buttons, it's remarkably easy to get comfortable with and only enhances the experience. Whether using stealth to creep past enemies or encountering them head-on, it's surprising how solid *Assassin's Creed* is on every level and a credit to Gameloft. Not only a great game in its own right, but also proof of the potential the iPhone has of being a gaming platform.

Ratings

Longevity	Fun factor	Practicality	Value
★★★★☆	★★★★☆	★★★☆☆	★★★★☆

Overall Rating ★★★★☆

■ Tracks get progressively harder, as do your opponents. Controls are easy to use and great fun.

■ Racing through a tunnel, you only have two more cars to overtake to make it into the lead.

Price: £2.99/$4.99 **Developer:** Chillingo

GTS World Racing

Race on tracks all over the world with your iPhone

On your marks. Get set. Tilt! *GTS World Racing* is a racing game that uses the iPhone's accelerometer to control every aspect of gameplay. You tilt the phone forwards to accelerate, back to brake, and left and right to steer. The controls are very intuitive and the game maker has built in a fail-safe to stop people having the phone tipped too far forward when accelerating, which comes in the form of a pink screen with a 'Too Flat!' warning.

There are a wide range of gameplay options: Single Race, Challenge Cup featuring 16 circuits, Challenge Tour that will have you racing a total of 64 times, and Championship that will have you battling it out 16 times. There are also four difficulty levels that not only increase the competitiveness of your opponents, but make each track that bit trickier too. You can also race head-to-head with a friend over Wi-Fi in this fun-filled game.

Ratings

Longevity	Fun factor	Practicality	Value
★★★★☆	★★★★★	★★★☆☆	★★★★☆

Overall Rating ★★★★★

Price: £1.19/$1.99 **Developer:** Freeverse

Moto Chaser

Ride like the wind, punch like a hard nut

This was one of the first games to be made available on the App Store, and at the time it was £5.99. But the price has now been dropped considerably, so it really is worth the money. It's another good example of accelerometer gaming, requiring players to control a motorbike by moving the iPhone in the direction they want to steer. The gas button provides the option to open the throttle and give it a good handful. *Moto Chaser* plays out on a time-trial basis, and as well as very cool cut-away jump sequences you also get the opportunity to punch others off their bikes in a very *Road Rash* kind of way. Our only gripe is that the learning curve is quite steep: we found the levels got quite difficult straight away without giving us enough rewards in the early stages. That said, it could be because we're rubbish at motorbike games. *Moto Chaser* offers good gameplay with great graphics.

Ratings

Longevity	Fun factor	Practicality	Value
★★★★☆	★★★★☆	★★☆☆☆	★★★★★

Overall Rating ★★★★☆

■ The graphics are great and you really get the feeling of speed as you play, but that does make the controls tough.

■ Select from several racing locations, some of which need to be unlocked as you play.

Health & Fitness

Being healthy is easy if you have the right tools to help you stay that way. The iPhone has many such tools which can genuinely change your life for the better

Price: £0.59/$0.99 **Developer:** Mastersoft Mobile Solutions

My Last Cigarette

Can a simple software program really help you to give up the weed? Yes...

It is very easy to dismiss tools which claim to help you give up smoking as nothing more than gimmicks, but in the right hands they can be extremely powerful tools. It is important to remember that will power is required above all else in such a situation and that extra tools can only act as guides to help you achieve your ultimate goal. My Last Cigarette from Mastersoft Mobile Solutions is based on medical fact and uses a variety of useful methods to help keep you off cigarettes for as long as possible; everything from cost savings to the harmful effects are covered and crucially it acts as a reference point for you to wallow in your success by recording your progress. This is an important part of giving up any habit and the better you feel about yourself, the more likely you are to stay away from tobacco in future.

The graphical interface works by showing you how long you've managed to go since you last had a cigarette as well as providing

■ Daily pictures highlight how much damage can be done through continued smoking.

■ You can check to see how much money you have saved whenever you like.

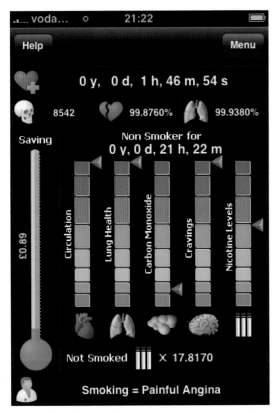

■ The interface is clean, concise and very effective.

you with medical information, including your carbon monoxide, nicotine and circulation levels. Straight off the bat you are presented, in a highly obvious manner, with a whole list of effects smoking has on you and as you keep off the cigarettes, so you will see the levels drop. It is a simple and visual method, but one which works incredibly well in practice. It goes further by showing daily pictures of parts of the body and how they are affected by smoking as well as implementing a simple savings calculator. Seeing how much money has been saved offers an extra spur in which you can reward yourself for giving up one of the most addictive drugs in the world.

My Last Cigarette may sound like a bit of a gimmick, but it's really not and it doesn't promise miracles, but its presentation and professionalism offer a truly effective method of curing yourself, and for that we have to recommend it highly. Having such a positive and helpful tool with you all of the time makes it all the more useful and if you are feeling weak, simply start up the application and look at what you have achieved so far as it should get you right back on track. It would be a shame to give up on your success, just as it would be to pass up this app.

Ratings

Longevity	Fun factor	Practicality	Value
★★★★☆	★★★★☆	★★★★★	★★★★★

Overall Rating ★★★★★

Price: £0.59/$0.99 Developer: SoftwareX Ltd

Two Hundred Sit-Ups

Get the six pack you always wanted with an app and effort

Sit-ups are arguably the most dreaded of all exercises and many people cringe at the idea of even doing one. Two Hundred Sit-Ups takes a pragmatic approach to this by offering a plan which builds up your daily sit-up regime to the point at which you can boast about doing 200. Not only does it present you with a daily sit-up count to undertake, but it also includes information on how to do a sit-up properly. You can check your progress by looking at the timeline graph or by simply looking at your stomach. No matter how you check your progress, Two Hundred Sit-Ups is a simple app which can help you provided you're prepared to make the effort to help yourself. Sometimes just having a record of your achievement is enough to keep you going and trying to reach the next goal, and this app takes all of the complexity out of building a belly to be proud of.

Ratings

Longevity	Fun factor	Practicality	Value
★★★★☆	★★★☆☆	★★★★☆	★★★★☆

Overall Rating ★★★★☆

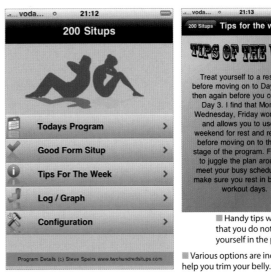

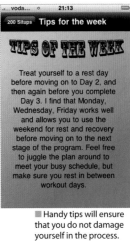

■ Handy tips will ensure that you do not damage yourself in the process.

■ Various options are included to help you trim your belly.

Healing Cards

Price: £2.39/$3.99 Developer: Oceanhouse Media, Inc

A beautiful and healing pack of cards dealing out lots of positivity

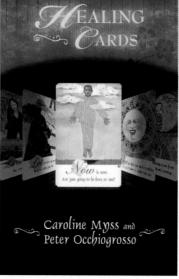

■ Lots of attention has been paid to the design of each card.

■ The scrolling card wheel is a beautiful introduction to the app.

The secret behind staying positive and happy in life is to embrace the concept of helping yourself. Beyond that the simplest of tools can be beneficial and Healing Cards from developer Oceanhouse Media is a good example of a simple app which can have a positive effect on you and your life. Healing Cards is simply a set of 50 cards which contain inspiring messages and descriptive reasoning on the back of each to help you stay in a positive frame of mind. The entire setup is beautiful to look at and the accompanying sounds add to the enchantment. The cards can be used as wallpaper or emailed to your friends to give them a lift as well, and taking the time to view one a day will soon become habitual, in a positive way of course. It is a simple concept and not the cheapest app in the App Store, but Healing Cards certainly has merits which could help you in a variety of ways.

Ratings

Longevity	Fun factor	Practicality	Value
★★★☆☆	★★★★☆	★★★☆☆	★★★☆☆

Overall Rating ★★★★☆

Price: £5.99/$9.99 Developer: Wolfgang Held

B.iCycle

Serious about cycling? B.iCycle is the ideal tool for your travels

You can buy devices which help you track cycling trips, but they tend to be dedicated to performing only one function. B.iCycle, on the other hand, takes the process of tracking your cycling trips to a whole new level and offers more stats than you can imagine alongside GPS tracking on moving maps and even the ability to receive trips via email for testing yourself. The B.iCycle interface is very clean and the map view is particularly impressive, which adds to the fun and usefulness. Over 70,000 people are apparently mapping bike trails around the globe so you should easily be able to use this app to explore new cycle routes whenever you like. It is of course an app designed for keen cyclists, but it includes almost every conceivable feature you could need. Please remember to take care when using an app like this on the move, and to ensure that your iPhone is secured properly before you start peddling.

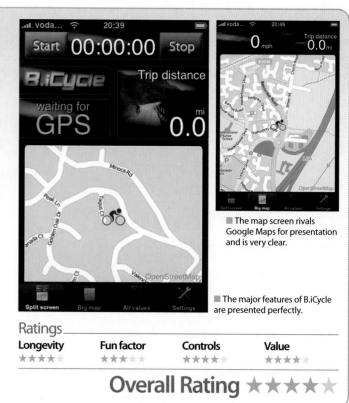

■ The map screen rivals Google Maps for presentation and is very clear.

■ The major features of B.iCycle are presented perfectly.

Ratings

Longevity	Fun factor	Controls	Value
★★★★☆	★★★☆☆	★★★★☆	★★★★☆

Overall Rating ★★★★☆

Price: £0.59/$0.99 **Developer:** made-up software

Track your weight loss daily to see how successful your diet really is

True Weight

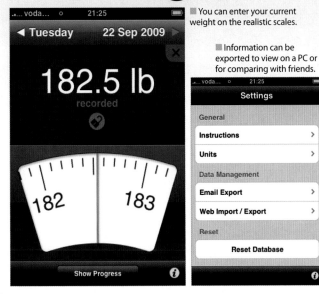

■ You can enter your current weight on the realistic scales.

■ Information can be exported to view on a PC or for comparing with friends.

Dieting is possibly the most common health activity we undertake in the Western world, but it is one that we are seldom particularly good at. One reason for this is that we do not track how successfully our changed eating habits are affecting us and therefore it is easy to lose track of where we are going wrong. True Weight lets you track your weight loss every single day and builds into a database which you can use to see which foods affect your weight. Checking each day also means that you will remember where you have gone wrong and this will benefit you further along in your diet regime. It is a simplistic application which offers basic monitoring, but with exporting capabilities built in you should not need much more. It is not a miracle diet aid, but it is a start and one which will help some people lose those precious pounds.

Ratings

Longevity	Fun factor	Practicality	Value
★★★★	★★	★★★	★★★

Overall Rating ★★★★★

101 Stress Busters
Price: Free **Developer:** Samir Roy

Reduce your stress with some concise advice

Few apps on the App Store are as simple as Samir Roy's useful 101 Stress Busters, but that does not mean that the software has little merit. It is in essence a list of short sentences which offer tips on how to reduce your stress levels, and these range from simple tasks to more fundamental changes. The simplicity is what makes it so effective and just reading one piece of advice from the app every day may have a positive effect on your outlook. Advice like 'Avoid tight fitting clothes' sounds rather bizarre, but when you consider it for a moment there is merit in such a statement. With an emphasis placed on letting the text shine through, there is little to see here and that is ironically what makes it such a worthwhile download. You may not use this app for long, but, on the other hand, you may well gain a nugget or two of useful advice for the future and with it being free who are we to complain?

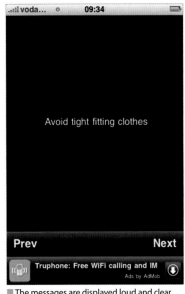

■ This app is as simple as it can be, but it has a certain charm.

■ The messages are displayed loud and clear.

Ratings

Longevity	Fun factor	Practicality	Value
★★	★★★★	★★	★★★★

Overall Rating ★★★★★

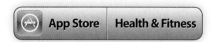

App Store | Health & Fitness

■ Input your data honestly for the most accurate result.

■ Seeing how long you have left to live can be slightly depressing.

Price: Free   **Developer:** Richard Rockhold

LifeCalc

Do you really want to know how long you have left to live?

Richard Rockhold's LifeCalc app will either be seen as a bit of fun or something that you will never ever want to look at. It uses data that has been inputted by you to guess how long you have left to live. Information such as smoking habits, how much alcohol you drink and how active you are each day is used alongside more specific details, such as where you live and your gender, to give you an estimate in countdown form, and the results will not always be what you want to hear. For example, in our first test the writer of this article was given a rather precise 26 years and 343 days to live, which was quite a shock as he has not even reached 40 yet! This could be seen as depressing or taken with a pinch of salt, but can also act as a trigger for you to improve your lifestyle with one of the other apps mentioned in this section. It is free and good for a simple check, unless you really do not want to know.

Ratings

Longevity	Fun factor	Practicality	Value
★☆☆☆☆	★☆☆☆☆	★★☆☆☆	★★★★☆

Overall Rating ★★☆☆☆

Price: Free   **Developer:** Plum Amazing

Natural Cures

Throw the tablets away and try the natural approach

No one likes to take too much medication if they can help it, but you are likely to be offered tablets or medicines when visiting the doctor as a first resort, no matter what the problem is. Natural Cures presents alternative therapies which are known to help out in certain circumstances and which should ultimately do less damage to your body in the long run. All manner of problems are covered, from acne to Alzheimer's disease, and the solutions offered do seem to make a lot of sense. Treatments are supplemented by background information, and for some issues even preventative measures are included which makes this an app which really deserves a place on your iPhone just in case a problem crops up. You should of course not rely on natural cures for more serious ailments, but for the little niggles that can get in the way of your life the options presented here are certainly worth a try. And even better, Natural Cures doesn't cost a penny.

Ratings

Longevity	Fun factor	Practicality	Value
★★★★☆	★★★☆☆	★★★★☆	★★★★★

Overall Rating ★★★★☆

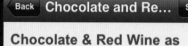

■ You may be surprised by some of the options on offer.

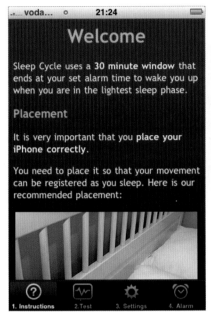

■ It is much more than an alarm clock and brings a fresh approach to waking up.

■ An explanation of how Sleep Cycle works is included with instruction images.

Price: £0.59/$0.99 **Developer:** LexWare Labs AB

Sleep Cycle Alarm Clock

This app really can take the grouch out of your mornings

We all know how it feels to wake up when we are in the middle of a deep sleep, and it is not a nice feeling because your mind and body need to take time to adjust to being awake. Developed by LexWare Labs AB, Sleep Cycle Alarm Clock takes a new approach to alarms by waking you up slowly when you are in your lightest sleep phase, and it does this in a physical and audible way. 30 minutes before your alarm is set to go off the app starts to gently wake you up by sensing movement and then emits a small sound each time you move. Simply place your iPhone on your bed and away you go. Of course you need to be careful where it is put to stop damage, but in our tests it really does work. It is a strange feeling the first time you use it, but even with limited sleep this app can help you start the day in a much better frame of mind and for only 59p Sleep Cycle Alarm Clock is well worth picking up.

Ratings

Longevity	Fun factor	Practicality	Value
★★★★★	★★★★☆	★★★☆☆	★★★★☆

Overall Rating ★★★★☆

Price: Free **Developer:** Tamtris Web Services Inc

Free Menstrual Calendar

Keep track of your body with this simple and effective tool

Menstruation affects everyone, female and male, and being able to predict when your next period is due can make all of the difference to your activities over that period of time, whether it's planning a holiday or planning for a baby. Free Menstrual Calendar is dominated by a simple calendar view which offers an easy to view method of tracking what is coming and also your menstrual history. Included is the ability to input how heavy a period has been and this can be useful for medical appointments in the future. The colour-coded method of input also caters for fertility predictions and ovulation so the benefits could be far more worthwhile than just tracking what has happened in the past. The style of the app may not be pleasing to all, but as a simple and free tracker it does what it needs to very well and keeps the menu options and unneeded extras to a minimum.

Ratings

Longevity	Fun factor	Practicality	Value
★★★★☆	★★☆☆☆	★★★☆☆	★★★★☆

Overall Rating ★★★☆☆

■ The app can be personalised for your cycle.

■ The interface is easy to read and even easier to learn to use.

Price: £0.59/$0.99 **Developer:** Tesla Audio Sciences

Brain Power

Sync your mind and improve your brain

Brain Power from Tesla Audio Sciences is a rather unusual app in that it serves two purposes – one of which is probably unintended – quite well. The idea behind Brain Power is to help you relax, meditate, focus or sleep depending on the situation you are in. There are 11 preset music tracks included, which loop forever and most of which are very easy on the ear. Listening to one of these on its own will no doubt produce a relaxing effect on you, but throw in some entertainment effects and you can start to really feel the benefits. These background beats have supposedly been designed for specific situations and even though there is little medical evidence behind Brain Power, there was little doubt that it had a positive effect on us when we tested it out. For the interface and music tracks alone it is a very decent value app, but if the effects work for you it will turn out to be an absolute bargain at 59p.

Ratings

Longevity	Fun factor	Practicality	Value
★★★★☆	★★★★☆	★★★☆☆	★★★★☆

Overall Rating ★★★★★

■ The included songs are easy on the ear.

My Health Coach Manage Your Weight

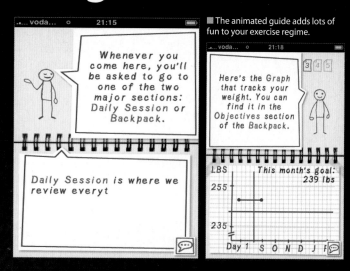

■ The animated guide adds lots of fun to your exercise regime.

Price: £0.59/$0.99 **Developer:** AppZap

Vision

Keep your eye out for this great application

Looking after our eyes is not something we tend to take very seriously or do particularly well and a gentle nudge can be useful in reminding us just how important they are to us. Vision offers a selection of guides which will help you look after your eyes as well as treat them should you have a problem. Throw in a long list of visual tests which analyse everything from colour recognition to retinal function and this is a good option for checking your eyesight whenever you need to. Tracking your eyesight over time is crucial to analysing deterioration and this is something we rarely do with normal eye tests so it could be argued that this app has more potential than most others on the App Store. Finally, if your eyes are starting to feel a little tired just open up the 'eye exercise' section and follow the instructions on screen. Vision is beautifully presented and extremely beneficial for almost everyone.

Price: £0.59/$0.99   Developer: Gameloft SA

A friendly and helpful health coach in your pocket

Gameloft is known for producing high-quality games on the iPhone platform, but the developer has dabbled in other areas and My Health Coach is an example of what is possible given lots of commitment. When you first start it up it almost feels like a mini Nintendo Wii title and the animation and sounds lead you into a welcoming environment which is perfect for encouraging you to keep your exercise regime going. The animated figure is a joy to behold and will even stick its tongue out at you from time to time, which adds to the fun. The tasks included are interactive and often involve wearing your iPhone to ensure that you have completed them properly. Statistics are built up over time and the advice given while you use the app makes it a fun and complete solution for getting healthy over long or short periods of time. And at 59p this app is difficult to fault.

Ratings

Longevity	Fun factor	Practicality	Value
★★★★★	★★★★★	★★★★☆	★★★★★

Overall Rating ★★★★★

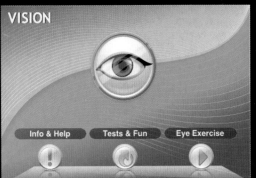

VISION

■ Vision is presented in an eye-catching manner which welcomes you in.

Info & Help   Tests & Fun   Eye Exercise

Back   Vision and computers

Ratings

Longevity	Fun factor	Practicality	Value
★★★★	★★★★	★★★★	★★★★

Overall Rating ★★★★

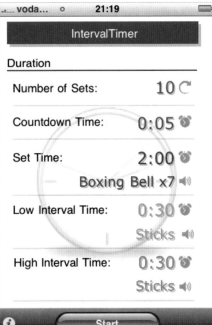

■ You can customise almost every part of the timer.

Price: £0.59/$0.99   Developer: Plain and Simple Software

Interval Timer

A simple timer which has a multitude of potential uses

Plain and Simple Software's Interval Timer is little more than a simple timing mechanism at heart, but this doesn't mean that it won't have plenty of benefits. There are many activities which require timing and being able to pre-programme your regime before you start is obviously beneficial. You can set the countdown time, interval times and even the type of sound which will audibly alert you at the correct moment. From weight training to jogging to cooking, there could be a million and one different uses for Interval Timer and therefore it could be suitable for more people than most other apps on the App Store. There is little to get really excited about when it comes to Interval Timer's interface or the implementation, but do you really need fancy graphics and a bloated app to do the simplest of tasks? All in all, Interval Timer works well, comes at a reasonable price and is handy to have tucked away for when you need it.

Ratings

Longevity	Fun factor	Practicality	Value
★★★★	★★	★★★★	★★★

Overall Rating ★★★★☆

Lifestyle

Lifestyle iPhone apps cover a multitude of uses, which are only limited by your imagination

Price: £0.59/$0.99   Developer: Hand Carved Code, LLC

Occasions

The perfect way to manage all of your special occasions

Managing birthdays and special events is a staple task for any smartphone, but Occasions brings a new twist to the party. Besides dealing with the core function of reminding you when an occasion is approaching, it can also be used to profile the person involved. Their zodiac sign, birthstone and likes can be included with a listing and you can include a photo of the individual for that extra personal touch. Occasions can also retrieve birthdays and important dates from the Contacts application to reduce the setup time and the ability to call or email from an Occasions contact highlights how well it is integrated with the core iPhone functions. With push notifications

including home screen badge counts, a selection of themes and the ability to show fun facts related to the date in question, there really is nothing missing here. Custom entries can be built, you can include a specific ringtone for each contact and the search mechanism is very fast so you could soon find yourself using this app as a replacement for the standard Contacts app. It looks better and is more fun, but is probably best dedicated to the people who really

■ You can store personal details for each contact easily.

■ The included themes add a touch of class to proceedings.

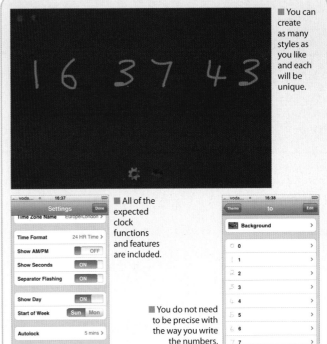

■ You can create as many styles as you like and each will be unique.

■ All of the expected clock functions and features are included.

■ You do not need to be precise with the way you write the numbers.

Price: £0.59/$0.99 **Developer:** Yarg

Doodle Clock

Take the turmoil out of time by adding some personality

There are many clock replacement apps in the App Store and many that can manage alarms and offer a pleasing display, but none offer the unique ability to personalise the clock like Doodle Clock does. Besides including alarms, time zones and a couple of themes, you get the ability to create your own clock style. You draw the numbers, AM and PM and the days and then choose a suitable background to display them on. Photos can be chosen and it works even better if one of your children draws the numbers for you as a reminder of your priorities when you are away from home. It is simple to use, quick to set up and offers just the right balance between usability and fun to create an app that you are highly likely to use for a long time to come.

Ratings

Longevity	Fun factor	Practicality	Value
★★★★★	★★★☆☆	★★★★★	★★★★★

Overall Rating ★★★★☆

---

matter in your life. The interface and presentation are as good as has been seen on an iPhone to date and it is overall a joy to use. The list of features is impressive and they are tied in well with the presentation to create a polished looking piece of software.

Every app has faults, but we have struggled to find any here and at its current price it excels in the value stakes as well. The only limitation is that you have to have the iPhone data connected for the push notifications to work, but to get around that Apple will need to open up the built-in alarm functions to developers. You will never miss an important occasion again and because you can use the app to buy presents related more specifically to the individual, you now have no excuse not to make everyone's birthday special.

Ratings

Longevity	Fun factor	Practicality	Value
★★★★★	★★★★☆	★★★★★	★★★★★

Overall Rating ★★★★☆

The Day I Was Born
Price: £0.59/$0.99 **Developer:** Unusual Things

Who was born on the same day as you, and who died?

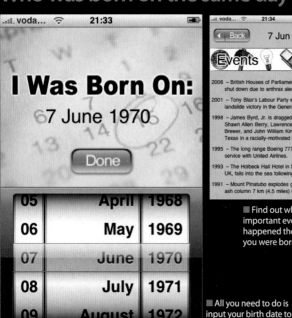

You can buy books that detail historic happenings on the day you were born, but these tend to be something you read once and never look at again. The Day I Was Born uses the same concept and includes some fun facts, but is much cheaper than a book and can be used for anyone you know. Once you have input your date of birth it presents you with a list of sectioned events pertaining to the Zodiac, holidays, events, births and deaths. It has little practical use but is designed as a bit of fun that can quickly tell you more about what happened on your birthday and really proves its worth when sharing with others. As a quick reference guide it works well and serves its purpose, but the longevity of an app like this is quite obviously questionable once you have shared information with all of your friends. It's a fun little app nonetheless and for its cheap price, can prove entertaining.

■ Find out what important events happened the day you were born.

■ All you need to do is input your birth date to get started.

Ratings

Longevity	Fun factor	Practicality	Value
★★☆☆☆	★★★☆☆	★★☆☆☆	★★★☆☆

Overall Rating ★★★

Price: £0.59/$0.99 **Developer:** NobleBug

Everything a wannabe chef needs in one app

Chef

■ Search a huge range of delicious recipes online.

■ Start off by selecting the groceries you need.

Chef takes the cookbook idea and throws in many more ingredients to make an app that is perfect for anyone who likes to cook. You can add your own ingredients, which are automatically broken down by aisle, and also include a database of your own recipes. This performs the basics you will need to buy your produce and then cook it in the way you want, but there is much more here that will lead you to experiment with recipes submitted by others. You can search online for recipes using various indicators such as the origin of a dish (American, Chinese and so on) and the type of meal you want to prepare (main course, dressing, starter or whatever) – you are then presented with a wide choice of meals and recipes in every category. These can be saved or emailed to friends and the entire process works without fuss and to great effect. So if you fancy yourself as hot, pan-boiling stuff in the kitchen, this is a useful tool.

Ratings

Longevity	Fun factor	Practicality	Value
★★★★☆	★★★★☆	★★★★★	★★★★★

Overall Rating ★★★★★

Find Free Parking

Price: £1.79/$0.99 Developer: Red C

Take the pain, and the price, out of car parking

Being able to navigate to a destination using your iPhone is, of course, advantageous for 99 per cent of the journey, but what happens when you arrive? Chances are that you will have to spend some time finding the nearest parking area and that you will end up spending a lot of money for the privilege of leaving your car in a designated area for a few hours. Find Free Parking is designed to find the nearest parking areas to your current destination and also offers up the price for each car park. Directions can be obtained from within the app and you can also view the results on a map for quick reference. The GPS antenna is used to good effect or you can search ahead of time to ensure a hassle free journey. Our tests suggest that this app is very much London-centric, but hopefully it will be expanded to cover more areas in time. Nevertheless, for the areas it covers, it's a great app.

Ratings

Longevity	Fun factor	Practicality	Value
★★★★☆	★★★☆☆	★★★★★	★★★★☆

Overall Rating ★★★★☆

■ Pricing and congestion charge areas are all included.

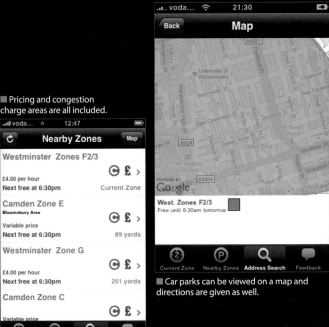

■ Car parks can be viewed on a map and directions are given as well.

Price: £0.59/$0.99 Developer: My Diary, Inc.

Now you can keep multiple diaries updated with ease

My Diary

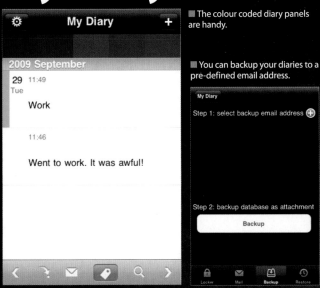

■ The colour coded diary panels are handy.

■ You can backup your diaries to a pre-defined email address.

Keeping a diary can be a time-consuming business and it is all too easy to sometimes forget to enter new entries on a daily basis. My Diary makes the process of adding new entries as quickly as possible by using a clutter free interface and colour tabs to define each separate diary.

You can enter information into five diaries, which are annotated with individual colours at the top – simply tap each colour to be taken to that diary. Adding a new entry is as easy as tapping '+' and then typing the entry, and you can also backup and restore all of your information by saving it as an email attachment or as a database on a specified web server. My Diary makes little attempt to include fancy graphics and looks rather basic, but for functionality alone it does very well. So for the perfect way to keep your thoughts and musings on record, look no further than My Diary on the iPhone.

Ratings

Longevity	Fun factor	Practicality	Value
★★★★★	★★★☆☆	★★★★☆	★★★★☆

Overall Rating ★★★★☆

Price: Free **Developer:** Ocado Limited

Ocado

Get your groceries delivered straight to your door without touching a computer

Supermarkets have struggled for the past few years to offer an online ordering experience that is hassle free, but things have gradually improved. Ocado is a service that brings the online grocery shopping experience to your iPhone and we have to say straight away that the user experience is exceptional. You can search for any item and we found that vague descriptions still brought back accurate results. You then add the item to your basket and it will appear as an image on the basket screen along with your other selections. The use of images in the app works well to highlight that you are buying groceries and brings a lifelike feel to every part of the program. Everything from booking a delivery slot through to multi-buy savings is included, and the app is a joy to use in almost every way. Expect to see other supermarkets follow suit in the future but for now, online shopping really has peaked with Ocado.

Ratings

Longevity	Fun factor	Practicality	Value
★★★★☆	★★★☆☆	★★★★★	★★★★★

Overall Rating ★★★★★

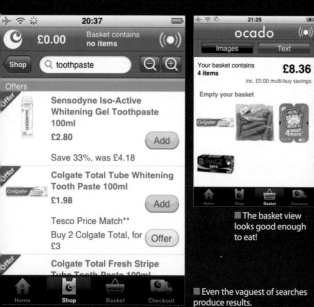

■ Even the vaguest of searches produce results.

■ The basket view looks good enough to eat!

Price: Free **Developer:** Masayuki Akamatsu

Banner Free

Grab people's attention without saying a word

How many times have you wanted to catch the attention of someone in a busy place or when you are unable to physically talk to them? The answer is probably not often, to be honest with you, but there are times when a method of talking to someone without speaking is rather useful and this is where Banner Free comes in.

This app does little more than scroll the words you type across the screen in very large dot matrix lettering. This can be used for fun or for more serious purposes, but it does indeed work very well for what it is. There is a paid version available, which includes more customisation options, but for the amount of times you will actually need to use it, the free version is most likely the way to go.

Banner Free does not do a lot really, but it works in a quirky kind of way and is free, so what have you got to lose? Get typing away now!

Christmas Countdown

■ The main image is a tad cheesy, but very 'Christmas'.

■ The tree gets larger as you approach the big day.

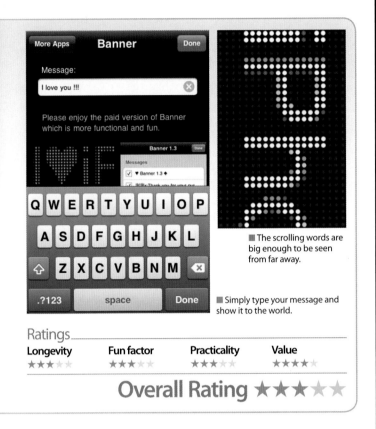

■ The scrolling words are big enough to be seen from far away.

■ Simply type your message and show it to the world.

Ratings

Longevity	Fun factor	Practicality	Value
★★★☆☆	★★★☆☆	★★★☆☆	★★★★☆

Overall Rating ★★★★☆

Price: Free **Developer:** Energize Software

Look forward to Christmas every single day

One special part of Christmas that is not often talked about is the naff side, which involves Christmas card styles from decades ago that do not look right in your house, music that can only be listened to at Christmas, and a huge tree that dominates your lounge and generally makes everything look pretty bad. Christmas Countdown encompasses everything that is naff about Christmas in one free app and does a sterling job of making you want to check back each day to see how long is left until that special day.

With a tree that grows larger as you get nearer to 25 December, dreadful music that is played when you touch the screen and a countdown option, there is little else you could wish for in an app that celebrates all the silly bits of Christmas. It is just a bit of harmless fun, and for that reason alone it is worth a download.

Ratings

Longevity	Fun factor	Practicality	Value
★★☆☆☆	★★★☆☆	★★☆☆☆	★★★★☆

Overall Rating ★★★☆☆

Price: £1.19/$1.99 **Developer:** Nikolay Nachev

9000 Awesome Facts

Impress your friends with thousands of weird facts

"The human tooth has about 55 miles of canals in it." That is just 1 of 9,000 facts included in 9000 Awesome Facts and is an example of how fascinating the majority of the content is. A list of facts would normally not warrant a price above free, but the selection included here make for an interesting read, which you will come back to time and time again. Each fact can be scrolled through with ease and you can click a star in the corner to mark it as a favourite. The problem is that so many of the facts are so interesting that you will end up with a very long list of favourites. The interface is clutter free and you only get to change the settings when you rotate the screen, which is a useful touch. All in all it is a great selection of facts that are displayed perfectly.

Ratings

Longevity	Fun factor	Practicality	Value
★★★★☆	★★★★★	★★★★☆	★★★★☆

Overall Rating ★★★★☆

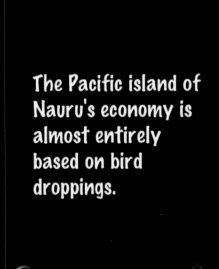

If you look carefully

■ Simply scroll through as many facts as you like or just tap the screen.

Price: Free **Developer:** R.B. Designs

My Baby's Name

Choosing a baby's name used to be a tad difficult

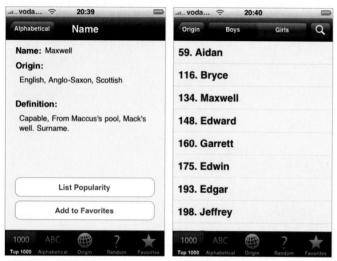

 Choosing a baby's name is not a simple process because it will obviously affect your child for the rest of its life, but help is at hand if you have the time to scroll through a huge list of names in this helpful iPhone app. They are sorted by popularity in a particular year, but can also be searched alphabetically or by their origin. The clean interface makes perusing names an enjoyable experience and tapping on one will bring up the origin and definition of the chosen name. You can also add a name as a favourite or check to see how popular it is in a particular year. It may be that you do not want a name that is too popular and this is a good way to double check, especially if you have a popular surname too. This app includes a wealth of information and is logically laid out, which should make the process of name choosing for your offspring so much easier.

■ Origin, popularity and definitions are available for every name.

Ratings

Longevity	Fun factor	Practicality	Value
★★☆☆☆	★★★★☆	★★★★☆	★★★★★

Overall Rating ★★★★☆

Price: Free **Developer:** Starburst Software Ltd

Fat Fingers

Find eBay items no one else can with Fat Fingers

 Finding true bargains on eBay is not all that easy these days because so many people use the service and most of these people are well aware of how much items are worth. Fat Fingers is an app that searches for misspelt listings and which will bring up a list of all items that match your search criteria, making bargain hunting that little bit easier.

In our tests it did bring up long lists of items, many of which had no bids on them at all, which suggests that there are some genuine benefits to this app. You can search eBay sites in many different countries, too, and also do a standard search without spelling mistakes included, but the true worth is in finding items that have been listed incorrectly.

For a free app, Fat Fingers has carved a niche for itself and will be very useful for anyone who purchases on eBay on a regular basis or for those wanting to dip their toes into the auction site.

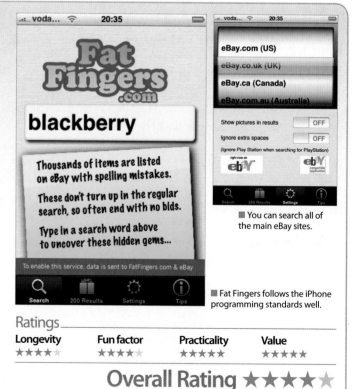

■ You can search all of the main eBay sites.

■ Fat Fingers follows the iPhone programming standards well.

Ratings

Longevity	Fun factor	Practicality	Value
★★★★☆	★★★★☆	★★★★★	★★★★★

Overall Rating ★★★★☆

Build Confidence With Andrew Johnson

Price: £1.79/$2.99 **Developer:** Michael Schneider

■ If you get interrupted, just click the pause button.

Building confidence is now easy

Building confidence may feel like a task that is impossible if it is something you are lacking in, but the process for increasing your confidence levels is surprisingly easy. It is all about your state of mind and this app is just one of a number which claims to help you on your journey to becoming a more confident person. When you consider that the normal price of these products usually hovers around £10, the iPhone app method is without doubt the best value way to help yourself. Andrew Johnson focuses on dispelling negative thoughts and opening yourself up to positive suggestion – it will not work for everyone, but then again there is some logic to this approach and if it works for you the price will feel inconsequential. This app is basically an MP3 file housed in an interface, but that is all you need to get started.

■ A few settings are all you need.

Ratings

Longevity	Fun factor	Practicality	Value
★★★☆☆	★★☆☆☆	★★★★☆	★★★☆☆

Overall Rating ★★★☆☆

iStylist Makeover

Price: £0.59/$0.99 **Developer:** Styler Design

Check your style with the tap of a finger – it really works!

Choosing a style that suits you is a case of trial and error and that is obvious when you walk through any town in Britain. iStylist Makeover offers you the opportunity to try a selection of outfits by using a photo from your iPhone. It includes a variety of hats, hairstyles, glasses, make-up and other items to ensure that you can find the right look for you. It is without doubt aimed at the female side of the population, but the iPhone is a genderless creation and is used by all walks of life. You can even upload your style and browse the styles of others at which point ratings can be offered. This can be a cruel process but serves as a useful double-check to make sure your style really does stand out from the crowd. iStylist covers all of the bases well and is expandable with new packs so the options really are unlimited, making this one lifestyle app really worth checking out.

■ Once you have your photo you can try hundreds of different styles.

■ You can use a new photo, an old photo or a model to check your style.

Ratings

Longevity	Fun factor	Practicality	Value
★★★★☆	★★★★★	★★★★☆	★★★★☆

Overall Rating ★★★★☆

Price: £0.59/$0.99 Developer: AppMania

DreamBook

What do your dreams mean? Maybe it's time to find out

■ Get started by inputting what you saw in your dream.

The science of translating dreams is somewhat controversial and opinions range from true believers to those who feel that it is all nonsense. DreamBook attempts to translate your dreams by letting you list objects or events you saw in a recent dream, and then offering an explanation as to what it may mean.

We tested a few people and the results ranged from logical to completely off the wall, but it still left us with the feeling that there is some merit in what is being offered. You can keep a record of your dreams using the automatically populated calendar and you can also choose which sources you want to use for the explanations offered.

Whether you believe or not is not really important because this is a competent offering that provides an interesting view point on what your dreams really do mean.

Ratings

Longevity	Fun factor	Practicality	Value
★★★★☆	★★★☆☆	★★★☆☆	★★★★☆

Overall Rating ★★★★☆

Price: £1.79/$2.99 Developer: mFactory Systems, LLC

Body Talk

Your body talks to people, it really does…

As you may know communication is not dominated by the words you speak, but rather a combination of words, facial expressions and body movements. Body Talk offers a guide to this often bypassed language and even includes video demonstrations of the movements. Did you know than an exposed neck is a submissive gesture and that it also shows that you are listening? You click on the name of the movement, at which point you are presented with a full description of the movement and a link to a video too.

This is an app that will be useful to many people, but also one that is interesting enough for everyone to learn from and we certainly had fun finding out what each movement means. It's an informative and useful little app, just be careful that you don't get too engrossed and start monitoring every movement you make.

■ Full descriptions are included to make sure you fully understand.

■ The included videos make for a fun point of reference.

Ratings

Longevity	Fun factor	Practicality	Value
★★★☆☆	★★★☆☆	★★★★☆	★★★☆☆

Overall Rating ★★★☆☆

Kidtivities

Price: £0.59/$0.99 Developer: Double TapApps

Keep the little 'uns entertained with this great app

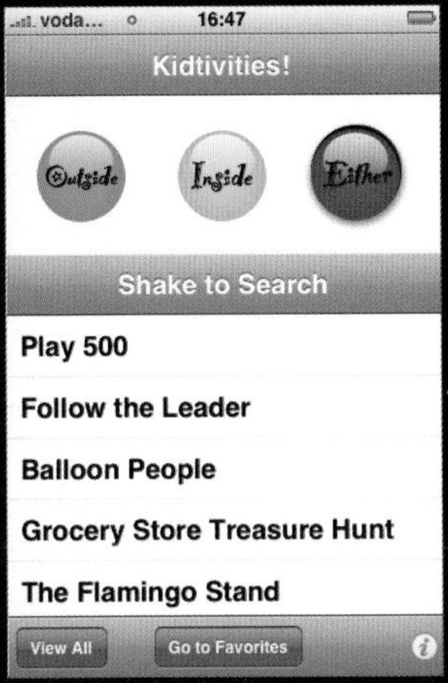

Indoor and outdoor activities are included, which is useful with our weather.

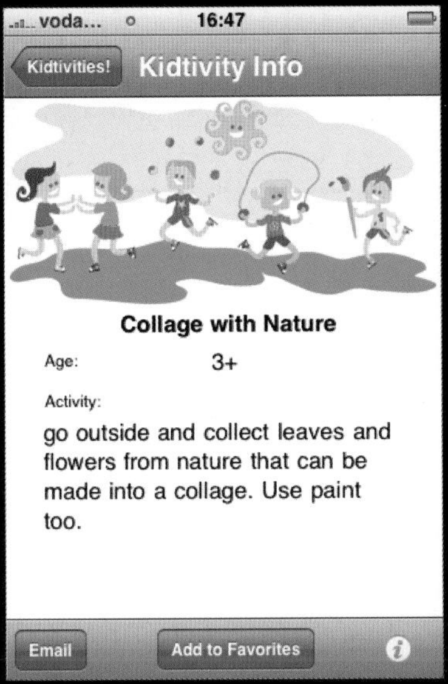

The ideas are simple and on the whole cost no money to do.

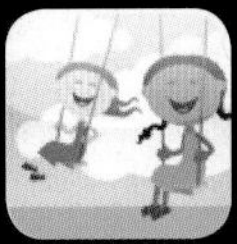

Keeping children happy on a rainy day is akin to trying to nail jelly to a ceiling. It is difficult to continually come up with new ideas and so any help is wholeheartedly welcome. Kidtivities attempts to offer a selection of simple ideas that will help you pass the hours, and on the whole does a very good of offering up ideas that cost little money to do.

Some of the activities are, admittedly, quite obvious but if they manage to plant the idea in your head that is certainly not a bad thing and hopefully more will be added over time. This app is novel and will be of help to busy parents and at its current price point is without doubt good value for money. You can also give your iPhone to your children, if you dare risk it, and they can look up the activities for themselves. A fun app to help entertain your little loved ones.

Ratings

Longevity	Fun factor	Practicality	Value
★★★☆☆	★★★★☆	★★★☆☆	★★★☆☆

Overall Rating ★★★☆☆

Amazing X-Ray FX2 Pro

Price: £0.59/$0.99 Developer: WebArtisan

Can an iPhone really X-ray your body? No.

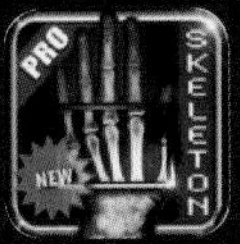

We would like to make it clear that this application does not actually X-ray parts of your body before we start. Firstly, it would be dangerous to continually do such a thing and secondly, that would be impossible. What it does do, however, is simulate X-rays by offering moving images of various parts of your body, which if used correctly could fool people. It takes some practice, mind, but once you are used to it some people will be fooled by the show on offer. The sounds and customisation options mean that you can set it up to suit the individual that you are scanning – you can also make the X-ray screen appear smaller for children and larger for big people and that is about it really. Some will see it as a gimmick and that is quite understandable, but it could pass away a few minutes in the pub when the conversation has dried up. We are not sure it's worth paying for, but it's fun nonetheless.

Ratings

Longevity	Fun factor	Practicality	Value
★★☆☆☆	★★★★☆	★★☆☆☆	★★★☆☆

Overall Rating ★★★☆☆

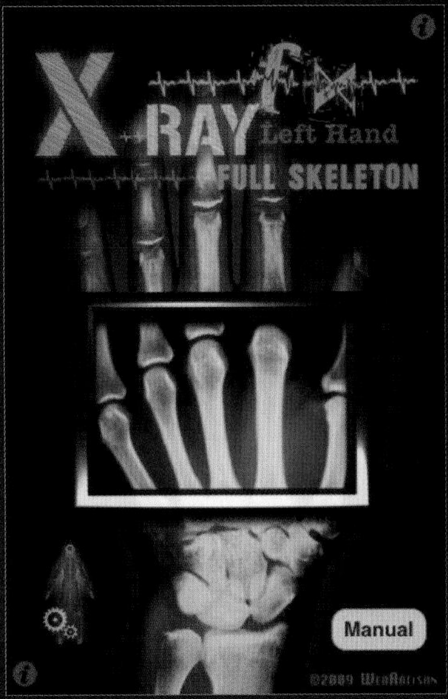

The Amazing X-ray app is extremely eye-catching and difficult to not notice.

The graphical representations should fool some of your friends.

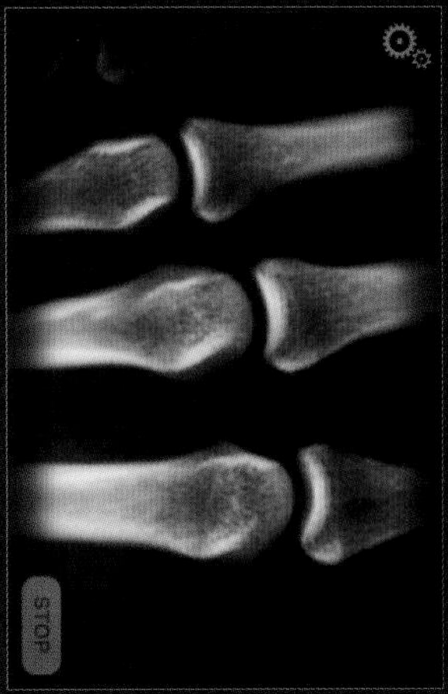

Medical

Medical apps are not just for students, anyone can learn from them…

Price: £0.59/$0.99 Developer: Jose Barrientos

Color Skeletal System

Understand every bone in your body

The skeleton is an endless source of fascination to children and adults alike, but on the whole we know surprisingly little about the bones that keep us standing upright. Color Skeletal System takes a visual approach to enlightening us as to what is inside our bodies, and does a good job of displaying complex detail on a small screen.

The images are clear, 3D and colour coded for maximum effect, and are easy to understand by anyone who takes the time to see what is inside. You can zoom in an out with a thumb and finger and also move the image around the screen to view in finite detail each part of the body, and the speed of the app is impressive considering the detail included. Detailed descriptions are also included so that you can understand the nature of each bone, and it quickly acts as a source of reference that makes for a fascinating and enjoyable experience. The colour codes work as part of the navigation system and tapping one colour will bring up that specific area with key markers annotating each individual bone and full descriptions below.

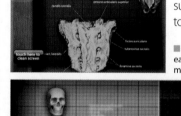

It cannot be easy to display such detail in a friendly and easy to use manner, but Color Skeletal

■ The app allows you to zoom in to view each part of the skeleton in great detail, making it easy to see.

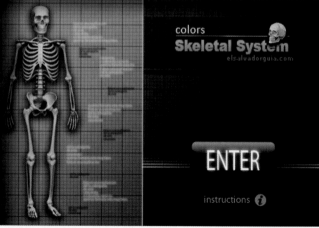

■ The included information is very accurate and beautifully presented, making this a brilliant app you will want to use again and again.

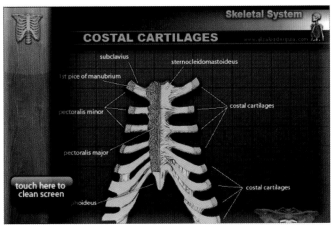

Tapping an area will bring up detailed images and text, and you can zoom in and out with your thumb and finger.

The navigation system takes a few seconds to understand but it is fairly usable once you get used to it.

System manages the task with ease. Crucially the information is deadly accurate and this builds confidence in the images you are viewing and the text you are reading. The price is low for medical detail of this level and as such it is difficult to not wholeheartedly recommend it. It can also be used for trivial matters such as pub quizzes or just impressing your friends with your newfound knowledge, which is always fun to do.

It won't turn you into a Doctor, but understanding your own body is not a bad thing by any measure. This app is unusual in that it will appeal to medical students, children and adults with an inquisitive mind in equal measure. It strikes the right balance between offering the detail you need but explaining (and showing you) information in a way that will make sense to everyone. A great medical app that will educate and entertain.

Ratings

Longevity	Fun factor	Practicality	Value
★★★★☆	★★★★★	★★★★★	★★★★★

Overall Rating ★★★★☆

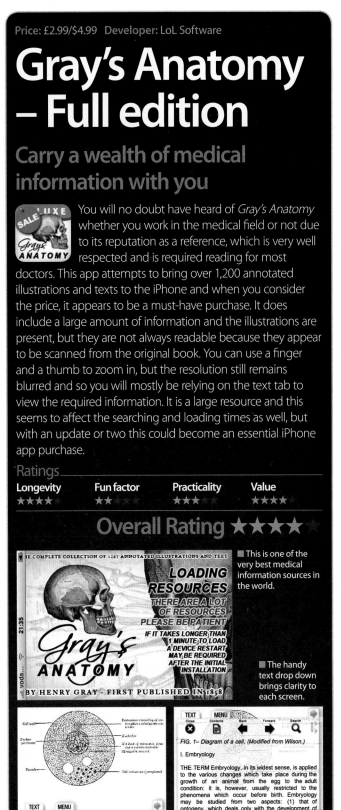

Price: £2.99/$4.99 Developer: LoL Software

Gray's Anatomy – Full edition

Carry a wealth of medical information with you

You will no doubt have heard of *Gray's Anatomy* whether you work in the medical field or not due to its reputation as a reference, which is very well respected and is required reading for most doctors. This app attempts to bring over 1,200 annotated illustrations and texts to the iPhone and when you consider the price, it appears to be a must-have purchase. It does include a large amount of information and the illustrations are present, but they are not always readable because they appear to be scanned from the original book. You can use a finger and a thumb to zoom in, but the resolution still remains blurred and so you will mostly be relying on the text tab to view the required information. It is a large resource and this seems to affect the searching and loading times as well, but with an update or two this could become an essential iPhone app purchase.

Ratings

Longevity	Fun factor	Practicality	Value
★★★★☆	★★☆☆☆	★★★☆☆	★★★★☆

Overall Rating ★★★★☆

This is one of the very best medical information sources in the world.

The handy text drop down brings clarity to each screen.

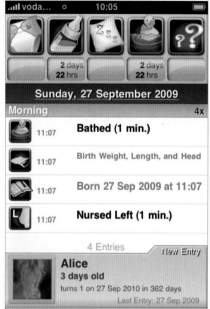

■ You can record every activity in minute detail.

■ This information could prove vital for health visits, as all the usual questions will be answered by the app's monitoring.

Price: £2.99/$4.99 **Developer:** ANDESigned

Total Baby

Record every moment of your baby's start in life

Babies cannot talk, obviously, and so it can be somewhat difficult for new parents to understand the needs of their child and how they are reacting to food and drink on a daily basis. Total Baby is an app that enables you to monitor the main aspects of a young child's development: feeding, sleeping, bathing and nappy changing. It does so by using large buttons that are easily pressed when your hands are full, and you can time each activity to the second with the ability to add notes and categories for each event. It is US-centric and uses words like diaper instead of nappy, but this should not put you off because it is a complete solution. Allergies, vaccines, doctor visits and growth measurements can also be set so you really are gaining a full overview of your child's development at every step. A great little iPhone app for new mums and dads.

Ratings

Longevity	Fun factor	Practicality	Value
★★★★☆	★★☆☆☆	★★★★★	★★★★☆

Overall Rating ★★★★☆

Price: Free **Developer:** Michael Quach

Mental Illness

This brings to the fore a subject some don't like to talk about

Mental illness is responsible for a high percentage of sick days, and can also have a detrimental effect on physical health too. Mental Illness offers an overview of the various illnesses and their associated medications, which act as a pointer to understanding any issues you may have or are recognising in others. The detail is not extensive by any means and this could not be used in the medical field as a primary source of information, but it appears to be accurate and will be of use to those interested in the subject as well as sufferers. The interface is as simple as it could be and is only dispersed by the scrolling adverts at the bottom, but the information is what is most important here and in this area it displays what you need to know quite effectively. It may not be for everyone, but certainly has a place and could prove very useful for some iPhone users.

Ratings

Longevity	Fun factor	Practicality	Value
★★★★☆	★★☆☆☆	★★★★☆	★★★★★

Overall Rating ★★★★☆

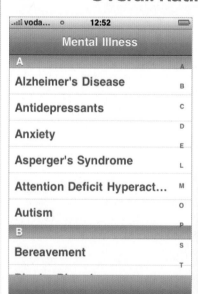

■ The detail is minimal, but acts as a good starter.

■ The range of topics covered in this app is really quite extensive.

iCandy

▢

🔒

‖ O2-UK ▪

13:32

Monday, 26 November

iCandy
iPhone 8GB

slide to

Apple iPhone 8GB
It doesn't take much to make the iPhone look good, but
this shot shows off the awesome beauty of its touch screen

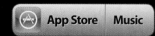

Music

Music is fun, educational and enlightening when you bring it to the iPhone

Price: £5.99/$9.99 Developer: IK Multimedia

GrooveMaker Hip-Hop

You will be amazed at how quickly you can create great sounds

 The number of mixing apps available to you on the App Store grows every week, but some still stand out from the crowd for their ability to offer layers of content and usability which makes them accessible to more than just musicians. GrooveMaker Hip-Hop is an excellent example of an app which includes a seemingly endless amount of riffs and sounds for you to experiment and play around with, but which crucially enables you to mix them together without needing to watch every second for the right moment to layer them. It works in real-time which allows you to experiment audibly and this is what makes it as fun as it is productive. It does not stop at simply providing a range of sounds and letting you play with them because you can also create new layers to add to your song, which is always playing, and choose from up to eight tracks to combine together.

One interesting aspect of GrooveMaker Hip-Hop is that the songs never sounded cluttered even when we loaded them up with many sounds and with experimentation we were able to produce tracks which we would never have dreamed of being able to create just an hour before. Once completed songs can be saved and exported to either a Mac or PC as high-quality WAV files and then used in any way you choose. Everyone from DJs who need some filler music to those who require background music

■ The interface looks confusing, but is easy to use.

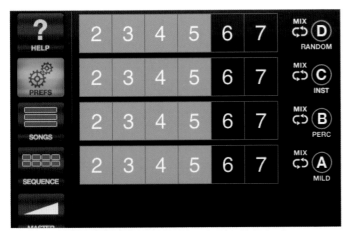

■ Multiple settings are included to guide you.

Touch any of the A-D Random Mix buttons to start creating grooves

Pad

The tracks will be filled with random loops and start playing together to create a groove. Each time you click a Random Mix button a new groove will be generated.

■ Handy hints pop up to help you get started quickly.

Price: Free   Developer: Spotify Ltd

Spotify

Spotify brings a whole new world of music to the iPhone

The appearance of Spotify gave birth to a raft of headlines when it was first announced because it is obvious competition to Apple's iTunes service. However, it finally arrived and has now found its way onto the App Store so now we can all use it. The service streams music to a desktop, but can now also stream any title in one of your playlists direct to your iPhone. These playlists can be changed on the iPhone and this will be shown on your main account as well and it works and plays in a very similar fashion to the main desktop-based software. You will need a premium Spotify account to use the iPhone version, but the killer feature is that you can listen to tracks offline when you have no access to Wi-Fi. This offers a whole new way to enjoy music on your iPhone and adds a lot to the value of the service. Few apps will have such an effect on your iPhone usage as this one.

Ratings

Longevity	Fun factor	Practicality	Value
★★★★★	★★★★	★★★★★	★★★★★

Overall Rating ★★★★★

■ Enter your username and password and away you go.

■ The interface is perfectly laid out for the iPhone.

for presentations can take advantage of the technology included in GrooveMaker Hip-Hop, and despite the daunting interface which looks quite specialised at first, you will quickly find yourself jumping around the various icons with ease as you look for more tweaks to add to your creation.

Most music mixing apps are designed to simply create music, but the content is so listenable in GrooveMaker Hip-Hop that you may find yourself quite happily listening to the included tracks and adding bits here and there for no other reason than to pass some time on your bus journey to work, for example. No matter how you use this app, it is a perfectly executed piece of programming on the iPhone which reaches out to more people than it should, and gives everyone the confidence to create something special in under an hour.

Ratings

Longevity	Fun factor	Practicality	Value
★★★★☆	★★★★★	★★★★★	★★★★★

Overall Rating ★★★★★

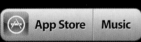
App Store | Music

Price: £14.99/$24.99   **Developer:** Baracoda Media

SonoRizr
10,000 DJ mixes for the price of a double CD

SonoRizr holds little content on the iPhone, but is more of a gateway to thousands of DJ mixes which are constantly updated. With claims of over 100,000 DJs adding new mixes to SonoRizr every day, the potential for discovering new music is in theory unlimited. It is broken down into 16 moods and these range from Sensual to Electro Party so you shouldn't have any trouble finding tracks that are suitable for every occasion. Wi-Fi is the best method of connection to this app and if used to its full potential it has a multitude of uses from background music in shops to getting people on the dance floor at a party. Although it's rather expensive, SonoRizr claims to be dedicated to professional use in public spaces and therefore could be a huge money saver for people who like to play music to their customers throughout the day. It is elegantly put together and one of the best services of this type that we have seen so far.

Ratings

Longevity	Fun factor	Practicality	Value
★★★★★	★★★★☆	★★★★★	★★★★★

Overall Rating ★★★★★

A huge catalogue of music is now at your disposal.

Price: £1.19/$1.99   **Developer:** Junpei Wada

FingerPiano
Cheat your way to piano-playing excellence

Learning the piano naturally takes many hours of practice and that is not something we all have the time to do. You can, however, cheat your way to playing some basic tunes with FingerPiano. It comes with a large selection of well-known tunes which you can play with both hands or right-handed, and chances are that you will know most of the tunes, which will also help the learning process. The notes are displayed above the piano keys and following them is child's play – within a minute you will be playing tunes. For those that cannot play the piano or have never had the chance to try, the experience is hugely satisfying. The tunes can also be played in real-time by the app and you then follow along to ensure you are at the correct pace. The keys are well sized and it all works perfectly – definitely an app for those wanting to play the piano, but can't.

Lady Gaga –
Walmart Soundcheck Concert

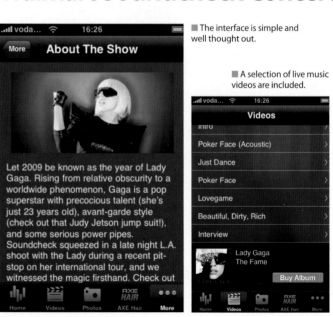

■ The interface is simple and well thought out.

■ A selection of live music videos are included.

Let 2009 be known as the year of Lady Gaga. Rising from relative obscurity to a worldwide phenomenon, Gaga is a pop superstar with precocious talent (she's just 23 years old), avant-garde style (check out that Judy Jetson jump suit!), and some serious power pipes. Soundcheck squeezed in a late night L.A. shoot with the Lady during a recent pit-stop on her international tour, and we witnessed the magic firsthand. Check out

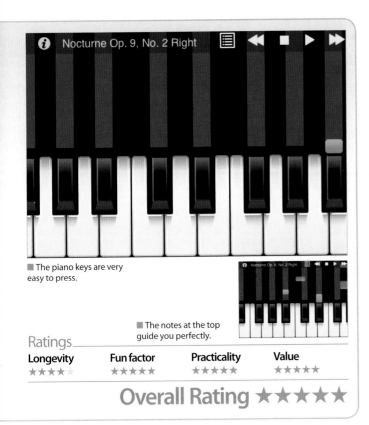

The piano keys are very easy to press.

Nocturne Op. 9, No. 2 Right

The notes at the top guide you perfectly.

Ratings
Longevity	Fun factor	Practicality	Value
★★★★☆	★★★★★	★★★★★	★★★★★

Overall Rating ★★★★★

Price: Free   **Developer:** Lunchbox

Check out Lady Gaga for free – decent content included

This app has one intention in mind and that is to sell more Lady Gaga records and to promote Walmart, but don't let that put you off. The app is also free and includes a healthy amount of content which will satisfy any Lady Gaga fan. You get six performance videos plus a video interview, a selection of photos, unusual facts about the singer and details of the live show in question. Apps like this are, as we said, primarily promotional pieces, but they also serve the purpose of pushing more free content to the fan which cannot be a bad thing. As this genre of app continues to become more popular with more artists, which it is already doing, we are likely to see them grow in content and still remain free of charge. You do need to be a fan to really enjoy what is on offer here, but it is still a fun distraction for those looking for an introduction to this much-talked-about artist.

Ratings
Longevity	Fun factor	Practicality	Value
★★☆☆☆	★★★★☆	★★★☆☆	★★★★★

Overall Rating ★★★★☆

SoundGrid

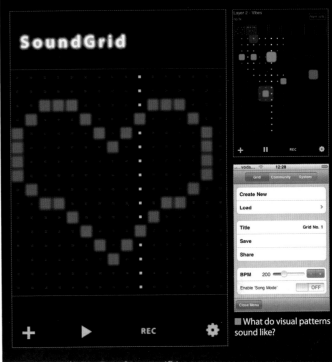

What do visual patterns sound like?

Price: £1.19/$1.99   **Developer:** mifki

SoundGrid
Anyone can make good music, even if they are tone deaf

SoundGrid is an example of a Marmite application – you will either love it or you will hate it. In our opinion, it opens up a whole world of music creation to those who either lack the talent or the patience to make a tune which others will want to hear. It works using a simplistic board which is split into separate layers, and in those layers you can then add different types of instruments and effects at any point during the tune. Drums, vibes, muted bells and a selection of other instruments and noises are included, and in no time at all you should be able to create a passable tune. You can record your creations, save a half-finished piece of work and also change the speed of the tune to suit your mood and the style of music you have chosen. This culminates in an interesting app which takes five seconds to dive into and which will take up many more seconds of your life as you explore the possibilities available to you.

Ratings
Longevity	Fun factor	Practicality	Value
★★★★☆	★★★★★	★★★☆☆	★★★★★

Overall Rating ★★★★★

3D Drum Kit
Price: £1.19/$1.99
Developer: Benjamin McDowell

The most realistic drum kit to reach the iPhone yet

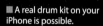

■ A real drum kit on your iPhone is possible.

Drums have been a continuing theme in the world of iPhone music apps and it can't be easy to come up with a new and exciting angle to entice potential purchasers. 3D Drum Kit offers a 3D view of a drum kit which sounds like a bit of a gimmick at first, but it helps an awful lot when you're trying to make a decent rhythm in a small space – you do need to seat the iPhone in the right place, though, and plenty of practice will produce some surprisingly positive results. Add to this the fact that you can record your performances, load over 50 demonstrations and even play along with music that's already playing on the iPhone and we are looking at a solution which is as good as, if not better than, most of the competition out there. You can even change the colour of the drums and customise the sounds to make your tracks as unique as possible, which takes it to an even higher level.

Ratings

Longevity	Fun factor	Practicality	Value
★★★★☆	★★★★★	★★★★☆	★★★★☆

Overall Rating ★★★★★

Price: £2.99/$4.99   Developer: Sound Trends LLC

Looptastic Electro Edition

Mix sounds by simply dragging your finger

■ The interface is very futuristic looking.

Looptastic Electro Edition brings the world of mixing to your fingertips, literally. It comes with an ample selection of techno sounds which you drag into the main play area to listen to – you can then move them around and add as many others as you like until you find a techno mix that you really like. Looptastic is as simple as it could be to use and you can also save your mixes for playing again later to show off to your friends, for example. 100 loops are included which can be embedded into ten remixable tracks and once you start, the process becomes somewhat hypnotic. Your mixes can be exported to a PC or a Mac and you have an infinite number of tracks that you can create because of the variety of included content. This is not a serious music mixing tool, but is more suited to those who want to dabble in the mix world and have a bit of fun while doing so.

Ratings

Longevity	Fun factor	Practicality	Value
★★★☆☆	★★★★☆	★★★★☆	★★★☆☆

Overall Rating ★★★★☆

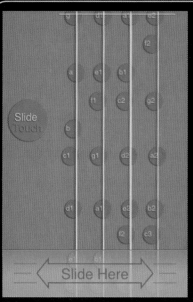

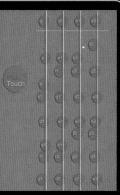

■ You can remove the slider and just tap the keys.

■ The slider at the bottom helps to re-create the violin-playing experience well.

Price: £1.19/$1.99 Developer: Phyar Studio

Real Violin

The iPhone can even turn into a violin

Never in a million years could you seriously expect a mobile phone to emulate a violin, but with the huge number of iPhone apps available it was bound to happen eventually. Real Violin from developer Phyar Studio attempts the impossible by making you hold your iPhone just like you would a violin to play all of the possible notes. The easiest method is to slide your finger at the bottom of the screen and press the desired notes, and the process is quite similar to how a violinist would play. If this doesn't work for you you can also get rid of the slide bar and just tap the notes, but this doesn't offer the same feel as the default setup. The violin sounds are realistic enough, as we discovered by some of the awful noises we managed to make, and for a bit of fun it works extremely well. It is debatable as to how well it could be used by musicians, but for those of us without a violin at home it has some potential.

Ratings

Longevity	Fun factor	Practicality	Value
★★★	★★★★	★★★	★★★

Overall Rating ★★★

Price: Free   Developer: Exabre Ltd

BandStalker

Find comprehensive information on multiple artists

There are many iPhone apps which offer biographical information and the latest news on specific music artists, but BandStalker takes the process a stage further by offering up information on many different artists. Once you have chosen the artist you want to read about, you are presented with a Bio, the latest news, videos, concerts and the relevant Twitter feed for said artist. The news and Bios are up to date and will be of particular interest for fans, but the video content can be low in number and quality because it is derived from YouTube with seemingly little planning put into the implementation. This is a free app and it offers a great deal of information so it would be churlish to knock it too much. It has huge potential and is already worthy of downloading, but a few more artists and better video content in the future would be welcomed and would make BandStalker a must-have app.

Ratings

Longevity	Fun factor	Practicality	Value
★★★★★	★★★★	★★★★	★★★★★

Overall Rating ★★★★★

Get the latest news, videos and tweets for your favourite artists

■ BandStalker offers information on multiple music artists.

■ The interface is reminiscent of any six-string guitar.

■ The green bar on the slider in the middle indicates perfect tuning.

Price: Free **Developer:** Mauvila Software

TyroTuner

Let your iPhone tune your guitar simply by listening

Mauvila Software's TyroTuner takes an unusual approach to guitar tuning by 'listening' to the notes you are playing, using the microphone, and then indicating whether you need to tune a particular string up or down. You tap each string and then play a note on your real guitar at which point a needle will move to the level it believes the string is tuned to. From there you can change the tuning and try again until it reaches the green middle section which represents perfect tuning. It is designed for six-string guitars and in our tests it proved to be accurate, which is, of course, the most important aspect here. Excitement is minimal with just a representation of the guitar to view, but as a basic app which delivers on its promise TyroTuner succeeds in every area. The real advantage is that it is quick to use and ideal for those times when you need to get in tune in a hurry.

Ratings

Longevity	Fun factor	Practicality	Value
★★★★☆	★★★☆☆	★★★★★	★★★★★

Overall Rating ★★★★☆

Price: Free **Developer:** Prodisky

PhotoMV Lite

Make a music video on your phone without the editing hassle

If you have ever tried to make a personal video summary of a holiday and wanted to add background music and effects, you will probably be aware that the process is time-consuming and often requires a steep learning curve to even get started. PhotoMV Lite takes away that hassle by offering a basic selection of features which come together enabling you to create mini masterpieces on just your iPhone. You can include your own photos and choose background music which suits the content as well as including song lyrics and a script. This is the Lite version and is therefore more of a stab at demonstrating what the main app can do, but even so it offers some fun and you may well find yourself engrossed in the creation of new projects in no time at all. Video creation does not need more than a few basic features and PhotoMV exploits that well.

Ratings

Longevity	Fun factor	Practicality	Value
★★★☆☆	★★★★☆	★★★★☆	★★★★★

Overall Rating ★★★★☆

■ Add some photos for the slideshow.

■ Choose a background song for extra mood.

Anthem Pro

Price: £0.59/$0.99 Developer: YJ Soft

Become an anthem know-it-all for just a few pennies

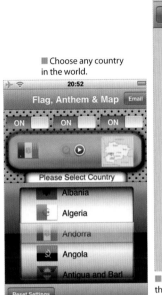

■ Choose any country in the world.

We hear many national anthems throughout the course of our lives, at sporting events and the like, but rarely can we remember any of them. With the Anthem Pro app from YJ Soft you can listen to the anthems of all of the countries in the world and also become familiar with their official flags. A map of each country is thrown in for good measure as well, and this information could be useful in a number of instances; pub quizzes, showing off to your friends and all sorts. You have to use an internet connection to listen to the anthems and while this would normally be a downside, at least you get to save some space on your iPhone by not having them pre-loaded along with the app. National anthems are not usually the kind of material most people want to carry around with them, but a little bit of knowledge goes a long way and for that the app held our interest well.

■ Flags and maps are included alongside the national anthems.

Ratings

Longevity	Fun factor	Practicality	Value
★★★☆☆	★★★★☆	★★★☆☆	★★★★☆

Overall Rating ★★★☆☆

Price: £1.19/$1.99 Developer: Linhoole

aRelax Sleep iSmooth Wave

Create a mix of sounds for the perfect relaxing background noise.

■ The app's interface is relaxing on its own.

aRelax Sleep iSmooth Wave from developer Linhoole is one of a growing number of apps designed to help you relax or to get a better night's sleep. It contains the expected rain and weather sounds, but also includes a number of different noises such as crickets at night and a frog song. The sounds can be chosen by length and you can also set up playlists which can include more than one sound at different volumes. This customisation ability makes aRelax Sleep different in that you can choose what you want to listen to and once you have found the right mix, just plug your headphones in and send yourself to another place before bedtime. The interface and selection of sounds will suit the majority of users and we found it to be one of the best available in this category. It is without doubt worth a try to see if it works for you, and we suspect that it will.

Ratings

Longevity	Fun factor	Practicality	Value
★★★★☆	★★★☆☆	★★★★☆	★★★★☆

Overall Rating ★★★★☆

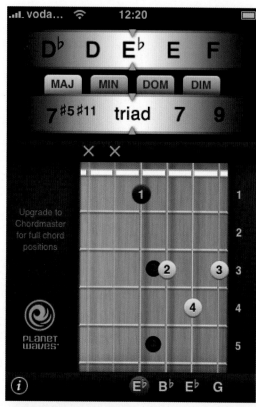

.ιΙ. voda... 🔋 12:20

Dᵇ D Eᵇ E F

MAJ | MIN | DOM | DIM

7 ♯5♯11 | triad | 7 | 9

× ×

Upgrade to Chordmaster for full chord positions

PLANET WAVES

ⓘ

Eᵇ Bᵇ Eᵇ G

■ You can strum any chord using the on-screen strings.

Chordmaster
Price: £1.19/$1.99
Developer: Planet Waves

Every chord you need in the palm of your hand

Chords are the staple diet of guitarists, but few people can claim to know them all. Chordmaster from Planet Waves brings together over 7,000 chords and conveniently puts them into one app and also throws in the fingering needed to play these chords on a nicely laid out guitar-based interface. The notes are displayed alongside every possible combination of physical and theoretical notation so you know that you are playing the correct chords, and this can be of huge benefit to any guitarist at any level of expertise, from beginner to advanced. The chords can be strummed on the screen and the realistic sounds are a testament to how well made the Chordmaster app is. Both left and right-handers are catered for and any guitar player will be hard-pressed not to see the benefits here. This is one app which truly pulls off its purpose and we cannot think of many ways to improve it.

Ratings

Longevity	Fun factor	Practicality	Value
★★★★★	★★★☆☆	★★★★★	★★★★☆

Overall Rating ★★★★★

Price: £0.59/$0.99 **Developer:** Helmes Innovations, LLC

60 songs in 60 minutes? You bet

Gone In 60

■ This is a whole new way to play music in bite-sized chunks.

■ Add some songs or go for the random approach.

🛪 ⬆ 21:05

Songs | Done

Add All Songs ⊕

A

Ad #3
Signature - Tom Munch ⊕

Addicted
Back To Black (Deluxe Edition) [CD1] - ... ⊕

Alfie
Alright, Still - Lily Allen ⊕

All I Need Is Time
I'm Still In Love With You - Roy Orbison ⊕

All I Want Is You
Greatest Hits Live - Carly Simon ⊕

All Over the World
All Over the World: The Very Best of EL... ⊕

All We Have Is Now

Playlists | Artists | Songs | Albums | More

Gone In 60 is a one-trick pony which does nothing particularly special, but the trick it performs works very well indeed and is one you will likely come back to time and time again. In its default setting you can play 60 random songs in one hour, but the music you play can be selected and also the length of each song changed as well. Gone In 100 is another setting on offer where you can choose 100 songs in, yep, you guessed it, 100 minutes. The playback can be paused at any time and the on-screen dialogue shows the number of songs played and the time remaining. It may all sound rather basic, but once you have used it once, it quickly becomes a whole new way to enjoy your own music. It's a great way to pass time on the train to work, for example, as before you know it your hour will be up. The only improvement we would like to see, though, is a smoother transition between tracks which are just cut off halfway through in this version.

Ratings

Longevity	Fun factor	Practicality	Value
★★★★	★★★★	★★★	★★★★

Overall Rating ★★★★

Blind Test

Price: £0.59/$0.99 Developer: Dworld Services

How well do you know your own music?

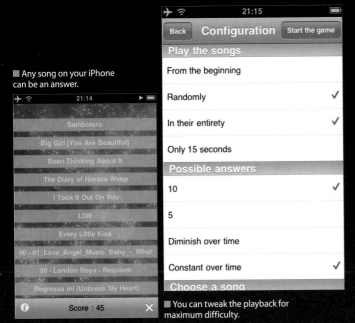

■ Any song on your iPhone can be an answer.

■ You can tweak the playback for maximum difficulty.

The best games are almost always the most simple ones and Blind Test is an excellent example of an app which you can enjoy on your own or with friends. It offers up a list of songs on your iPhone and plays one of them – all it asks you to do is tap the correct song name to gain points, which are made up as follows: ten points for choosing the right one within ten seconds and a point lost as each ten-second unit passes. You also lose a point for each incorrect guess. It really could not be simpler, but is most enjoyable when played with a group of people to test their music knowledge. One thing we did notice was how few tracks on our test iPhone we recognised straight away which suggested that a lot of it is rarely listened to, and you will probably find the same issue. This app is great fun and to maximise the longevity of Blind Test all you need to do is change the music on your iPhone regularly!

Ratings

Longevity	Fun factor	Practicality	Value
★★★★☆	★★★★★	★★★☆☆	★★★★☆

Overall Rating ★★★★☆

Album Covers

Price: £1.19/$1.99 Developer: Andrea Vettori

Use your album covers for more than just decoration

Developed by Andrea Vettori, Album Covers looks like little more than a fancy screen saver when you first power it up, but there is a bit more beneath the surface which makes it an entirely different beast. After a day's use you may find yourself using it to manage the music you are playing each day on your iPhone. The album covers already loaded on your iPhone are used to produce a spiralling screen saver which can then be manipulated to play particular albums or to add and delete selected covers. Covers can be resized and rotated and your selections can then be saved to form a visual playlist of your favourite albums. Tracks can be played at random and after you have become familiar with the interface, it soon becomes a useful and interactive tool which brings a touch of fun to the otherwise mundane process of playing music and selecting which tracks to listen to next.

■ You can resize any album cover.

■ Your album covers spin as the music plays.

Ratings

Longevity	Fun factor	Practicality	Value
★★★★☆	★★★★☆	★★★☆☆	★★★★☆

Overall Rating ★★★★☆

Navigation

With all the big players finally making their way to Apple's mighty device, it's time to let your iPhone take you in new directions…

Price: £59.99/$99.99   **Developer:** TomTom International BV

TomTom UK & Ireland

The in-car navigation giant comes to the iPhone

Of all the turn-by-turn navigation apps to have appeared recently, TomTom For iPhone is probably the most eagerly awaited. Interface-wise, TomTom has done a nice job integrating the familiar look and feel of its established range of personal navigation devices with the iPhone's own unique control system, so that anyone who has spent time using either device will quickly feel at home.

The inclusion of the latest IQ route calculation algorithms is a welcome plus, but there's a distinct lack of some of the more standard features that you might find on a dedicated device, such as lane guidance, map share, custom POI, road speed warning alarms, and motorway

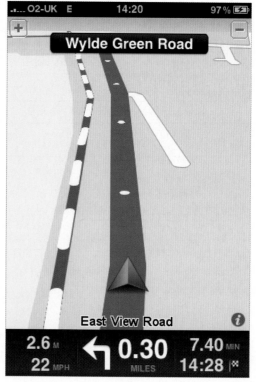

The app will work in both portrait and landscape modes.

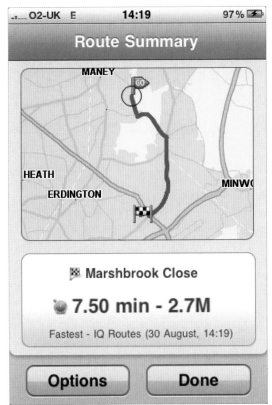

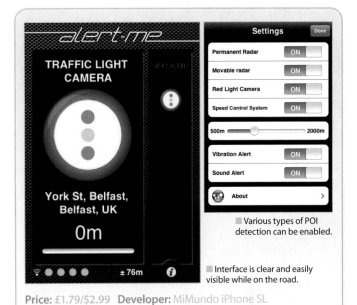

■ Useful route summary page displays your intended route.

junction views. You do, however, get a safety camera database, the ability to call POI from the interface and the option to use an iPhone address book contact as a destination, together with an A-B route planner and real-time route simulation.

Out on the road, initial route calculation was swift, but the app's use of the iPhone's GPS receiver was somewhat patchy. Promising to boost GPS reception significantly by way of its own built-in GPS antenna, this also offers a secure windscreen suction mount, car stereo support and hands-free calling capabilities. With a steady signal, the map display lagged slightly behind our vehicle's actual road position, but the voice directions were consistently clear and precise and the plentiful on-screen information was well laid out and clearly legible in typical TomTom style.

In summary, the app works well as a basic satnav, but TomTom aficionados may be left feeling disappointed by the apparent lack of more advanced features. The forthcoming car kit may well improve any performance issues, but the eye-watering combined price of £160 makes the system a more expensive option than some of the company's standalone devices, and with the current feature set you have to wonder whether it's worth it.

Ratings

Longevity	Fun factor	Practicality	Value
★★★★	★★★	★★★★	★★

Overall Rating ★★★☆☆

■ Various types of POI detection can be enabled.

■ Interface is clear and easily visible while on the road.

Price: £1.79/$2.99 **Developer:** MiMundo iPhone SL

Speedcams UK: AlertMe

Europe's top speed camera detection app comes to the UK

This speed camera detector can be set to detect both fixed and mobile speed cameras, as well as traffic light cams and speed control systems. It can sometimes be a little over-sensitive, detecting cameras that aren't actually on the road you're on, but it's better that it reports ghost ones instead of missing them.

Audible warnings are loud and clear, although it would be nice to be able to turn the volume down a bit. When there are no cameras around, you get a cool rotating radar scanning effect, but as you approach a camera, you get an audible warning, a description of the type of camera and a display of the speed limit you should be obeying, alongside a range indication of how far away the camera is. Other than a six-LED display of GPS signal strength, that's about it, but considering how much cheaper this is than a dedicated unit, it works impressively well.

Ratings

Longevity	Fun factor	Practicality	Value
★★★★	★★★	★★★★	★★★

Overall Rating ★★★★☆

Price: Free **Developer:** Route Buddy Ltd

RouteBuddy Atlas

Offline map viewing, but you have to purchase maps separately

Route Buddy allows online viewing of two popular online mapping services, OpenStreetMap and OpenCycleMap, and also stores Ordnance Survey maps for viewing offline, but there's one huge catch. Although the app itself is free, it only comes with two offline maps for demonstration purposes. If you want any Ordnance Survey maps, you have to buy them from the RouteBuddy website at anything from £10 per sheet upwards. The online maps require a network connection, but although the app will automatically cache them allowing you to view them offline, they're nowhere near as detailed as the OS maps available. Syncing purchased maps to the phone is also a bit of a palaver, so we'd like to see an in-app purchasing system with a considerable drop in map prices. An app with a lot of potential but let down by a business model that's sure to put off a lot of buyers.

Ratings

Longevity	Fun factor	Practicality	Value
★★☆☆☆	★★☆☆☆	★★★☆☆	★★☆☆☆

Overall Rating ★★★★☆

■ Main interface displays both online and offline map options.

■ Uses GPS to display and track your location and movements.

Price: Free **Developer:** Graphiclife

POI Warner Lite

Get advance warning on speed and safety camera locations

When you first launch this app, it can be a bit puzzling, as initially the interface of three polished glass blobs and a compass dial appears inert. It only comes alive out on the road, when the largest of the three blobs reveals itself to be a speedometer. When a camera appears in range, the unit beeps and a 'distance to camera' countdown bar appears at the top of the screen. The current speed limit is displayed in one of the smaller blobs, while the third blob displays the type of POI being detected. In our tests, the speedometer always seemed to be a couple of seconds behind, but the camera detection proved fairly accurate.

This free version contains a database of over 20,000 fixed speed and red light cameras, but a Pro version can be had for £3.49 that includes details of an additional 22,000 mobile speed cameras.

Ratings

Longevity	Fun factor	Practicality	Value
★★★☆☆	★★★☆☆	★★★★☆	★★★★★

Overall Rating ★★★★☆

■ Green speedo turns red if the limit is exceeded.

■ Red bar at the top displays distance to camera.

Price: £52.99/$89.99 **Developer:** Navigon

Mobile Navigator British Isles
Full turn-based navigation app

Of the clutch of turn-by-turn navigation apps to hit the App Store this summer, Navigon was the first to show its colours. As these apps go, Mobile Navigator is an extremely capable solution, good on all the important points such as quick load time, fast GPS lock, clear interface, well-timed announcements and good route calculation. There are a couple of handy add-ons such as lane assist and realistic motorway junction views, and iPod control is also well integrated, with music lowered nicely while directions are being announced. All of the UK and Ireland is covered for your 53 quid and while it may not currently leap out from the pack, a raft of promised updates, including text-to speech, live services and full seven digit UK postcode entry (a surprising omission from the current version) should make this a worthy contender for the iPhone satnav crown.

Ratings

Longevity	Fun factor	Practicality	Value
★★★★☆	★★★☆☆	★★★★☆	★★★☆☆

Overall Rating ★★★★☆

■ Stylish menu system includes useful 'Take Me Home' button.

Price: £0.59/$0.99 **Developer:** Zach Waugh

Meter Maid
Avoiding parking tickets is what this app was 'maid' for

Meter Maid lets you set a parking meter time of up to eight hours, then alerts you with a push notification 15 minutes before your time is up, after which it can guide you back to where you parked your wheels via GPS. The countdown timer runs in the background, and the app works perfectly well for the purpose for which it was designed, but many UK car parks now employ a ticket method which relies on remembering the actual expiry time rather than the period of time purchased, and that's where this app falls down.

You can set the time remaining on the meter with ease, but you can't simply enter a "paid until" expiry time, so if you're parked by one of those machines, a bit of mental arithmetic is often required to work out what you need to enter into the app, and on the whole that kind of defeats the purpose just a little bit.

Ratings

Longevity	Fun factor	Practicality	Value
★★★★☆	★★☆☆☆	★★★☆☆	★★★★☆

Overall Rating ★★★☆☆

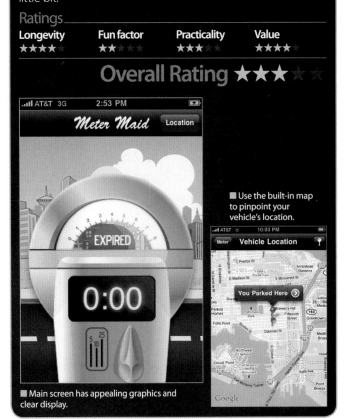

■ Use the built-in map to pinpoint your vehicle's location.

■ Main screen has appealing graphics and clear display.

Price: Free   Developer: sendmetospace

London JamCams

Check out traffic hotspots in the capital at any time

London JamCams captures traffic camera feeds from major roads in the London area and relays them to your phone so that you can check in advance whether it's worth leaving work in time to hit Hanger Lane at 5pm on a Friday. The app is easy to use and although the images are not live, we never found one that was more than a few minutes old. You can store a favourite sequence of cameras along a particular route if there's one that you need to check regularly, but the selection of 179 available cameras could be improved, as there are some areas not covered. Every now and then an image was unable to be displayed for technical reasons, but that's probably more the fault of Transport For London's camera network than this app. For a free app, you can't really complain, and if you're a working Londoner you'll be surprised how often you'll end up checking this.

■ Camera images are zoomable, but not by a huge amount.

Ratings

Longevity	Fun factor	Practicality	Value
★★★★☆	★★☆☆☆	★★★★☆	★★★★★

Overall Rating ★★★★☆

Price: £52.99/$89.99   Developer: NNG Global Services kft

iGO MyWay 2009 – Western Europe Edition

One of the best-looking options

iGO's MyWay turn-based navigation system includes maps of all of Western Europe, with free quarterly map updates until December 2010, but the payoff is that the app takes ages to start up. Once loaded though, the satellite lock is quicker than most, and this is the only app of its kind with configurable vehicle markers and 3D models of famous landmarks and display of the surrounding terrain. It doesn't yet have a speed camera database, however, and we had the occasional screen blackout. The bongs before each announcement also get old very quickly, but the voice instructions themselves are plentiful and clear, route recalculation is swift, and the lane guidance feature is a useful plus. There are also some improvements in the pipeline.

■ Usual level of flexible route settings are available.

■ 3D renderings of local landmarks aid at-a-glance navigation

Ratings

Longevity	Fun factor	Practicality	Value
★★★★☆	★★★☆☆	★★★☆☆	★★★☆☆

Overall Rating ★★★☆☆

Geocaching

Price: £5.99/$9.99   Developer: Groundspeak Inc

Love treasure-hunting? This is the app for you…

■ The interface has an evocative retro military feel.

Geocaching is a 21st Century global treasure-hunting game, where participants hide small objects, or 'caches', at outdoor locations and log the co-ordinates online so that they can be discovered by anyone with a GPS system. It's great fun, and is developing quite a following, with nearly a million geocaches hidden globally. This official app of the geocaching.com website combines regular GPS functions with a dedicated database of geocache locations and access to the website at which users can log their finds. Let it know your location and it displays a list of all known nearby caches, together with a map, description and co-ordinates for each one. A free intro version is available, limited to your three nearest caches, but this paid version allows access to all caches in your immediate vicinity. The app integrates well with the website, and made finding our first cache easy and fun.

■ All your nearest geocache locations are displayed in list format.

Ratings

Longevity	Fun factor	Practicality	Value
★★★★☆	★★★★☆	★★★☆☆	★★★☆☆

Overall Rating ★★★★☆

G-Park

Price: £0.59/$0.99   Developer: Posimotion

Find your way back to your car… or someone else's

Guiding you back to where you parked your car is a popular application of the iPhone's location-based services, and G-Park is Posimotion's answer to this problem. While the basic premise is excellent, unfortunately the spectre of bad GPS reception tends to get in the way of what should be a simple process.

The idea is you press the 'Park Me!' button once you've parked your car, take a photo or add some notes if you wish, then continue on your way. However, the app took ages to get a GPS fix on our location, leaving us loitering beside our car until we gave up and entered the car's position manually. When we wanted to return, the app frequently failed to locate our current position properly, and often calculated a ridiculously circuitous route back to the stored location. We so wanted to like this app, but unfortunately it just didn't work for us.

■ Use the Park Me! button to acquire a GPS fix.

■ Get Google Map directions back to your car.

Ratings

Longevity	Fun factor	Practicality	Value
★★☆☆☆	★★☆☆☆	★☆☆☆☆	★★★★☆

Overall Rating ★★☆☆☆

■ The recent update adds iPhone keyboard functionality throughout the app.

Price: £25.99/$42.99
Developer: ALK Technologies

CoPilot Live UK & Ireland

Can CoPilot steal a march on its more expensive counterparts?

CoPilot Live offers full turn-based navigation at literally half the cost of its three main rivals. The Navteq map system loads very quickly, and there's full 3D display with speed-variable zoom, safety camera alerts, full postcode entry, lane guidance, and much more. The 'Live' tag refers to weather information and roadside assist, but sadly not traffic updates or fuel prices as-of yet; these are to be a forthcoming paid update.

CoPilot combines a clear and concise menu system with a smart, easily legible map display, although the voice commands can sound like you're being shouted at through a kazoo. On-road performance is sound and it holds the GPS signal well, although it tends to announce turns late and it doesn't always find the best route. That said, with this many features at this price, CoPilot Live is hard to fault. Great value for such a feature-packed app.

Ratings
Longevity	Fun factor	Practicality	Value
★★★★	★★★	★★★★	★★★★★

Overall Rating ★★★★☆

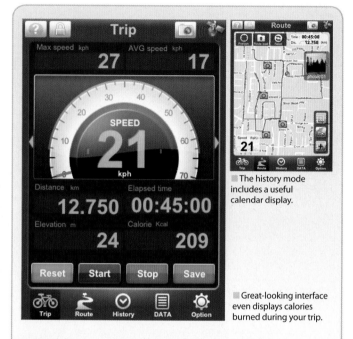

■ The history mode includes a useful calendar display.

■ Great-looking interface even displays calories burned during your trip.

Price: £1.79/$2.99 **Developer:** ZeroOne MIA

BikeMate GPS

Keep track of your cycling routes and exercise data

BikeMate GPS is an advanced cycle computer, route tracker and exercise log, aimed primarily at serious cyclists. The app consists of a trip mode with speedometer, elevation meter and trip computer, a route mode that records your movements and a history section to archive stored trips. You can also take photos within the app while en route. The speedo function looks fantastic, but unfortunately it lagged behind our test bike's onboard computer both in response time and displayed speed. The Route mode did a good job of tracking and displaying our route, although it would also be good if it featured a way to keep your blue dot centred on the map while riding. This app is packed with features, so the comprehensive built-in help system is a big plus, and a free version appeared on the store as we went to press, providing an excellent way to try before you buy.

Ratings
Longevity	Fun factor	Practicality	Value
★★	★★★★	★★★	★★★

Overall Rating ★★★☆☆

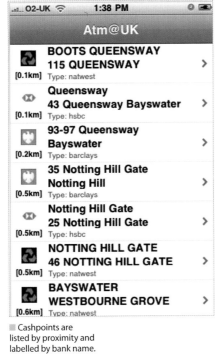

Show in Maps Application

Email Location

Cancel

■ Cashpoints are listed by proximity and labelled by bank name.

Price: Free   **Developer:** Wees Wares

Atm@UK

Run out of money? Quickly locate the nearest cash dispenser

Atm@UK is a free app that uses the iPhone's GPS capability to highlight the location of nearly 6,000 NatWest, Barclays, HSBC and HBOS cash machines across the UK.

It asks to use your location and subsequently offers a list of nearby machines, listed by proximity with the closest at the top. From there, you have the option to view your selected machine's location on a map, or launch the iPhone's Maps app to guide you to the location. You can also email the co-ordinates to a contact if you wish. In our tests, results were accurate and up to date, and we couldn't really fault it.

It's free, so you have to endure the inevitable banner ads at the bottom of the screen, but this is a relatively small price to pay for such a useful app. This could certainly come in very handy on your next night out.

Ratings

Longevity	Fun factor	Practicality	Value
★★★★☆	★★★☆☆	★★★★☆	★★★★★

Overall Rating ★★★★☆

■ The app certainly packs a lot into a small space.

■ Add new cameras as and when you find them.

Price: £0.59/0.99   **Developer:** Atoll Ordenadores

aSmart HUD 3D + Speedcams UK

A real bargain!

This app is a sort of in-car GPS Swiss army knife, comprising a speedometer with limit warnings, compass, real-time GPS map display, weather information, iPod music controller and speed camera detector – all for 59 pence! It also has a head-up display mode that inverts the display so that you can place your device on your dashboard, read its reflection in your windscreen and pretend to be a jet pilot. Although it's a cool idea, the HUD mode only really works properly when it's fully dark, as the screen just doesn't go bright enough to use in daylight, and even then you tend to get a double reflection which makes it hard to read. Nevertheless, everything else works pretty well. You do get a lot for your loose change, and the fact that all of this is crammed onto a single screen and remains usable is a credit to the designers.

Ratings

Longevity	Fun factor	Practicality	Value
★★★★☆	★★★☆☆	★★★★☆	★★★★☆

Overall Rating ★★★★☆

App Store | **News**

News

From celebrity gossip to hard hitting headlines, there's an application to will satisfy your hunger for news

Price: £0.59/$0.99   Developer: 8080 srl

Frontpages

Hold the front page! Turn your iPhone into a virtual newsstand!

Many news apps provide links to specially formatted digital editions of your favourite newspapers but reading a digital version of a newspaper is like browsing a website. Your favourite paper can lose its character and identity when viewed in its iPhone-formatted edition. This lovely app re-connects you with your newspaper by downloading the latest 'hot off the press' front page directly to your iPhone. This is akin to popping into your local newsagents and treating it like a library as you read through all the front pages (though you don't have to worry about the annoyed glare of the shopkeeper as you get your free hit of headline news).

This is a great app if you need a quick news fix and don't have time to wade through a whole paper. If you're on holiday it's nice to be able to get a taste of what's going on at home. You can pinch to zoom in to read the small newsprint and pan around the paper by dragging your finger on the screen.

Frontpages is designed to look like a traditional newsstand. Simply search through the list of papers (or browse by typing a country into the search field)

You can browse via paper or country to choose your favourite front page.

Zoom and pan the front page to read its contents.

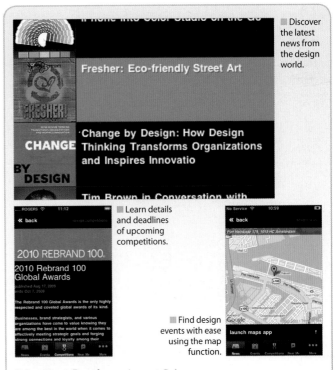

Price: Free **Developer:** Levent Ozler

Dexigner

Discover news and events from the world of design

This app is based on the comprehensive Dexigner website and it puts that site's resources in the palm of your hand. If you're a creative person then Dexigner will keep you up to date on the latest news and trends from the world of design.

As well as sharing design news the app excels at telling you about local design-related exhibitions and events courtesy of its Near Me tab. After reading the blurb about an event you can click on a location link to view the venue on a map. The map displays the location from within Dexigner so you don't have to leave the app to view the location in the iPhone's Maps app. Also, the Competitions tab reveals opportunities for you to showcase your skills. All in all a practical and well-designed app!

and choose your favourites. The selected paper's latest edition will then be displayed as a folded newspaper in the main newsstand graphic. You can swipe your finger to browse through multiple shelves of papers. If a particular headline intrigues you and you need to know more then there's an icon that will take you to the website edition of that paper in Safari. You can also open PDF versions of the front pages in Safari too, for sharper looking text and brighter image colours.

On the downside there's only a few UK papers to peruse but this should change over time. Occasionally you'll get a closed shutter graphic saying 'Image Not Available', which is frustrating. You only need to buy this app once and the latest front pages of your favourite papers can be within reach wherever you are.

Ratings

Longevity	Fun factor	Practicality	Value
★★★★☆	★★★☆☆	★★★☆☆	★★★☆☆

Overall Rating ★★★☆☆

Ratings

Longevity	Fun factor	Practicality	Value
★★★★☆	★★☆☆☆	★★★★☆	★★★★☆

Overall Rating ★★★★☆

Price: Free   Developer: The Financial Times Ltd.

Financial Times

Follow changes in the markets and get sound money advice

To get more from this app you'll need to register.

Money makes the world go round, so financial news is important. This app is the digital edition of the respected pink paper that's seen folded under the arm of commuters as they head for the city. The app is free to download, but you get a limited amount of articles to read per month. You can increase this amount by registering for free, but to really benefit from the app you'll need to subscribe for £2.99 per week.

As well as breaking financial news from around the world you can use the app's Market tab to compare the performance of your currency with any other country's cash to help you get the best exchange rate when going on holiday. There's also a handy currency converter to stop you being ripped off! You can also customise it to set up a personalised portfolio to watch your share process rise or fall. It could be a sound investment to download this app.

Ratings

Longevity	Fun factor	Practicality	Value
★★★★☆	★☆☆☆☆	★★★☆☆	★★★☆☆

Overall Rating ★★★☆☆

Price: Free   Developer: Russell Berry

HonestJohn Motoring Advice

Need a motor? Ask Honest John

Honest John used to be a motoring columnist for the *Daily Telegraph*. He can now dispense expert car-related advice directly from your iPhone. This is a great app for those who love cars and want to read road tests of specific models so that they can make an informed purchase. It's also handy for those who are thinking of buying a new car but don't know their axle from their engine.

You can search the app's Back Room for answers to specific topics and read expert advice. To ask your own question you need to log on to HonestJohn.co.uk, but there are plans to make this function accessible via the application.

There's also a link to video Road Tests that open in the iPhone's YouTube app. The video production values aren't that of *Top Gear* but the clips are very informative. Put your foot down and download this useful app.

■ Read in-depth road tests of multiple makes and models.

■ Get the latest car-centric stories from the app's news tab.

Ratings

Longevity	Fun factor	Practicality	Value
★★★★☆	★★★☆☆	★★★☆☆	★★★★☆

Overall Rating ★★★★☆

iHotUKDeals

Price: Free   Developer: DiddleySoft 2009

Grab a bargain courtesy of this credit-crunch clobbering app

The app's users share high street deals that they spot.

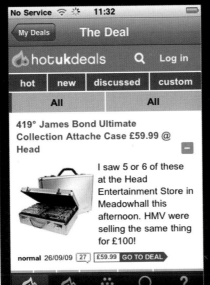

In the current financial climate we all appreciate the value of money and this handy app can help us cut costs. You can browse for deals by Categories (like Entertainment and Groceries for example) or type in the goods that you're looking for using the app's Search function. The Freebies section is well worth a look as it lets you discover deals like the fact that Comet are throwing in a free a Samsung D60 camera with every Mac purchased. You can even log in and ask for advice on where to buy specific items and you'll get a host of helpful hints and tips from other users.

Many of the links will take you to various vendor sites in Safari (like Play.com) so you'll need to re-launch the app to continue browsing, which can prove annoying at times. The hottest deals are red with a high temperature rating so you can spot a bargain with ease.

Ratings

Longevity	Fun factor	Practicality	Value
★★★★	★★★★	★★★	★★★★

■ Bag yourself a bargain with this free app.

Overall Rating ★★★★

KickScreen Movie Trailers

Price: £1.19/$0.99   Developer: k5 Softwa

KickScreen gives you a Hollywood hit whenever you need one.

The great thing about movie trailers is that they're designed to entertain. A boring film can look great when viewed as a truncated trailer. You could search for trailers using your iPhone's YouTube app but you may miss some new films. There are podcasts that collect and play movie trailers but these are not always up to date and take longer to download and sync.

KickScreen presents you with quick and easy access to trailers for the latest releases. They're listed by the day that they were released so you won't miss a thing. Click a link to play the trailer in your YouTube app. You can also browse trailers for upcoming movies and discover what's just out on DVD. On the other hand, apps like Flixster also show movie and DVD trailers and throw in local cinema times for free, so the asking price of £1.19 may be viewed as a bit steep.

■ Get a flavour of each trailer before streaming i

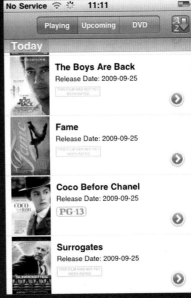

Ratings

Longevity	Fun factor	Practicality	Value
★★★★	★★★	★★★	★

■ Find trailers for what's showing or what's

Overall Rating ★★★

Price: Free Developer: Stepcase Limited

Lifehack

Learn to stay human in a technology-centric world

There are many news apps out there vying for attention, so each app needs a unique selling point to make it stand out from the crowd. As its name suggests, Lifehack combines tips on living a fulfilling life with ways to manage technology. The app is crammed full of interesting self-help articles (like Dating, Living and Being Your Best Self), but it also has articles with a technology-related twist like 10 Basic Tech Tips (which covers good working practices like making backups and organising your workflow).

The app's bias towards technology is clear from the presence of its Productivity and Technology tabs. A Comment link lets you share your thoughts on any article via the Stepcase Lifehack website, though, as this is displayed within the app's interface, you don't need to use Safari. This self-help app is a great way to improve both your personal and technology-related life!

Ratings

Longevity	Fun factor	Practicality	Value
★★★	★★★	★★★	★★★★

Overall Rating ★★★★

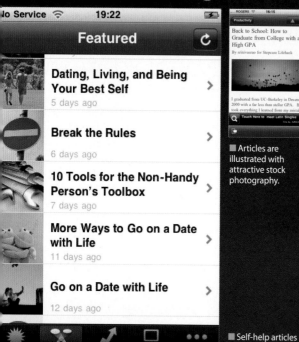

■ Self-help articles help you develop as a person.

■ Articles are illustrated with attractive stock photography.

Price: Free Developer: Kosmix Corporation

meeTV

Catch up with the latest news from your favourite programmes

We all have 'must see' TV programmes to look forward to, but we may lack the time to dig up the latest plot developments and rummage through rumours. This free app trawls blogs and news sites for stories relating to our favourite shows and delivers them to the iPhone for you to enjoy.

The meeTV app could be accused of being biased to American shows like *Lost*, *Dexter* and *American Housewives* but with the wide availability of cable and satellite TV you'll probably be familiar with most of the 50 shows listed in this app.

The app is customisable so it's easy to choose which shows to display using the Customize tab. You can then browse news relating to your chosen programmes in the My Shows tab. The app is a bit hit and miss when it comes to finding relevant stories so you may have to wade through irrelevant content to find the pertinent points, but overall it's a great app.

MissionClock

■ Now you can follow the build up to an impending mission launch.

■ The app is light on looks but heavy on mission information.

Price: £0.59/$0.99 **Developer:** James Leung

News Feed (UK)

The perfect portal to multiple news sources

 This invaluable app lets you gather all of your favourite news providers under one roof. News sources are grouped into handy categories, like British News or Technology News, so you can find what you fancy with ease. Each source is symbolised by an icon, so the app can cram lots of links into the iPhone's screen to minimise scrolling. You can tell the app to assign labels to each icon if you're unsure what they represent. Collapse any categories that you're not interested in to speed up access to those that you are. To make full use of the iPhone's screen the navigation bar only pops up when summoned.

The app is fully customisable so you can drag favourite news sources to the top of the scrollable stack. Once you click an icon the content is formatted to fit your iPhone's screen and you can click the back icon to continue browsing other sources. This amazing app is a one stop news shop!

Ratings
Longevity	Fun factor	Practicality	Value
★★★★☆	★★☆☆☆	★★★★☆	★★★★☆

Overall Rating ★★★★☆

■ Browse top tales from the world of TV.

■ Chose the shows you're a fan of with a tick!

Ratings
Longevity	Fun factor	Practicality	Value
★★★☆☆	★★☆☆☆	★★☆☆☆	★★★☆☆

Overall Rating ★★★☆☆

Price: £2.99/$4.99 **Developer:** Latency: Zero

Get a front seat in Mission Control with this hi-tech app

 When the Apollo missions blasted off in the Sixties the eyes of the world followed every development with fascination. In the 21st Century we take rocket launches for granted. Luckily there are news apps like MissionClock for those with their eyes on the stars.

Most people tune in when the countdown to a rocket launch gets to ten but with MissionClock you can prepare for lift-off hours before the event. You can also count down to key events like arrival of the crew.

You don't have to be a rocket scientist to enjoy MissionClock, but it won't appeal to the casual app user. It takes knowledge of space terminology for granted and uses lots of acronyms. You can also follow the status of current missions on the International Space Station and even be alerted to key developments like a launch abort by Push Notifications. An app that's out of this world.

Ratings
Longevity	Fun factor	Practicality	Value
★★★★☆	★☆☆☆☆	★★★☆☆	★★★☆☆

Overall Rating ★★★★☆

■ Drag your favourite feeds to the top to see their icons first.

Price: £1.19/$1.99 **Developer:** LeapBound

Push News

Get the latest news headlines to pop up on your screen

 We all like to know what's happening as soon as it happens, which is why so many TV news channels have a scrolling 'Breaking News' caption to keep us hooked. But to keep up to date on breaking news via the iPhone we need to tap on a news app's icon. Not any more! This clever app lets you subscribe to the news feed of a variety of sources like the BBC or the *New York Times*. You can then browse through the latest headlines. If a new story breaks you'll hear an alert and receive a Push Notification that will appear in a text message-style box. Tick View to go straight to Push News. If the alert sounds prove annoying, then you can turn them off via the Settings menu. On the downside, though, you may get annoyed when a message pops up while you're using another app and multiple beeps can be distracting when you're trying to work. Despite this, though, it's a useful news app.

Ratings

Longevity	Fun factor	Practicality	Value
★★★★☆	★★★☆☆	★★☆☆☆	★★★☆☆

Overall Rating ★★★★☆

■ News headlines pop up text-message style.

■ Click on a link to get the full story.

Price: £0.59/$0.99 **Developer:** Hassan Hosam

Tech Fuse

A sleek, well-designed way to enjoy technology news

 Many apps do a similar job of collecting themed news sources and providing links to their websites, however, some of these sites are not designed to be viewed specifically on the iPhone, so you have to double tap to make the text readable and slide the content around to read it. Tech Fuse does provides exclusive access to iPhone-formatted versions of popular technology sources like Engadget, Ars Technica, TechCrunch and Mashable. It also features 20 other technology related sites to peruse.

Tech Fuse combines good looks with functionality. You can summon site icon links with a shake, then shake again to banish the icons so you can enjoy the stories you've summoned. Swipe left or right to browse through the collection of news sources. You can also copy and insert an email link to an interesting story with a tap. A technology news app that makes full use of the iPhone's technology!

Ratings

Longevity	Fun factor	Practicality	Value
★★★☆☆	★★☆☆☆	★★★☆☆	★★★☆☆

Overall Rating ★★★★☆

■ Shake your iPhone to summon or banish the navigation strip.

■ Browse tech apps by tapping on an icon.

Price: Free Developer: Missing Ink Studios Ltd.

The Independent

Enjoy your news via this slickly designed digital newspaper

The sayings 'content is king' and 'looks aren't everything' certainly apply to apps. Some have amateur graphics but are rich in content while others are all style but no substance. The Independent is the mobile version of the British newspaper that manages to combine style with content. The main page's colourful logos are against a white background so you can quickly find your favourite news category in a tap. Each icon displays the number of unread stories.

Once you dip into a category you can scroll through the text-based headlines until you find something you want to explore. All the content is formatted for the iPhone's screen so there's no need to double tap to zoom (and you can tweak font size from the Settings menu). The font colour of each headline changes to grey once you've clicked it, so you know which articles have been perused. An attractive and practical digital newspaper.

Ratings

Longevity	Fun factor	Practicality	Value
★★★★☆	★★★☆☆	★★★★☆	★★★★★

Overall Rating ★★★★★

■ Colourful icons against a clean white interface make browsing quick and easy.

Price: £1.19/$1.99 Developer: Navjot Kailay

Tick Talk

Wake up to the future of news delivery with this hi-tech app

Sometimes you get hold of an app with enough novelty factor to show off to everyone. Tick Talk is this type of app, as it turns your iPhone into a talking robot. Your iPhone-dwelling droid will wake you up in the morning, greet you by name and read you your favourite news site's latest stories in a suitably sci-fi sounding voice

The interface looks great as the robot wakes from its slumber, its eyes aglow. You can tell your robotic servant to snooze or start reading the news. You can get Tick Talk to read news from any site that has a valid RSS feed and type in a personalised greeting for it to speak. You can wake the robot from his sleep with the swipe of a finger so he'll start reading you the news whenever you desire. On the downside the app needs to be running to wake you up so you'll need to pop it in a dock, but this a minor drawback on an exceptional app.

Ratings

Longevity	Fun factor	Practicality	Value
★★★☆☆	★★★★★	★★★☆☆	★★★★☆

Overall Rating ★★★★☆

■ The droid will read the latest newsfeed out loud.

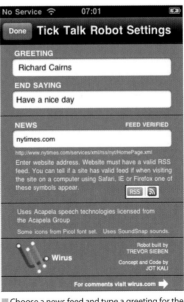

■ Choose a news feed and type a greeting for the robot to read.

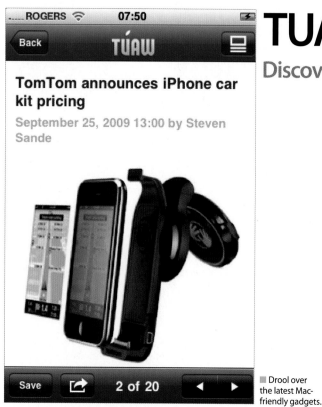

ROGERS 07:50

Back TÚAW

TomTom announces iPhone car kit pricing

September 25, 2009 13:00 by Steven Sande

Save | 2 of 20 | ◀ ▶

■ Drool over the latest Mac-friendly gadgets.

TUAW
Price: Free Developer: AOL

Discover news with an Apple flavour

The iPhone may be the first Apple product you've ever owned, but there are many out there who have been consuming Apple products their entire life. If you're obsessed with all things Macintosh then the Unofficial Apple Weblog is well worth a download (especially as it's free). You can gorge yourself on the latest Apple-related news, indulge in speculating about the next batch of juicy Apple products (from the Rumors tab) and even wallow in nostalgia by browsing through old pictures of Macs from the past. There's also blogs on the latest Apple accessories like the Blur Tripod that lets you take better pictures with your iPhone. The app is also a valuable source of Apple-related tips and tricks. We were especially interested in the technique of shooting magnified photos through a water droplet placed on the iPhone's lens (but have yet summon up the courage to try it!).

Ratings

Longevity	Fun factor	Practicality	Value
★★★☆☆	★★★☆☆	★★★☆☆	★★★★☆

Overall Rating ★★★☆☆

Price: Free Developer: Reed Business Information

Keep tabs on the latest media industry news

Variety

O2-UK 3G 06:46

VARIETY

Today

Malkovich saddles up for 'Secretariat'
John Malkovich is set to join "Secretariat," the Randall Wallace-directed drama for Disney.Malkovich will play Lucien Laurin, the…
22 September 2009 03:00:00

CBS collars Sony TV crime shows
RedlichTolanCBS is developing two more crime-themed hourlo…
22 September 2009 03:00:00

Turteltaub extends tube deal at CBS
TurteltaubJon Turteltaub's Junction Entertainment has sig…
22 September 2009 03:00:00

Visible MEASURES TRAILER BLAZING! OR TRAILER TRASH?

News Reviews Photos Videos Search

■ Browse by categories like News, Reviews and Photos.

■ Enjoy pro shots of the stars via the Photos tab.

ROGERS 17:09

VARIETY

'Mad Men' lead actress nominee Elisabeth Moss arrives at the 61st Primetime Emmy Awards held at the Nokia Theatre on September 20, 2009 in Los Angeles, California.

The Variety app is the digital incarnation of the famous weekly entertainment magazine that's been around for decades, so it has a respectable pedigree. This app is a one-stop-shop for news from the entertainment industry, providing comprehensive coverage of stories from the world of film, TV and even the games industry. It's rich in content and as well as breaking industry news, it boasts a wealth of well considered reviews of the latest Hollywood and independent films.

If star spotting is your thing then the Photos tab will take you to paparazzi-sourced pictures of celebrities as they grace the red carpets at recent awards ceremonies. The Video tab is intriguing, with links to new movie trailers. Sadly the videos aren't compatible with the iPhone's YouTube app, which loses it a Practicality star. The adverts don't fade out like they do in other apps, leading to a rather cluttered interface.

Ratings

Longevity	Fun factor	Practicality	Value
★★★☆☆	★☆☆☆☆	★★☆☆☆	★☆☆☆☆

Overall Rating ★★☆☆☆

Weird News

Price: Free   Developer: Joey Susbilla

Explore the weird wide web with this quirky news app

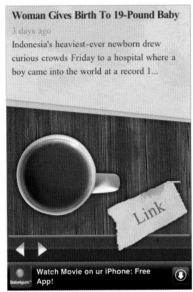

Woman Gives Birth To 19-Pound Baby

3 days ago

Indonesia's heaviest-ever newborn drew curious crowds Friday to a hospital where a boy came into the world at a record 1...

Link

◀ ▶

Watch Movie on ur iPhone: Free App!

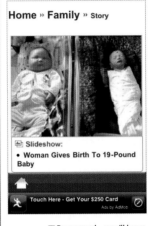

Home » **Family** » Story

Slideshow:
- **Woman Gives Birth To 19-Pound Baby**

Touch Here - Get Your $250 Card
Ads by AdMob

■ Be warned – you'll keep clicking to find more strange tales.

Many TV news broadcasts end the show with the words 'And finally…', before finishing off with a light-hearted or unusual feature like a skate-boarding duck. If you fancy a taste of the weirder side of life then this app will point you in the right direction.

Weird News presents the latest quirky headlines from around the world in an attractive interface that features a coffee-stained desktop (implying you can enjoy browsing this app during your tea break). Each headline (like Woman Gives Birth To 19-Pound Baby) is followed by a brief strapline that gives you the first few lines of the story. If the strap hooks you then press the Link graphic to view the full story from its source website. As the site is displayed within the Weird News browser you can click the Home icon to continue browsing other weird news items without the hassle of relaunching the app.

Ratings

Longevity	Fun factor	Practicality	Value
★★☆☆☆	★★★☆☆	★★★☆☆	★★★☆☆

Overall Rating ★★★★☆

Price: £1.19/$1.99   **Developer:** David Earnest

A comprehensive collection of links to digital news sources

World Newspapers

.....ROGERS 🛜   08:25

ℹ️ **World Newspapers**

Favorites   ›

Regions

The United States   ›

Europe   ›

The Americas   ›

Asia   ›

The Middle East   ›

Africa   ›

■ The content makes up for the app's lack of style.

ROGERS 🛜   08:25

World Newspapers **Europe**

☪ Turkey

Turkmenistan

Ukraine

United Kingdom

Uzbekistan

Vatican City

■ Scroll through countries and tap to find their online papers.

Most news-related apps tend to feed news from a very small collection of big-hitters like Reuters or the BBC. If you want to broaden your search (or focus on a specific country or region), however, then this appropriately named app is certainly for you. It's packed with links to almost 4,000 online newspapers from all over the planet.

If you're working abroad and want to know what's going on in your home town then you'll probably find a link to the local rag's online edition here. Each country is broken up into regions so you can find specific papers with ease. By clicking on a link you'll view the relevant site's webpage from within the app, so there's no need to waste your time jumping back and forth between World Newspapers and Safari. The interface looks a little amateur from a design point of view but it does exactly what it says on the tin.

Ratings

Longevity	Fun factor	Practicality	Value
★★★★☆	★☆☆☆☆	★★★★☆	★★★★☆

Overall Rating ★★★★☆

Photography

Enhance your iPhone's camera, turn photos into paintings, share shots on Flickr and turn the iPhone into a lightmeter!

Price: £1.19/$1.99 **Developer:** Snapture Labs

Snapture

Software that dramatically extends your iPhone camera's functionality

One of the annoying things about shooting photos with the iPhone is the fact that you have to tap a tiny part of the screen to take a picture. This can cause you to miss photo opportunities if you miss the button. Snapture turns the entire iPhone screen into a giant button so you can tap anywhere to capture a killer shot.

At first glance the app looks quite complex with a series of pop-up icons to master. Simply hold your finger down on an icon to see what functions it performs and tap it to change settings. There's also a full explanation of each icon's function when you press the 'i' icon.

▌You can mail a shot before saving it to share photos fast.

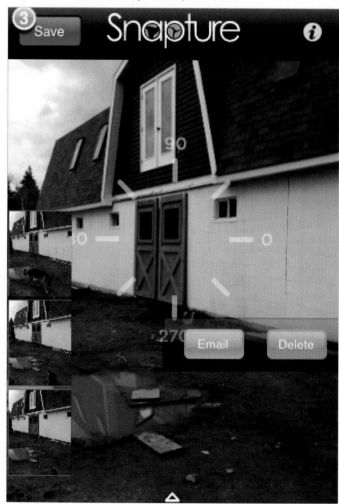

■ The Level Aid overlay helps you stop horizons from tilting.

Snapture soups up your iPhone's camera in many ways to makes it much more versatile. You can tap the screen several times to take consecutive shots without waiting for it to process and save them one at a time. Your shots are displayed as Quick View thumbnails on the screen so you can preview them before deciding whether to save or delete them. You can spread the thumbs out or stack them to save space (or turn them off). Flip a thumbnail to the side and you can delete it or mail it to a mate without having to exit Snapture. This makes Snapture one of the fastest ways to shoot and share! You can also make the iPhone behave as if it has a zoom lens by pinching the screen.

The Save button tells Snapture to process and pop shots into the iPhone's library while you carry on shooting. Snapture also helps you with image composition by offering to overlay a Level Aid graphic that helps you get your horizon looking straight. If you're shooting action then you can get Snapture to take three consecutive shots with one tap using its Multishot function, increasing your chances of capturing a decent shot.

Snapture streamlines the photo shooting, processing and sharing workflow so that you can get much more from your iPhone's camera. It's worth every penny!

Ratings

Longevity	Fun factor	Practicality	Value
★★★★☆	★★☆☆☆	★★★☆☆	★★★☆☆

Overall Rating ★★★☆☆

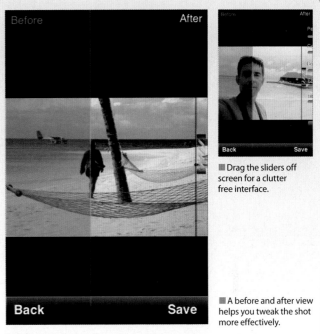

■ Drag the sliders off screen for a clutter free interface.

■ A before and after view helps you tweak the shot more effectively.

Price: £1.79/$2.99 **Developer:** Athentech

Perfectly Clear
Create shots with more contrast and colour

 Many apps let you apply filters to a shot to improve its colour or tone. These changes are often made in a linear way so you can't undo the colour change once you've made a tweak to the contrast. The beauty of Perfectly Clear is the fact that you can change the photo's colour and tonal attributes as much or as little as you like until it's perfect. If it suffers from flat tones boost the Contrast slider. Brighten up under-exposed shots with the Exposure slider. Boost weak colours with the Vibrancy slider and so on.

This app's interface is a bit like a cut-down version of the Adobe Camera Raw editor so if you're a Photoshop fan then you'll feel at home here. Unlike most other photo-fixing apps you can see a before and after version of your shot so you can see how your editing is shaping up. All in all, it's a well-designed and practical app.

Ratings

Longevity	Fun factor	Practicality	Value
★★★★★	★★★★☆	★★★★★	★★★★★

Overall Rating ★★★★★

■ Browse through a variety of filters with thumbnail previews.

■ Choose a shot to edit from your iPhone's library.

■ Choose an effect and preview it using a rather handy thumbnail.

■ Modify attributes like brush size and softness for more effective editing.

Price: £0.59/$0.99 **Developer:** macphun.com

Price: Free **Developer:** Janos Barkai

101+ PhotoEffects

Produce amazing creative images with this filter-filled app

Many iPhone apps let you apply a handful of filters to your shots to grade their colours and produce different looks. This incredible app blows the competition out of the water as it's packed full of Photoshop-style filters. You can make conventional photo-fixing adjustments using filters like More Contrast or Vivid Colors and there's even a handy Crop tool with the ability to rotate and straighten a shot.

The app is also bulging with artistic filters. You can turn a photo into a pencil sketch or make it look like a vintage sepia photo on crumpled paper. It's easy to use too. Simply select a shot, scroll through the list of filters and apply them. By clicking 'Set as current' you can apply a new filter to an already filtered shot, enabling you to combine a variety of filtered effects without having to export and re-import the filtered photo. Incredible value for money.

Ratings

Longevity	Fun factor	Practicality	Value
★★★★★	★★★★☆	★★★★☆	★★★★★

Overall Rating ★★★★★

Effect Touch Lite

Make creative and selective adjustments to your photos

Many photography apps in the iTunes Store let you change a photo by just slapping an effect over the whole image. The great thing about Effect Touch is that it allows you to make selective adjustments. Although the app allows you to produce quite complex creative results, it's very easy to use. Import a shot and then choose a source file from your library (or snap one there and then using the iPhone's camera). Browse through a scrollable selection of effect thumbnails like Color Change or Pixelate and tweak attributes using sliders.

Once you've set the effect up, start painting it onto the screen using your finger. This lets you turn the background black and white to draw attention to an object by leaving it in colour, for example. You can also zoom into your shot, which gives you more control when applying the effect. A clever and creative image-editing app.

Ratings

Longevity	Fun factor	Practicality	Value
★★★★☆	★★★★☆	★★★★☆	★★★★☆

Overall Rating ★★★★★

■ Discover which camera settings will produce the best results.

■ LightMeter evaluates the lighting in the shot as a whole.

Price: £1.79/$2.99 **Developer:** Ambertation

LightMeter

Get a second opinion about a scene's light levels

 Capturing a well-balanced exposure can be a challenge, even using a sophisticated digital SLR with a built-in light meter. If there's contrasting lighting then your SLR may struggle to capture detail in both the shadows and the highlights. Your SLR may be using spot metering to capture detail in a specific part of the scene. This could cause other parts of the scene to be incorrectly exposed.

LightMeter lets you shoot the subject with the iPhone's camera. It then measures the average lighting of the scene and recommends the best aperture, shutter speed and ISO settings for your SLR camera . This enables you to capture detail in the whole shot. If you want to create a wide depth of field you can scroll the aperture wheel to a narrow f-stop like f22. LightMeter will then tell you the appropriate shutter speed and ISO settings to use. Recommended for photography pros only.

Ratings

Longevity	Fun factor	Practicality	Value
★★★☆☆	★☆☆☆☆	★★☆☆☆	★★★☆☆

Overall Rating ★★★☆☆

■ Tap the shots that you want to share on Flickr.

Price: Free **Developer:** Green Volcano Software

Flickit

Upload iPhone photos to Flickr on the move

 Yahoo's online photo gallery, Flickr, is one of the most popular places to share your shots via the web. Although Yahoo's slickly designed Flickr app lets you browse Flickr galleries, it doesn't make it all that easy for you to actually upload your photos to Flickr via the iPhone.

Flickit on the other hand makes it a breeze to blast your iPhone photos off to Flickr. You need to set up a Flickr account to send shots to Flickr from the iPhone, but once that's sorted Flickit will get your photos online in seconds.

Simply tap on the Camera icon to take a shot, or tap the Library icon to select a series of photos from your library. Selected photos appear in a fun filmstrip icon. You can add details like a Title and Description to each queued shot. Click the chunky Upload icon and off they go! And efficient photo uploading app.

Ratings

Longevity	Fun factor	Practicality	Value
★★★★★	★★★☆☆	★★★★★	★★★★★

Overall Rating ★★★★★

■ Big buttons make this Flickr-friendly app easy to use.

■ Add a photo and use Effects to enhance it.

■ Pick a postcard design from a wide range of frames.

Price: £2.99/$4.99   **Developer:** RogueSheep Incorporated

Postage – Postcards

Turn pictures into personalised postcards to share with friends

When you're on your hols it's the tradition to scribble out a 'wish you where here' style postcard and pop it in the post. It's also the tradition to get home before your postcard does. Postage – Postcards lets you create and share personalised postcards in minutes.

As well as presenting your holiday snaps in a variety of attractive designs you can edit your shots to improve their colours and tones. Type in a greeting and change the font, style and text colour to suit the postcard's design. The Share button lets you upload the shot to Facebook or pop it in your library.

The app may seem pricey, but it'll pay for itself in the long run as you'll save on the cost of buying real postcards and postage. It's beautifully designed, full of attractive frames and postcard templates, easy to use and packed full of functions. The perfect professional postcard producer.

Ratings

Longevity	Fun factor	Practicality	Value
★★★★	★★★★	★★★★	★★★★

Overall Rating ★★★★★

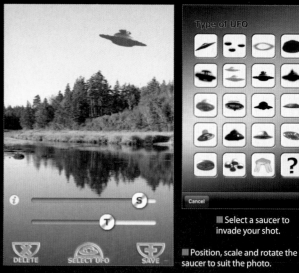

■ Select a saucer to invade your shot.

■ Position, scale and rotate the saucer to suit the photo.

Price: £0.59/$0.99   **Developer:** GK Project

UFO Camera Gold

Prove that the truth is out there with this saucer-spotting app

The frequency of reported UFO sightings tends to follow fashion. During the time that *The X Files* ran on TV in the Nineties, reports of flying saucer sightings soared. Thanks to this clever and easy to use compositing app, the web should brace itself for a new wave of documented UFO sightings.

To add a UFO to any shot simply take a snap with the iPhone (or raid your iPhone's library for a suitable source file). Select a UFO from a generous range of saucer types and drag it into position with your finger. You can then use a slider to scale down the saucer. To make it blend more effectively with the source photo, reduce the UFO's opacity. There's a free Silver edition of the app but it lacks the Gold version's extra saucers and the ability to rotate them to fit landscape-oriented photos. This is a creative app that's out of this world.

Ratings

Longevity	Fun factor	Practicality	Value
★★★	★★★★★	★★★★	★★★★★

Overall Rating ★★★★★

■ Bathe a scene in a 'Hollywood ending' style golden glow.

■ Create classy looking movie graded shots in seconds.

■ Email a high-resolution image to your mates.

■ Let your mates see a precise map of your photo's location.

Price: Free **Developer:** Stephane Lunati

Photo+Map Lite

Add maps to your snaps to illustrate where they were taken

When you snap a photo with your iPhone's camera it uses GPS technology to assign your current location to the photo (if the Location services option is enabled in the Settings menu). The Photo+Map app is able to use this information to add maps to each photo to create a cool and informative souvenir that you can mail to family and friends.

You can choose to add one or four maps to your shot at its full resolution (which will create a healthy 2048 x 2048 sized image if you're using a 3GS). This enables you to produce decent size prints of your photo and map combination.

The app can't find a shot's location if it's been imported from iPhoto (even if it was originally captured on your iPhone), so it's best to assign maps to images before you export them to the Mac. An interesting way to enhance your iPhone photos.

Ratings

Longevity	Fun factor	Practicality	Value
★★	★★	★★	★★

Overall Rating ★★★★★

Price: £0.59/$0.99 **Developer:** Nexvio inc.

CinemaFX

Give your photographs a Hollywood-style makeover

With this app you can make shots look like screen grabs from the movies (without a blockbuster's budget!). In these digital days many filmmakers shoot on video, but they adjust their footage to give it a specific look. This colour and tonal grading process can make a shot look warm and inviting or cold and sinister.

The app is easy to use and produces attractive looking results in seconds. Filters like TWI.Poster produce deep clipped blacks and a subtle desaturated look that mimics the bleach bypass technique applied using traditional film processing, for example. You can use sliders to fine-tune each filter's look to suit your source photo and produce eye-catching results. Bathe a shot in a warm sunset glow using the Japanese Memory filter. CinemaFX may lack the amount of filters boasted by other apps but it's free of the cheesier filters padding out those apps.

Ratings

Longevity	Fun factor	Practicality	Value
★★★★	★★★	★★★★	★★★★

Overall Rating ★★★★★

Price: £1.79/$2.99 **Developer:** Jens Damgen

ProCamera

Need anti-shake and a self-timer? Here you go…

ProCamera does a similar job to Snapture. Both apps have a level indicator designed to help you get your horizons looking horizontal. Both cameras let you zoom in for a close-up and trigger a shot by tapping anywhere in the screen. They also let you preview a shot before saving it (though you can tell ProCamera to AutoSave while you continue snapping).

Although ProCamera doesn't boast Snapture's ability to blast off three consecutive shots with one press of the button, it does outgun its rival thanks to several fabulous features. ProCamera's Tiltmeter is more sophisticated than Snapture's static horizon guide, as it rotates relative to the actual horizon. ProCamera also throws in a grid, which helps you get verticals looking vertical. ProCamera also features a handy self-timer that you can set to a maximum 20-second countdown. The camera also performs well in low light conditions. Both apps have their attractions but this one just has the edge.

Ratings

Longevity	Fun factor	Practicality	Value
★★★★★	★★★	★★★★	★★★★

Overall Rating ★★★★★

■ The interactive Tiltmeter helps you get horizons looking horizontal.

■ The anti-shake feature waits till the camera is steady before shooting.

Price: £1.19/$1.99 **Developer:** Cloudburst Research Inc

AutoStitch

Stitch multiple shots together to create a wide-angle view

The iPhone is stuck with one lens, so you'll end up with a cropped version of a wide landscape. SLR-owning photographers can pop a wide-angle lens on their camera to capture the whole scene. Thanks to this useful app, your iPhone can mimic a wide-angle lens and produce perfect panoramas.

Kick off by panning the iPhone and taking a series of shots of your landscape. Each shot must overlap the previous one so that Auto Stitch can merge them together into a seamless wide-angle image. As the iPhone is handheld, the edges of the panorama may not be aligned, so you can use the app's Crop tool to improve composition and straighten the edges. Auto Stitch lacks the onion-skinning function of stitching apps like Pano (which lets you align the shots as you capture them) but we got the app to work perfectly the first time we used it.

Pop Art Lite

■ Drag sliders to create darker shadows and lighter highlights.

■ Select a shot from your iPhone's library for the screen print treatment.

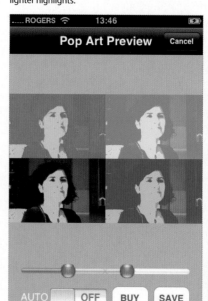

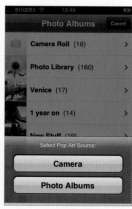

■ The shots will be stitched together as a wide-angle panorama.

■ Take three overlapping shots and import them into the app.

Ratings

Longevity	Fun factor	Practicality	Value
★★★★★	★★★☆☆	★★★★☆	★★★★☆

Overall Rating ★★★★☆

Price: Free **Developer:** Adam Freeman

Reproduce a Warhol-style screen print in seconds

 Screen-printing is a traditional art technique that was popularised by American artist Andy Warhol. By applying brightly coloured paint through cut-out stencils he produced stylised portraits of celebrities like Marilyn Monroe and turned ordinary subjects like tins of soup into iconic pieces of pop art.

Thanks to this free app you can give your own shots a pop art-style makeover without playing with paper and paint (or faffing around with filters in Photoshop). Simply launch the app, select a suitable source file, like a close-up portrait, and use the sliders to fine-tune the pop art effect. Genuine screen prints don't feature midtones so you can drag two sliders until the photo has a posterised look with tinted shadows and highlights. There is a paid version of Pop Art in the App Store but that only boasts extra colours, so isn't much better than the free version. A pop-tastic app!

Ratings

Longevity	Fun factor	Practicality	Value
★★★☆☆	★★★☆☆	★★★★☆	★★★☆☆

Overall Rating ★★★☆☆

Price: £0.59/$0.99 **Developer:** Hiray Information

Frames Tycoon

Frame your friends and family with this fun app

 By framing an image we're saying that it's good enough to hang on our wall. In these digital days our walls are more likely to be virtual rather than physical ones – like online albums in Facebook. This well-designed app enables us to make our favourite shots stand out from the online crowd by popping them in a picture frame.

The app boasts frame designs to suit a variety of subjects and events like family portraits or birthdays. You can even place your subject on a magazine cover. Tap the frame that you fancy then take a shot with the iPhone's camera or import a picture from your library. Pinch, pan and rotate the image with your fingertips until it fits inside the frame, then save it to your iPhone's Album or upload it to Facebook from within the app. A great way to make important pictures look even more special.

Ratings

Longevity	Fun factor	Practicality	Value
★★★★☆	★★★★☆	★★★★☆	★★★★☆

Overall Rating ★★★★☆

■ Pop your pals into a spoof magazine cover.

■ Whiten teeth automatically with a single click.

■ Face Salon can tackle multiple faces in one go.

Price: £0.59/$0.99 Developer: macphun.com

Face Salon Lite

Retouch your portraits to perfection in a few clicks

We all want to look our best, especially in a profile picture for a social networking or dating site. However, capturing a flattering shot is not always easy. If our skin is oily then the camera flash can create shiny skin, for instance.

This clever app can enhance portraits in a subtle way, without creating an artificial looking result. Open a portrait from your iPhone's library. The software works well with close-up shots but it may not recognise faces in long shots and refuse to work with them. It's not a fan of tilted faces either.

To enhance a feature, like whitening yellow teeth for example, simply click on the appropriate icon for instant improvements. You don't have to faff around selecting the teeth for the app to work its magic. You can also remove shiny hotspots from skin and enhance eye colour. A fabulous face-flattering app.

Ratings
Longevity	Fun factor	Practicality	Value
★★★☆☆	★★★☆☆	★★★☆☆	★★★★☆

Overall Rating ★★★★☆

Price: £1.19/$1.99 Developer: Black Frog Industries

iSwap Faces

Tease your friends with this cheeky image-editing app

iPhone photography apps tend to fall into two categories. There are those that help you improve your shots by tweaking colour and tone to make them look perfect (like Face Salon). Then there are those designed to edit your shots in more creative ways like UFO Camera. iSwap Faces falls into the latter category. This sophisticated pixel-pushing app enables you to choose two separate portraits of friends or family and indulge in a bit of *Face/Off* style shenanigans.

The app takes time to master but the results make it worth your while. You can define the areas you want to transplant by stretching, rotating and scaling a mesh. There are a variety of different meshes available to suit different face shapes. To make the transplanted faces blend with their new bodies you can use sliders to adjust skin tones. There's a free Lite version to try out but it won't let you save, so this is your best bet.

Ratings
Longevity	Fun factor	Practicality	Value
★★☆☆☆	★★★☆☆	★★☆☆☆	★★★☆☆

Overall Rating ★★★★★

■ Scale, rotate and colour the face to complete the photographic transplant.

iCandy
iPhone 3G

iPhone 3G 8 & 16GB

The choice is yours when it comes to the iPhone: 8GB in black or the 16GB in white or black? It's a difficult decision

Productivity

Use your iPhone or iPod Touch to get things done. We present you with the very best task management apps on offer

Price: £11.99/$19.99   Developer: The Omni Group

OmniFocus

Award-winning task management comes to the iPhone

 OmniFocus is the Award-winning granddaddy of the GTD (Getting Things Done) genre of apps, combining to-do lists with advanced task management. When you first launch the app, it can be tricky to figure out how to use it, as beneath the simple interface lies a depth that other apps of this type don't necessarily possess. Fortunately, the developer's website provides a downloadable PDF manual and a

smattering of excellent video tutorials outlining the basic functions to get you started. These introduce the concept of actions and contexts, which are the building blocks of the principle around which OmniFocus operates.

Tasks you find yourself needing to do can be entered into an inbox as you think of them. The inbox is like an initial catch net for your thoughts, from which point they can be

■ You can use the search feature to filter large lists of tasks.

■ Return to the main screen quickly with the home button.

www.iphonekungfu.com

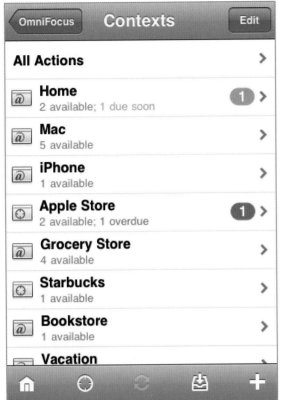

New contexts are easy to create and manage.

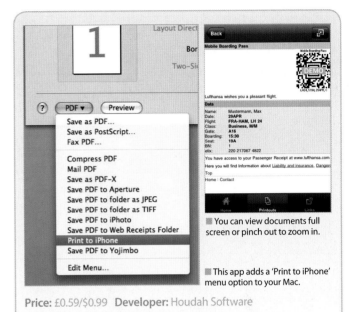

You can view documents full screen or pinch out to zoom in.

This app adds a 'Print to iPhone' menu option to your Mac.

Price: £0.59/$0.99 **Developer:** Houdah Software

ACTPrinter – Print to iPhone

Ever wanted to print to your iPhone? Now you can

Unlike many other iPhone printing apps, ACTPrinter enables you to print documents to your iPhone rather than from it. Once the app is installed on your phone, the developer provides a small helper app that needs to be installed on the computer you want to print from, adding a 'Print to iPhone' option to the generic print dialogue. As long as the two machines are connected to the same Wi-Fi network, the iPhone will appear as a menu choice in the helper app and the file is 'printed' to the device, where it can be viewed full screen or zoomed in.

It's a real shame that the helper app quits after each file is printed, as re-establishing the connection each time quickly becomes tedious if you have multiple files to process. That said, this is a neat little idea, the software is very easy to use and the basic premise works well, making ACTPrinter a great iPhone app to get the job done.

broken down into actions representing the steps that need to be taken to accomplish a particular goal. Each individual action is assigned a context relating to the situation you'll be in when you do each task. For instance, if you need to make a phone call, assign it to the 'Phone' context. If it's a web-related task like ordering something from a website, it belongs in the 'Online' context. New contexts are easy to create; you can have categories for home, office, even contexts related to individual people.

Combining the contexts function with the iPhone's location awareness, the clever Nearby Contexts feature can help you decide what to do next based on where you are, so if you're out shopping, OmniFocus can show you the location of the nearest shops and compile a shopping list.

Overall, the app does the job very nicely, although it's a bit slow to load, which unfortunately can make the spontaneous adding of new entries as you think of them a bit of a chore. The app also syncs wirelessly with its desktop counterpart, OmniFocus for Mac, keeping your OmniFocus data current on multiple Macs, and it's in this scenario that it really comes into its own. It may be a bit pricey, but it's well worth it.

Ratings

Longevity	Fun factor	Practicality	Value
★★★★★	★★★	★★★★★	★★★

Overall Rating ★★★★★

Ratings

Longevity	Fun factor	Practicality	Value
★★★★	★★	★★★★	★★★★

Overall Rating ★★★★

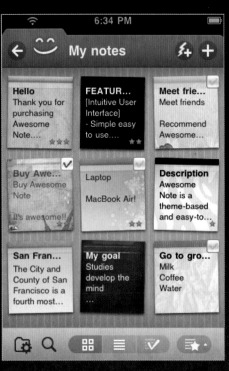

■ A classy interface makes the app a pleasure to use.

■ Notes can be viewed on a virtual chalkboard.

Price: £2.39/$3.99   Developer: BRID

Awesome Note

Note-taking on the iPhone just ramped up a notch

The somewhat confidently monikered Awesome Note is essentially a note-taking app on hyperspeed, with an added dash of to-do list functionality. It seems to have been conceived with the sole aim of eclipsing Apple's proprietary Notes offering, and the finished result comes pretty close. The interface is very classy, and the app is a pleasure to use, although some of the clickable areas are a bit on the small side. Notes are stored in folders according to subject, and new folders are easy to create. There are several views to choose from, including a corkboard-style gallery view, plain list and checkbox views. Notes can be sorted by title, priority, date created or modified, and fonts and backgrounds can all be altered at will. The key here is customisation, and it results in an app that's not only very nice to look at, but which absolutely bristles with very useful features.

Ratings

Longevity	Fun factor	Practicality	Value
★★★★★	★★★	★★★★	★★★★

Overall Rating ★★★★

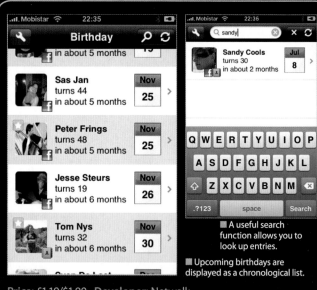

■ A useful search function allows you to look up entries.

■ Upcoming birthdays are displayed as a chronological list.

Price: £1.19/$1.99   Developer: Netwalk

Birthday Reminder

Never forget another birthday with this useful app

If you have a terrible memory for birthdays, this app will keep you being completely ostracised by family and friends. It pulls contact information from your address book and Facebook profile, or you can add new people directly. Entries are then displayed in a chronologically ordered list, displaying each person's photo, name, age, next birthday and the date this will occur. Of course, your contact's birth date has to be correctly entered in the Address book to start with, or when you first launch the app you'll find your friends all turn one next birthday. If you're the sort of person who needs this app, chances are that you won't have entered this data, but luckily Birthday Reminder allows you to edit the entries. The app will then email you a set number of days before the event, giving you time to sort out shopping for presents, getting cards posted and booking white limos.

Ratings

Longevity	Fun factor	Practicality	Value
★★★★	★★	★★★★	★★★

Overall Rating ★★★

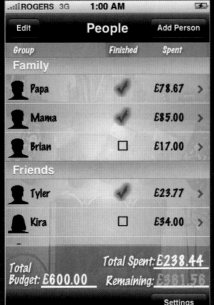

■ Check boxes denote whether a gift is pending or purchased.

■ People can be grouped into different categories for easy management.

Price: £0.59/$0.99   Developer: iDelux

■ Files can be downloaded via the built-in web browser.

■ A pleasant no-frills interface gets the job done without fuss

Price: £2.99/$4.99   Developer: Good.iWare

Christmas Shopping List (UK)

Get your Christmas shopping sorted with this dedicated app

You may wonder about the long-term appeal of an app called Christmas Shopping List but, in fact, when the app is installed, it appears on your phone merely as 'Shopping List'. The idea is to create a list of people you are shopping for, detailing the intended purchase, where to buy it from and how much it costs. You can allocate a budget to each person and keep track of it by entering the items as you shop. You can check off each purchase as it is made and the budget will let you know how much cash you have left. The decorative background wallpaper can be changed to suit the theme of your shopping expedition too. Festive functionality aside, as a standard shopping list app, this still has a lot going for it, and should by no means be dismissed as a seasonal novelty item.

Ratings

Longevity	Fun factor	Practicality	Value
★★★	★★★	★★★★	★★★★

Overall Rating ★★★★

Good Reader

Easily import, view, share and manage large documents

Good Reader may seem like a fairly inauspicious title for an app, but in this case it really fits the bill. Its primary function is viewing large PDF and TXT files, but this is really just the tip of the iceberg. Getting documents into the app is a breeze, either by USB cable, Wi-Fi or downloading from the built-in web browser, and a brilliant built-in help system guides you every step of the way. Large files of over 1GB are handled with no trouble at all, and documents can be zoomed up to 50x for detailed inspection and navigated via 'touch zones', different areas of the screen yielding different results when tapped. A touch of the Actions button allows you to select, copy, rename or email multiple or individual documents, and all this is wrapped up in a pleasantly functional interface. Deceptively deep, this could be the only document reader you'll ever need and comes highly recommended.

Ratings

Longevity	Fun factor	Practicality	Value
★★★★★	★★	★★★★★	★★★★

Overall Rating ★★★★

■ You can choose between text-only or graphical layouts.

Price: £2.99/$4.99 **Developer:** Marco Arment

Instapaper Pro

No time to read web pages? Help is at hand

Instapaper saves web pages to be read later offline, optimising pages for readability on the iPhone's screen. This is perfect for capturing long articles that you don't have time to read when you find them, so that they can then be read at other times. You simply register at Instapaper.com and copy a 'Read Later' bookmarklet to your browser's bookmarks bar. When you find something you want to read later, just click the bookmarklet and the page is synced to your phone. There is a free version also available, but that's limited to saving ten articles. It's a simple app to use and contains some nice touches. The Pro version adds the ability to change font size and invert the text to white on black, as well as the very classy tilt scrolling function, which allows you to scroll through an article one-handed just by tilting the phone back and forth. Instapaper Pro is elegant and effective.

Ratings

Longevity	Fun factor	Practicality	Value
★★★★☆	★★★☆☆	★★★★★	★★★★☆

Overall Rating ★★★★★

■ The white on black text option is easy on the eyes.

■ Computers whose login details you've stored appear on a menu.

■ Log in to your selected machine from this page.

Price: £17.99/$29.99 **Developer:** LogMeIn Inc

LogMeIn Ignition

LogMeIn gives the term Remote Control a whole new dimension

A full remote control for your desktop Mac, LogMeIn Ignition allows you to access your machine from anywhere. The setup is simple – you create a free account at LogMeIn.com, then add the login details for the computers you wish to control remotely. These then appear in a list when you launch the app on your phone, and within seconds you see your Mac's desktop in the palm of your hand.

In theory, anything you can do on your Mac, you can do with LogMeIn, although you need to pay for a Pro account to be able to transfer files and the target machine has to be powered up and connected to the internet, which is a tall order if you're going away for a few days.

It's very rare that an app leaves us slack-jawed with wonder, but that's the effect that LogMeIn Ignition has when you first use it. Expensive, but amazing.

Ratings

Longevity	Fun factor	Practicality	Value
★★★★☆	★★★☆☆	★★★★★	★★☆☆☆

Overall Rating ★★★★★

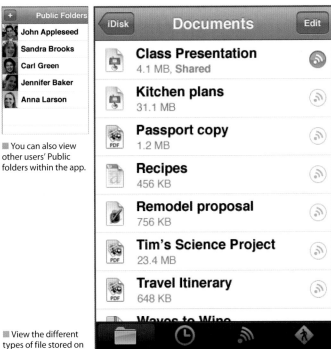

■ You can also view other users' Public folders within the app.

■ View the different types of file stored on your iDisk.

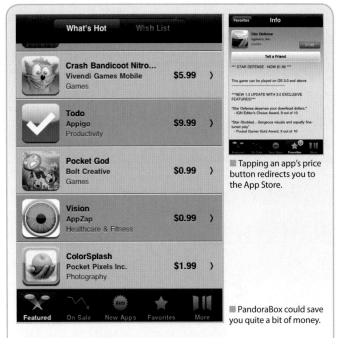

■ Tapping an app's price button redirects you to the App Store.

■ PandoraBox could save you quite a bit of money.

Price: Free **Developer:** Apple Inc

MobileMe iDisk

Official iDisk access from your iPhone is here at last

More than two years after the iPhone's launch, Apple has released an app that enables MobileMe subscribers to access their iDisk from the device. It's strange that this has taken so long to appear, but even though it's free, there are serious limitations. You can view the files on your iDisk, but you can't actually download them or store them on your phone. Uploading files isn't possible either, but you can email a link to the selected file that the recipient can use to download it. In terms of transfer speed, MobileMe in the UK has never been the quickest, and our 4 minute wait to view a 4MB file over Wi-Fi only serves to highlight this. The interface, too, is unusually basic – you expect something with a bit more visual oomph from Apple to be honest. For a free app, we shouldn't really grumble too much, but there are much better solutions out there than this.

Ratings

Longevity	Fun factor	Practicality	Value
★★✩✩✩	★★✩✩✩	★★★✩✩	★★★✩✩

Overall Rating ★★★✩✩

Price: Free **Developer:** AppZap

PandoraBox

Find 'on-sale' or free apps you wouldn't otherwise know about

Shopping in the App Store, particularly from the iPhone, can be a bit of an overwhelming experience – with such a huge variety of apps, where do you start to look? The conventional store display can only scratch the surface of the many thousands of available apps, and this is where apps like PandoraBox attempt to lend a hand, displaying apps that are temporarily free or have dropped their prices so that you can pick them up for peanuts.

What makes PandoraBox stand out from the crowd is the ability to view screenshots and descriptions without having to exit the app to launch the App Store. Unfortunately, a recent update has removed the star rating displays, which we miss, as one of the main criteria when app shopping is whether the app is actually any good, and without the star ratings it's impossible to tell.

Ratings

Longevity	Fun factor	Practicality	Value
★★★★✩	★★★✩✩	★★★★✩	★★★★✩

Overall Rating ★★★★★

Reference

For those who want knowledge and thousands of facts at their fingertips, this section has everything

Price: £0.59/$0.99   **Developer:** CrispyThinking

Birds UK

Birdwatchers rejoice, this could be the ultimate digital field guide and is the best you'll find on the iPhone

If you're a keen birdwatcher and you're also the proud owner of an iPhone, chances are you can now throw away your old, dog-eared traditional paper field guide, as Birds UK is a comprehensive visual and audio guide to identifying the 50 most common species of garden bird in the UK, as listed by the RSPB.

The app contains information about each bird's habitat, diet and also its predators, along with example images of the male, female and juvenile of each species. There are also audio samples of the song and/or call of each bird, so if you have a cat, you can use this to make it go mental, although obviously we don't advocate its use for that purpose!

Finding the bird you're looking for is surprisingly easy. It's done by simply scrolling through an alphabetical list of names accompanied by thumbnail images, although some sort of search feature would have made finding entries a little bit quicker, but this is only a small grumble. Audio files can be accessed either from the main list page, via buttons which are, it has to said, a bit fiddly, or from each bird's main directory entry page, from which the full-screen example photos can also be accessed. Information on each species is plentiful, and each bird's page also features a link

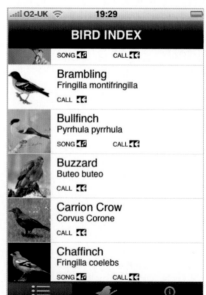

■ High-resolution photos used throughout the app are top-notch.

■ Birds are listed alphabetically along with thumbnail images.

■ Access birdsong audio recordings and Wikipedia pages from here.

to its Wikipedia page, so that you can discover more about each individual breed of feathered friend.

The only downside really is that many of the audio recordings contain artefacts that sound as if a noise-reduction plug-in has been overused, which tarnishes the app's otherwise Radio 4-esque sheen of classiness. Other than fixing this, the most obvious improvement to make to this app would be to add more species of bird, which is something that the developer states will be addressed in future updates. Overall, it's a charming, elegant and useful addition to the App Store, and one that UK twitchers will have been eagerly awaiting. It's great to see such a well-conceived and executed app fulfilling a genuine requirement, and with a small bill of only 59p, this is one app that really is going cheep!

Ratings_____

Longevity	Fun factor	Practicality	Value
★★★★★	★★★☆☆	★★★★☆	★★★★☆

Overall Rating ★★★★☆

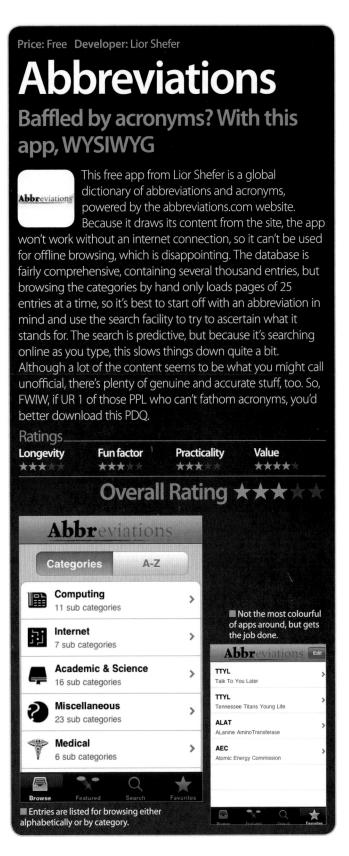

Price: Free   Developer: Lior Shefer

Abbreviations

Baffled by acronyms? With this app, WYSIWYG

This free app from Lior Shefer is a global dictionary of abbreviations and acronyms, powered by the abbreviations.com website. Because it draws its content from the site, the app won't work without an internet connection, so it can't be used for offline browsing, which is disappointing. The database is fairly comprehensive, containing several thousand entries, but browsing the categories by hand only loads pages of 25 entries at a time, so it's best to start off with an abbreviation in mind and use the search facility to try to ascertain what it stands for. The search is predictive, but because it's searching online as you type, this slows things down quite a bit. Although a lot of the content seems to be what you might call unofficial, there's plenty of genuine and accurate stuff, too. So, FWIW, if UR 1 of those PPL who can't fathom acronyms, you'd better download this PDQ.

Ratings_____

Longevity	Fun factor	Practicality	Value
★★★☆☆	★★★☆☆	★★★☆☆	★★★★☆

Overall Rating ★★★☆☆

■ Not the most colourful of apps around, but gets the job done.

■ Entries are listed for browsing either alphabetically or by category.

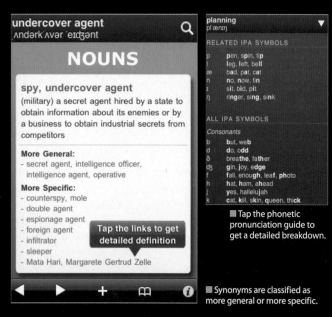

undercover agent
ˌʌndərkˈʌvər ˈeɪdʒənt

NOUNS

spy, undercover agent
(military) a secret agent hired by a state to obtain information about its enemies or by a business to obtain industrial secrets from competitors

More General:
- secret agent, intelligence officer, intelligence agent, operative

More Specific:
- counterspy, mole
- double agent
- espionage agent
- foreign agent
- infiltrator
- sleeper
- Mata Hari, Margarete Gertrud Zelle

Tap the links to get detailed definition

planning
pˈlænɪŋ

RELATED IPA SYMBOLS
p   pen, spin, tip
l   leg, left, bell
æ   bad, pat, cat
n   no, now, tin
ɪ   sit, bid, pit
ŋ   ringer, sing, sink

ALL IPA SYMBOLS
Consonants
b   but, web
d   do, odd
ð   breathe, father
dʒ   gin, joy, edge
f   fall, enough, leaf, photo
h   hat, ham, ahead
j   yes, hallelujah
k   cat, kill, skin, queen, thick

■ Tap the phonetic pronunciation guide to get a detailed breakdown.

■ Synonyms are classified as more general or more specific.

Price: £5.99/$9.99   Developer: jDictionary Mobile

Advanced English Dictionary & Thesaurus

A combined dictionary, thesaurus and encyclopedia!

This dictionary app claims to be unique in that alongside regular word definitions it also lists words that are related to the word being looked up. Its impressive word count boasts up to 250,000 entries covering 1.6 million words and 355,000 relations. Search for a word and the results include not only the definition, but also synonyms, antonyms, hypernyms and meronyms. The interface is simple yet effective and doesn't get in the way of things. All the info is clearly presented and stored locally on the device, so there's no need for an internet connection, and this also means that the app runs pretty swiftly. The 134,000 International Phonetic Alphabet pronunciation guides are content sensitive, so that tapping the guide for the selected word opens up a detailed breakdown of how each phoneme should be pronounced, and the way the app links to similar words makes this a useful tool for improving your English vocabulary.

Ratings

Longevity	Fun factor	Practicality	Value
★★★★☆	★★★☆☆	★★★★☆	★★★☆☆

Overall Rating ★★★★☆

Price: Free   Developer: Genetic Mistakes

Drinks & Cocktails

Drink and cocktail recipes at the spin of a dial

Drinks & Cocktails from developer Genetic Mistakes is an aptly named interactive collection of cocktail recipes. You can browse the list to discover new drinks or search for a specific one, but most impressive of all, you have the option to enter the ingredients you already have in your cupboards to refine your search to drinks you can make immediately. While this is a great idea in principle, each tick box took several attempts to tick, and the app interpreted pepper as peppermint schnapps in its determination to find something we could actually make. The list of available ingredients has a few omissions – it lists Jagermeister but not Jack Daniels, even though at least one recipe includes it. The units seem to be limited to US ounces, so we'd like to see an imperial measures option, but this is still well worth downloading. If you start to see two iPhones, though, it might be time to stop.

Lottery Results

■ Clear and colourful layout is easy to navigate and use.

■ Results are displayed with the most recent at the top.

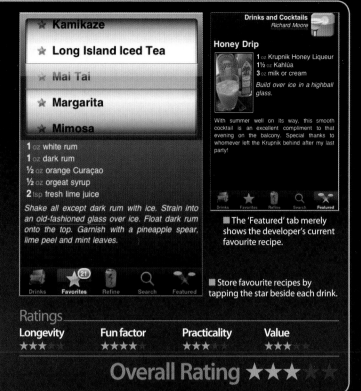

Drinks and Cocktails
Richard Moore

Honey Drip

1 oz Krupnik Honey Liqueur
1½ oz Kahlúa
3 oz milk or cream

Build over ice in a highball glass.

With summer well on its way, this smooth cocktail is an excellent compliment to that evening on the balcony. Special thanks to whomever left the Krupnik behind after my last party!

1 oz white rum
1 oz dark rum
½ oz orange Curaçao
½ oz orgeat syrup
2 tsp fresh lime juice

Shake all except dark rum with ice. Strain into an old-fashioned glass over ice. Float dark rum onto the top. Garnish with a pineapple spear, lime peel and mint leaves.

■ The 'Featured' tab merely shows the developer's current favourite recipe.

■ Store favourite recipes by tapping the star beside each drink.

Ratings

Longevity	Fun factor	Practicality	Value
★★★☆☆	★★★★☆	★★★☆☆	★★★☆☆

Overall Rating ★★★☆☆

Price: £0.59/$0.99   Developer: Craig Merchant

An easy way to discover whether you've hit the jackpot

If you play the UK National Lottery on a regular basis, you may be less than satisfied by how complicated it seems to be to simply check the results on the official website. This app makes things easier – as long as you have a wireless or cellular data internet connection – by displaying the most recent UK National Lottery, Thunderball, Lotto HotPicks, Dream Number, EuroMillions and Daily Play draws in a simple, easily accessible fashion. The list of available choices is made more visually appealing by the use of each draw's official logo, and the results pages, listed in reverse chronological order, are colourful and clear. There's also a rather handy random number generator for each type of draw that works offline for when you can't decide on your numbers but are in need of your next lotto fix. Perhaps a touch pricey for what it is, but handy nonetheless. At least the developer doesn't demand a cut if you win!

Ratings

Longevity	Fun factor	Practicality	Value
★★★★☆	★★★☆☆	★★★★☆	★★★★☆

Overall Rating ★★★★☆

Price: Free   Developer: Kevin Rye

planetFacts
Amazing astronomical facts at your disposal

If you're after a handy guide to facts about all the different planets, then Kevin Rye's interesting planetFacts is the app for you. Consisting of nothing more than a collection of planetary statistics, it could prove incredibly useful if you regularly find yourself being quizzed by inquisitive children about just how far the Earth is from the Sun and how hot it is on the surface of Mercury. You get the same set of facts for each celestial body, including rotation time, length of year, distance from the Sun, number of moons, diameter, mass, escape velocity, and so on. As you pick each planet from the list, the pertinent facts appear set against a backdrop picture of the selected object. planetFacts may be the sort of thing that you only need very occasionally, but it could prove to be a sound download if you want to build a reputation as the go-to guy for astronomical facts in your family. And most important of all, it's free!

Ratings

Longevity	Fun factor	Practicality	Value
★★☆☆☆	★★★☆☆	★★★☆☆	★★★★☆

Overall Rating ★★★☆☆

■ Facts are superimposed over images of the planets in question.

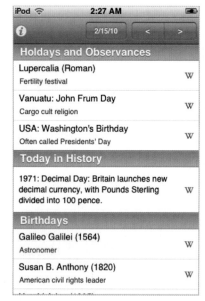

■ Tap the date button to choose a date to view.

■ Wikipedia entries open within the app.

Price: £1.79/$2.99   **Developer:** Jeremy Nixon

ThisDay - Today In History

Uncover historical events that correspond to today's date

ThisDay conjures up historical events and national holidays that correspond to the current date. The app contains around 500 historical events entries in all, together with around 1,100 famous birthdays. Some entries have disclosure buttons, indicating that more information is available within the app, and most also include links to Wikipedia articles, which open within the app for easy viewing, although access to these does require an internet connection. On launching the app, the information page for the current date is displayed by default, but you can use arrow buttons to scroll back and forth a day at a time, or enter an alternative date for viewing simply by tapping on the date button. There's quite a heavy US bias in the content, and the listed religious festivals and holidays seem centred around the Christian and Jewish religions, but this is an interesting and diverting app to dip into.

Ratings

Longevity	Fun factor	Practicality	Value
★★★☆☆	★★★☆☆	★★★☆☆	★★★☆☆

Overall Rating ★★★☆☆

Price: £1.19/$1.99   **Developer:** NZWidgets

UK Codes

Look up UK STD codes with this handy directory app

UK Codes is a two-way directory of British STD telephone area codes from NZWidgets, which enables you to find out the area code of a specific town or city in the UK by entering a place name, or by entering a code to unveil the name of the place it's allocated to. The main screen consists of an alphabetical list, with an index down the right-hand side of the screen for quick access to particular letters, similar to that which appears down the right-hand side of the iPhone 'Contacts' list. At the top are the 'search by name' or 'search by code' option buttons, followed by a search window for text entry. The only worry is that sometimes the database doesn't appear to be specific enough to recognise satellite towns. This could do with being revised so that, for example, entering 'Sutton Coldfield' will produce a result of 0121 rather than 'No results found'.

Ratings

Longevity	Fun factor	Practicality	Value
★★★★☆	★★☆☆☆	★★★★☆	★★★☆☆

Overall Rating ★★★☆☆

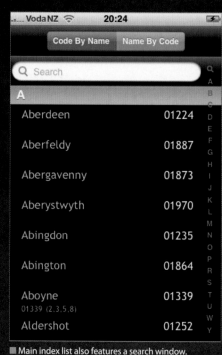
■ Main index list also features a search window.

Price: Free **Developer:** MyFonts

What The Font

Innovative tool for capturing and identifying fonts

This intriguing free app from MyFonts offers a unique service – it can capture a font from a magazine ad, poster or website via a photo and attempts to identify it by breaking up the individual characters and comparing them to the What The Font website database. Once you've taken and cropped your image, it's uploaded to the MyFonts.com website for analysis, and the results are displayed for you to check. Wrong character guesses can be deleted, and you can type the correct character into a box to confirm what it should be. Once you're happy that all the guessed characters are correct, the 'Identify!' button returns a selection of possible matches. In tests, it worked pretty well with high contrast, monochrome text, but struggled with picking out coloured text on a coloured background. It's very clever when it does work, though, and could come in fontastically handy if you're a designer.

Ratings

Longevity	Fun factor	Practicality	Value
★★★★☆	★★★☆☆	★★★★☆	★★★★☆

Overall Rating ★★★★☆

■ Fine-tune the character analysis before hitting the 'Identify!' button.

■ Either take a new photo or use an existing one.

Price: £1.79/$2.99 **Developer:** TranCreative Software

WordBook English Dictionary & Thesaurus

TranCreative's dictionary and thesaurus probed and tested

A combined dictionary and thesaurus, WordBook lets you search for words in the normal way, the predictive search narrowing down the possibilities as you type. Due to not requiring an internet connection for definitions, the app is generally fast and responsive. You can select from the standard dictionary definition, linked words, a thesaurus option which displays synonyms, and a web button that takes you to the Wikipedia entry. There are three choices of voice for audio pronunciation, one of which is very realistic, and the app seems to accommodate both UK and US spellings of contentious words, such as 'flavour' and 'centre'. The 'Featured' section picks random words of the day to keep your vocab skills up to scratch, and unusually for a dedicated dictionary app, this also contains a useful crossword-solving feature. A worthy contender in the battle for iPhone dictionary supremacy, and good value, too.

Ratings

Longevity	Fun factor	Practicality	Value
★★★★☆	★★★☆☆	★★★★☆	★★★★☆

Overall Rating ★★★★☆

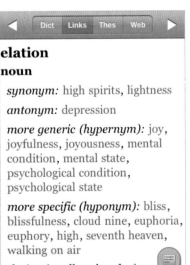

■ Shake the phone to get a new selection of 'Words of the Day'.

■ WordBook contains over 330,000 relational references.

www.iphonekungfu.com

Social Networking

Keep in touch with your mates, broadcast your thoughts and make new friends with ease with these innovative apps

Price: £0.99/$1.99   **Developer:** Meson Networks Ltd

Message In A Bottle

Throw your thoughts into the virtual ocean and make new friends

 Message In A Bottle provides a fun and easy way to get in touch with total strangers anywhere in the world and turn them into friends. Like other social networking apps you can use it to share your thoughts with the world and listen to the opinions of others. The beauty of the app is the way it packages this experience. Imagine you're a castaway and the iPhone is your island. You can write a message about anything you like, pop it in a virtual bottle and throw it into the cyber sea. The bottle will then be washed up on the digital shores of another iPhone running the same app. The recipient of your bottle can read your note, reply to you by email or lob your bottle back in the sea for another person to find it.

This is a great app if you're shy about meeting new people. Other apps feature profiles of thousands of strangers. With Message In A Bottle you can be as anonymous as you like and respond to people at your own pace. You only get a few bottles washing up on the shore throughout the day so each new

■ Tap on a washed-up bottle to read its contents… it's simple but effective, and keeps you entertained.

contact is more exciting and special than wading through lots of online profiles or tweets. Some bottles are on a world trip so you can add your name and location to the paper inside and lob the bottle back into the sea. Other bottles are from people looking for friends so you can keep those, begin an email conversation and re-use the bottles to send out your own messages.

The app's graphics are a little cheesy in a Nineties computer game sort of way, but you'll soon get into the spirit of the desert island experience. It's rewarding to wander down to the beach and tap on bottles to read their contents. When you launch your own bottle a 3D animation shows it spinning through the air to land in the sea. Check out the free version first, though you only get five bottles to kick off with. This is a fun, practical, safe and addictive way to meet new folk.

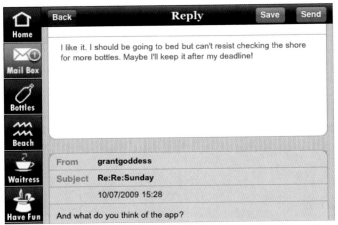

■ Send emails to people whose bottles you encounter and you never know, you might just make a few friends.

■ Pop your parchment in a bottle and throw it in the sea.

Ratings

Longevity	Fun factor	Practicality	Value
★★★★☆	★★★★☆	★★★☆☆	★★★★★

Overall Rating ★★★★☆

Price: Free   **Developer:** North One Television

Social Beacon

Update your Twitter or Facebook status without typing

If you don't update your Facebook status every now or then your status message reverts to a blank space. If you're too busy to type in your current status then this app provides a fun way to let people know you're still around. Social Beacon allows you to choose your current status from a selection of templates. Kick off by tapping a category like Travel, then click a subcategory like Holiday. Tap a third icon and your Facebook and Twitter status will be updated.

The app is designed to let you update your status without any typing. Flick left or right to choose different options and flick the phone forward to make a selection. Sounds great in theory but in practice this involves shaking the iPhone around like you're trying to swat a wasp so the 'fingerless functionality' isn't very practical! A good-looking, creative but altogether too gimmicky app.

Ratings

Longevity	Fun factor	Practicality	Value
★☆☆☆☆	★★★★☆	★★☆☆☆	★★☆☆☆

Overall Rating ★★☆☆☆

■ Keep tapping to refine your status or set up a custom message.

■ Choose a status message from a variety of common categories.

Price: £1.19/$2.99 Developer: Vurgood Applications

Black Book

Impress the ladies with a digital version of your little black book

The concept of a 'little black book' evokes thoughts of Seventies-era casanovas who flick through a well-thumbed paper record of their conquests before deciding on who to telephone for a night down the disco. This cheeky app has given the black book concept a digital spin.

The app's charm lies in its design. It launches showing an old-school leather black book which you tap to open. Meet a girl and you can whip out your iPhone, launch the app and write in her contact details. As well as storing phone numbers of ladies that you like you can save their Facebook page location and assign a photo to their entry. You can also assign a password to keep its contents safe from any prying eyes. On the downside a few bugs need ironing out. If you click to call a contact then chicken out, the Cancel button doesn't work, forcing you to reboot the app.

Ratings

Longevity	Fun factor	Practicality	Value
★★☆☆☆	★★★☆☆	★★☆☆☆	★★☆☆☆

Overall Rating ★★☆☆☆

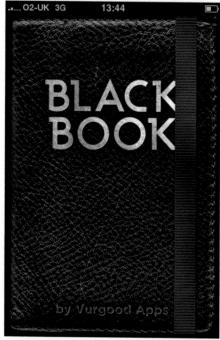

■ The app's splash screen helps set the mood.

eBuddy

■ Put friends from multiple networks under one roof.

■ Enhance conversations by dropping in emoticons.

Price: £0.59/$0.99 Developer: iApp Ventures LLC

Twitter Pro

Follow your favourite tweeters while on the move

No section on social networking apps would be complete without a Twitter-related review, and here it is! The microblogging site Twitter enables you to broadcast what you're up to as 'tweets' (or text messages) of up to 140 characters. This handy app lets you follow the tweets of people you're interested in or get news updates tweeted by the BBC, for example. You can also use the app to tweet out your own activities or opinions. Twitter Pro lets you search for famous tweeters to follow such as Stephen Fry and you can type out your own tweets wherever and whenever you like.

You can also use the app to find out who's following you, but brace yourself for some followers who are advertising products. The option to remove unwanted followers doesn't seem to work but all-in-all this is app provides an easy way to interact with the world via the ubiquitous Twitter.

Price: Free   Developer: eBuddy B.V.

Keep in touch with friends on a variety of networks

The problem with managing multiple mates is the fact that they are scattered over different networks. You'll have a crowd of Facebook friends you chat to using the Facebook app, but you could be neglecting family members who are signed up with MSN Messenger or AIM. eBuddy lets you gather multiple networks into a single app so you can chat with Facebook friends and natter with pals on MSN Messenger or Gtalk.

The app is easy to set up. Simply sign in to the networks you're interested in and it'll gather all your contacts into a single page. You can then see who's online on any of your networks and text chat with them. You can drop emoticons into your chats to enhance the conversation. After you exit the app it will even send you push notifications when someone wants to chat, so you won't miss a thing! Puts all your pals in one place!

Ratings

Longevity	Fun factor	Practicality	Value
★★★★★	★★★★☆	★★★★★	★★★★★

Overall Rating ★★★★★

■ The Directory lets you discover new tweet sources.

■ Keep tabs on your favourite tweeters wherever you are.

Ratings

Longevity	Fun factor	Practicality	Value
★★★	★★★	★★	★★★

Overall Rating ★★★☆☆

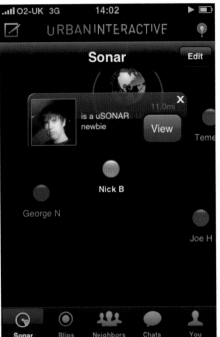

■ Local people appear as coloured dots relative to your location.

Price: £2.99/$4.99   Developer: Urban Interactive

uSonar

Scan your locality for friends or activities and make contact

This is one of the slickest looking apps in the social networking category. As soon as you fire it up a cool-looking radar animation sweeps your immediate location for other uSonar users, ongoing chats or local activities. Other users or events show up as colour-coded dots on the radar screen. Click on a dot to find out more about the person or event that it symbolises. You can then join in ongoing chats (symbolised by a green dot) or email Neighbors (purple dots) to start up a conversation.

To keep up-to-date on what's happening around you, simply shake the iPhone to refresh the screen. Your Neighbors on the radar have profiles for you to explore so you can work out if you have anything in common with them before deciding to make contact. Check out the free version of the app to sound it out before you cough up any cash, but it's definitely a good way to pass some time.

Ratings

Longevity	Fun factor	Practicality	Value
★★★	★★★	★★★	★★★

Overall Rating ★★★☆☆

Upload video from your iPhone to Facebook

Price: Free **Developer:** Sol Lipman

12mail Video Messenger

Your iPhone enables you to share video clips with friends via email, or pop them on a YouTube or MobileMe gallery for the world to see. If you have a Facebook account then your significant others are probably on there too, so this is could be the most useful place to share your footage. The Facebook iPhone app lets you upload photos but not video, so there's a definitely need for 12mail's services.

12mail also lets you upload footage to Twitter too, so it essentially covers the two biggest social networking outlets. Uploading footage to Facebook or Twitter is a breeze. Click the New Mail icon, title your clip and tag it with keywords. You can even add your GPS co-ordinates with a click so others can see the video's location on a map. Create a clip by hitting Record or select it from your Library and click Send. Hey presto, it's online! And it's free!

■ Type in a title and some tags for your video.

■ Send clips to individual Facebook recipients by ticking their contact icon.

Ratings

Longevity	Fun factor	Practicality	Value
★★★★☆	★★☆☆☆	★★★★☆	★★★★☆

Overall Rating ★★★★☆

Ping

Price: £0.59/$0.99 **Developer:** Gary Fung

Message your mates for free wherever they are!

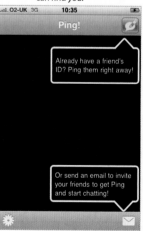

Text messaging is a popular way to stay in touch with other members of your social network, and you may be send hundreds of free messages each month. However, if you're a prolific texter you will start paying extra once you exceed your free allowance, and the cost can start to add up. If you send texts from abroad then each text will cost you more, leading to nasty surprises when the bill comes through your letterbox.

Ping works by allowing you to choose a unique Ping ID. You can mail the ID to a fellow Ping owner and then use the app to send free text messages, without any limits on the monthly quantity. If you use a hotel or café Wi-Fi connection while on your holidays then you can Ping away 'til your heart's content without caring about cost. Push notifications tell you when a new message comes through and it even works on an iPod touch!

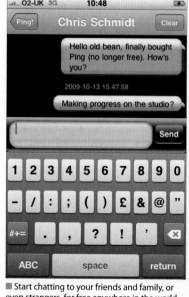

■ Mail your buddy your unique Ping ID so he or she can find you.

■ Start chatting to your friends and family, or even strangers, for free anywhere in the world.

Ratings

Longevity	Fun factor	Practicality	Value
★★★★☆	★★★☆☆	★★★★★	★★★★☆

Overall Rating ★★★★☆

Price: Free **Developer:** Padadaz

PhotoSwap

■ Shoot something interesting and blast it off to a random recipient.

Swap picture messages and see the world (for free)!

Many social networking apps are designed to put you in touch with new people so that you can forge friendships and exchange messages. This is not one of those apps. PhotoSwap is a fun distraction that lets you take a shot of something interesting using the iPhone's camera and send it to a random PhotoSwap user anywhere on the planet. In return you'll get a photo from another PhotoSwap user. You can only reply to that image by sending another photo. To find out where each shot comes from you simply have to click Show on Map.

This app offers tantalising insights into the lives of others without the need to engage in small talk. If anyone sends you unsuitable shots you can click the Report button to curtail their antics, though we didn't see anything unpleasant or naughty while reviewing this unusual app. On the downside you can't save the photos taken or sent (but you could take a screengrab).

Ratings

Longevity	Fun factor	Practicality	Value
★★★☆☆	★★★☆☆	★★☆☆☆	★★★☆☆

Overall Rating ★★★★☆

Price: £0.59/$0.99 **Developer:** SMALLMEDIUM

Avatar Creator

Make your profile picture stand out from the crowd

Many social networking apps give you the option of assigning a photo to your profile so prospective admirers can be drawn to your magnetic good looks! If you use a head and shoulders style composition for your avatar it may be impossible to discern as a tiny thumbnail.

Avatar Creator lets you design a stylised self-portrait that looks great as a thumbnail and promotes your online presence in a distinctive way. It reminds us of the old-school police ID kits that contained dozens of different eyes, noses, mouths etc. You could pick and mix between various facial features until you had a rough picture of the suspect! In this app you can swipe your fingers to select the appropriate features and colourise them with a click to suit your desired look. Friends will easily pick your digital avatar out from a line-up of postings. It's a sophisticated app but easy to use.

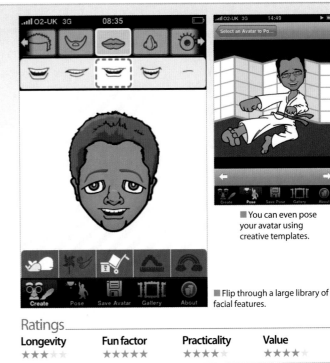

■ You can even pose your avatar using creative templates.

■ Flip through a large library of facial features.

Ratings

Longevity	Fun factor	Practicality	Value
★★★☆☆	★★★★★	★★★★☆	★★★★☆

Overall Rating ★★★★☆

Price: Free   Developer: Facebook

Facebook

Check out new features in this popular app's 3.0 upgrade

We took a look at the Facebook app in an earlier App Directory, but as the app's been radically revamped it's worth revisiting. The older version tried to give you access to everything via one page using tabs and scrolling menu bars, which created a cluttered-looking interface. Version 3.0 gives you more space to browse through your mates' News Feeds or scroll through posts on your wall as the key sections are now accessible by clicking on a homepage full of icons. Tap on Chat for example and the entire screen fills with the Chat window so you can natter to friends who are logged into Facebook. You can now rotate the phone and peruse Facebook in landscape format to make even better use of screen space. New notifications appear at the bottom of the front page so you can quickly keep up to date on who's doing what. It makes staying in touch with friends even easier.

Ratings

Longevity	Fun factor	Practicality	Value
★★★★★	★★★★☆	★★★★☆	★★★★★

Overall Rating ★★★★★

■ Find special friends faster by adding them to Favorites.

■ Icons take you to areas of interest in just a simple click.

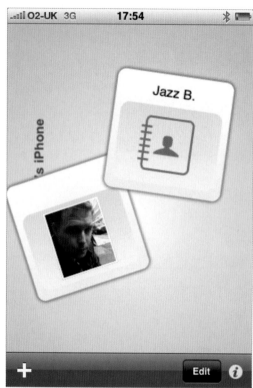

■ Simply flick the files towards the other iPhone to share them.

■ Choose what you want to share via Mover.

Mover
Price: Free   Developer: Infinite Labs

Share photos and contact details quickly and stylishly

We've all had the experience of meeting someone and having to rummage around in our bag or pockets for a pen and paper to scribble down their contact details. Typing contact details into an iPhone can also be a time-consuming fiddle and you may get their phone number down incorrectly. Even if you're organised enough to carry a card with your contact details printed on it you will still have to email your contact if you want to share an image from your iPhone's library. If you're both packing Mover on your iPhones then it's a doddle to share contact details and images without the hassle of having to pair them. When both phones share the same Wi-Fi connection, choose an image and flick it towards your friend's phone. It will magically slide into view on their screen and be saved automatically into the library! Mover+ adds Bluetooth functionality to the software.

Ratings

Longevity	Fun factor	Practicality	Value
★★★☆☆	★★★★☆	★★☆☆☆	★★★☆☆

Overall Rating ★★★★☆

Price: Free Developer: Skype Software

Skype

Phone friends and family on the cheap!

Many of us have Skype installed on our Mac or PC at home so that we can all call friends who also have Skype and have voice conversations with them for free. By installing the iPhone version of Skype you can see who's online and call them via their computer at no cost – though you must be using a Wi-Fi connection for this to work as you can't Skype people over the 3G network.

When you're abroad the cost of making regular calls back home can be very high, especially if you step out of Europe. By setting up an account with Skype and installing the Skype app on your iPhone you can pop your feet up in a local café, log onto its Wi-Fi connection and use Skype to call other mobiles or landlines back in Blighty at a fraction of what it would cost you using the 3G network. A practical money-saving app.

Ratings

Longevity	Fun factor	Practicality	Value
★★★★★	★★★	★★★★★	★★★★★

Overall Rating ★★★★★

■ Scroll through your contacts and then simply click to call.

■ Keep tabs on your Skype credits and update your profile.

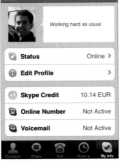

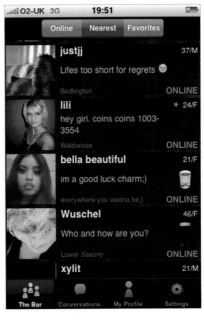

■ Break the ice by offering to buy someone a drink.

■ Check out who's in the bar and what they're drinking.

Price: Free Developer: Jim Young

TapRoom Casual Chat

Pop down the virtual pub and meet your mates

Many Social Networking apps provide the same service – they put you in touch with new people by creating an environment that's conducive to conversation. Some apps use a gimmick to make interaction more fun, from chucking letters into the sea (Message In A Bottle) to scanning the area with a radar (uSonar). TapRoom's gimmick is designed to appeal to social drinkers by letting them mingle in a virtual pub! Tap the Nearest icon to see who is drinking in your area and find out if they're online. You can start up a live conversation or send them a message if they're offline. You can even buy potential friends a virtual drink to break the ice. The interface is well designed and easy to interact with, but our nearest pub only contained a handful of locals. As you'd expect with a pub there can be some colourful language so it's not a suitable environment for kids to hang out in.

Ratings

Longevity	Fun factor	Practicality	Value
★★	★★	★★	★★★

Overall Rating ★★★★★

Price: Free **Developer:** Niftybrick Software

Hey Where Are You: Location Service

Pinpoint your pals' positions with this GPS-friendly app

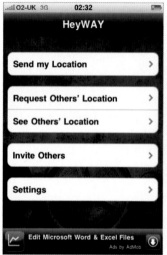

■ Ask a mate to broadcast their position.

In these digital days most of our friends and family will be carrying their mobile around wherever they go so we can contact them whenever we fancy. This handy app adds an extra dimension to our social networking experience by allowing us to see where they are!

If you need to hook up with mates in town or pick up the kids after a night out then send a request for their location using the app. Once your friend or family member broadcasts their location via their copy of HeyWAY you can zoom and pan the map to clarify exactly where they are.

We reviewed the free app and it worked well, but if you want one that's free of adverts or want to send custom messages when asking for a location then buy the Pro version for £0.59. You'll be notified by push notification when someone sends his or her location so the app doesn't need to be running.

Ratings

Longevity	Fun factor	Practicality	Value
★★★★★	★★★★★	★★★★★	★★★★★

Overall Rating ★★★★★

Price: Free **Developer:** SpeedDate.com

UK SpeedDate

Looking for love? You might find it on your iPhone!

More and more people are meeting their significant other through dating agencies and the internet. It's no longer a social stigma to say you met online as this is becoming a popular way to interact. The app is the mobile version of the SpeedDate.com website so you'll need to register with that to set up your profile. You can then search through the app's database of men or women by age, though you can't specify location or distance. If someone takes your fancy you can wink at them with the click of a button or send them a free message.

The dating game is big business and although this app is listed as free you will have to cough up some cash for Premium membership if you want to use SpeedDate's most useful features. Without the membership the app only lets you dip your toe in the water of online dating, but it's a great taster of the features on offer, and the people you could meet.

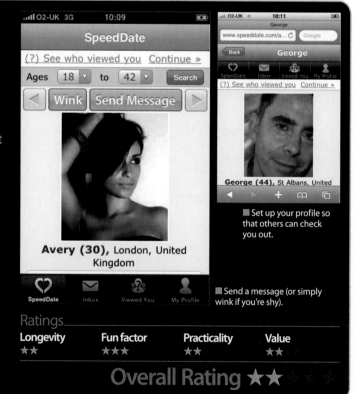

■ Set up your profile so that others can check you out.

■ Send a message (or simply wink if you're shy).

Ratings

Longevity	Fun factor	Practicality	Value
★★	★★★	★★	★★

Overall Rating ★★

Price: Free **Developer:** Said Marouf

Consult popular opinion before choosing a movie to watch

Movie Tweets

■ Browse movies via handy categories like Coming Soon.

■ Select a movie and delve into dozens of related tweets.

The problem with Twitter is that with thousands of people broadcasting their opinions into the digital ether, it's a challenge to find relevant content. This app helps you sort the tweet from the chaff by letting you browse movie-related tweets. The app presents you with categories like Top Ten Movies or Coming Soon. Delve into a category to find a list of movies and tap on a movie to read relevant tweets. As tweets are only 140 characters or less you'll not be getting an in-depth review of the film in question.

However, by skimming dozens of tweets you will get a general positive or negative opinion which will help sway your own movie-going choices. If you do find someone with a passion for film and a flair for encapsulating a movie in just a simple tweet then you can choose to add them to the list of people that you follow regularly. A quick way to sound out a movie and make sure you don't waste your hard-earned cash!

Ratings

Longevity	Fun factor	Practicality	Value
★★★☆☆	★★★☆☆	★★★☆☆	★★★☆☆

Overall Rating ★★★★☆

Price: £0.59/$0.99 **Developer:** Iconic Solutions

Facebook Picture Importer

Get shots off Facebook and onto your iPhone

Some folk like to keep a photographic record of their lives and upload dozens of images to their Facebook albums. They use Facebook to share exciting holiday locations with friends throughout the world or update them on the latest antics of their new pet for example. The Facebook app mentioned on page 142 of this guide lets you view Facebook photos with ease, but you can't save them to view them when you're offline. The sensibly named Facebook Picture Importer is a doddle to use. Log into Facebook and click Connect. Click the big shiny Import Album button and it will retrieve a list of all your Facebook contacts. Click on a friend and it will list all their albums. Tick a box by the albums you fancy and click Import Selected. The clever app will retrieve and save the photos. You can then use your iPhone's Photos app to view the shots in the usual way. Simple, fast and effective!

Ratings

Longevity	Fun factor	Practicality	Value
★★★★★	★★★☆☆	★★★★☆	★★★★☆

Overall Rating ★★★★★

■ The app won't win any design awards but it works well.

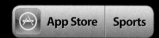
Sports

The iPhone can help athletes stay in shape, track their workout progress, or just keep in tune with their daily regiment without using a dedicated workout device

Nike+

Price: Free   **Developer:** Nike

Track everything you do with this great app from the sportswear giant

 It's rare when a free app provides so much utility that you wonder how you lived without it. It's even rarer when that app is included on the iPhone. Nike+ – which is included with the iPhone 3GS and requires that model – lets you not just track a rough estimate of where you go or what you do in a workout, it tracks every footstep you make. To use it, you'll need a pair of Nike shoes that have an insert for the Nike+ sensor. The sensor connects to the iPhone over a proprietary wireless network, which is why it won't work with the iPhone 3G. Once connected, you can track exactly where you run or walk during a workout. Yet, the real strength of the app has to do with

■ The Nike+ app helps you reach workout goals, one footstep at a time.

■ You can quickly choose a workout goal according to distance, time or calories burned.

accountability. Why accountability? With the Nike+ app, you can load your workout data – including distance, time, pace and your route – to the Nikeplus.com website. There, you can connect with other users who can offer advice and tips on your workout. Nike says about 2 million people use the service. The maps, interface, social networking features and tips on Nikeplus.com really enhance the utility. If you decide to skip the web service, you can still track your workout when you connect your iPhone to iTunes (look for the Nike+ iPod tab) and see your progress.

Of course, you can also use the Nike+ app to plan your workout. The app includes quick options for setting how long you will run or walk, the time you want to invest, and how many calories you want to burn. Then, you can create a playlist that is specific to your run. As you workout, the app provides spoken time and distance notices. The app provides a detailed history of each workout you do, and – if you do load the workouts to the Nikeplus.com site – you can see graphs and charts on previous workouts.

The Nike+ app accomplishes that rare goal of actually encouraging you to workout more and make progress, as opposed to just offering a few gee-whiz features.

Ratings

Longevity	Fun factor	Practicality	Value
★★★★★	★★★★☆	★★★★★	★★★★★

Overall Rating ★★★★★

Price: £1.19/$1.99   Developer: Maverick Software

TriCalc

Calculate time and distance variables for races and workouts

TriCalc is an absolutely brilliant app for two reasons: first of all it provides a simple scroll wheel for adjusting time (which makes it incredibly easy to use when you are ready for a workout) and, second, it also uses an interface that presents all of the workout and triathlon variables in a clear fashion. With TriCalc, there are three main tabs at the top of the screen and they are representative of time, distance and pace. You first select the tab that is most important to you. In other words, if you care most about time, you would select the 'time' tab, then enter the distance you want to run and the speed (or pace) to see how much time it will take. Or, you can select distance (and punch in the time and pace variables) or the speed (and punch in the time and distance variables). Not only is TriCalc an incredibly useful app for keeping track of your workouts, but it's also very reasonably priced and well worth picking up.

Ratings

Longevity	Fun factor	Practicality	Value
★★★★☆	★★★☆☆	★★★★★	★★★★☆

Overall Rating ★★★★☆

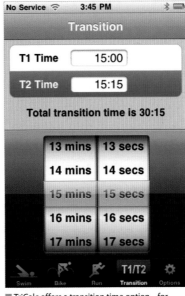

■ Plan a workout or race using time, distance or speed (pace).

■ TriCalc offers a transition time option – for triathlons and other races.

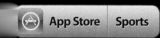
Price: £1.19/$1.99 Developer: GPP Software

The Bullpen

The ideal stats companion for baseball pitchers and coaches

Coaches trying to track pitcher stats will find a major ally in The Bullpen from GPP Software. The app provides a simple interface for tapping in balls, strikes and other pitching stats. Most importantly, it is designed for use during the actual baseball game, so the buttons are large and easy to press. There's an 'end appearance' button that allows you to quickly pause the pitching stats of one pitcher and move to the next bullpen pitcher. You can also add new pitchers just by pressing a plus sign. At the end of the game, The Bullpen shows you the stats for each pitcher during the game, including total number of balls and strikes. You can then email the pitching stats to your coaching staff or to the players. Since the chaos of a game can be a bit overwhelming, The Bullpen also offers an undo feature in case you press the wrong button (but forget which one you clicked erroneously). A useful app for those who'll need it and at a good price, too.

Ratings

Longevity	Fun factor	Practicality	Value
★★★★★	★★☆☆☆	★★★★★	★★★☆☆

Overall Rating ★★★★★

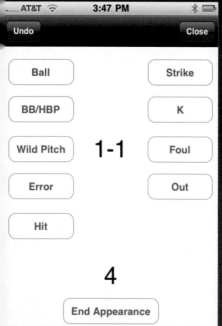

■ You can tap in the pitching stats easily for each pitcher.

Golfshot GPS

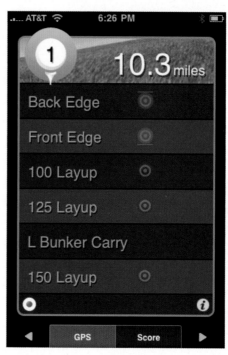

■ Line up your tee shot with a little help from the GPS inside your iPhone.

■ Let the Golfshot app suggest shots based on your current position on the course.

Price: £5.99/$4.99 Developer: Major League Baseball

At Bat 2009

Real-time baseball scores and live game footage in your palm

One of the best apps released for the iPhone, Major League Baseball's At Bat 2009 allows you to quickly see scores for all current baseball games – including post-season and the World Series – from one simple screen. More importantly, you can purchase, for just one dollar, the video for any game. The At Bat app also offers one free game video per day. Even if you do not watch the video, At Bat shows you real-time stats for any game, including the current pitch count, runners on base, and instantly updated score. Most games have an audio feed for free as well, post-game highlights, and condensed games that show you every pitch – minus all the boring bits. At Bat 2009 also features an alert system that tells you when a game you want to watch is starting. Best of all, the interface is extremely easy to use: you just click an arrow to see the game stats, or press and hold to see the video options. Obviously, At Bat 2009 will only appeal to fans of Major League Baseball, but for the price there is plenty here to get your teeth into.

Price: £17.99/$29.99 **Developer:** Shotzoom Software

Leave your caddy at home with this in-the-pocket GPS assistant

Golf is a game of persistence, patience and determination mixed with fairly regular stressful and frustrating moments. With Shotzoom Software's Golfshot GPS, you can take a little of the stress away. The app shows you GPS-rendered maps for your current location on the course and distance to the hole, which helps you decide which club to use. Golfshot GPS also lets you track your distance on shots, view aerial maps, keep score for any round and view stats for your finished rounds. A graph at the end of the round shows you how you shot (distance and direction) and also allows you to compare your round to other golfers for that specific course. The app includes about 15,000 different courses, and there is no extra charge for new course data. One important note: using GPS constantly out on the course will drain your battery quickly, so make sure you bring a back-up charger.

Ratings

Longevity	Fun factor	Practicality	Value
★★★★★	★★★★☆	★★★★☆	★★★★☆

Overall Rating ★★★★★

■ You can purchase game videos, but will also get one free video a day.

■ Track the stats for any current games – including post-season contests.

Ratings

Longevity	Fun factor	Practicality	Value
★★★★★	★★★★★	★★★★☆	★★★★☆

Overall Rating ★★★★★

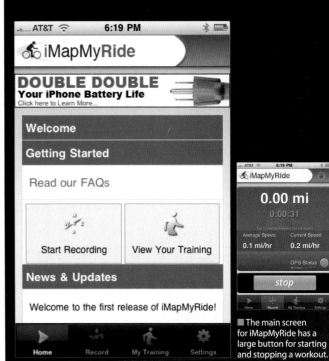

■ The main screen for iMapMyRide has a large button for starting and stopping a workout.

Price: Free **Developer:** MapMyFitness

iMapMyRide

Superb real-time tracking app that shows your workouts on a map

Like the Nike+ app, iMapMyRide allows you to track your actual progress in a workout. Instead of using a sensor in your shoes, iMapMyRide uses the GPS receiver in the iPhone to track your movement. For example, you can set up a bicycle ride, run or walk, then just click a large start button to have the app track where you go, how far you've travelled and also the distance. After the workout or race, you can see your actual GPS-tracked route in Google Maps. The app also lets you share routes with other users, emailing them or posting them to the MapMyRide.com site. Since other users can share routes and even hold racing events, there is an accountability factor with the app that encourages users to give you advice and share tips. Nike+ offers a few extra features, especially for setting calorie-burning data to plan a route, and the app will not work for indoor runs or walks because GPS is only really effective for outdoor use.

Ratings

Longevity	Fun factor	Practicality	Value
★★★★☆	★★★☆☆	★★★★☆	★★★★☆

Overall Rating ★★★★☆

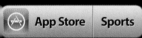

App Store | Sports

Price: Free   Developer: Timebom

Let's Parkour Lite

Cool app teaches you the basics of parkour – a fun urban activity

It's known as l'art du déplacement in France, but Let's Parkour Lite from Timebom is great fun in any language. The app provides a series of detailed how-to videos for the sport of parkour – an activity where you jump, juke and bound off walls and even rooftops. Be careful out there!) Each section of the app offers more advanced manoeuvres for you to try out, and the videos get straight to the point, showing you exactly what is involved without a lot of fluff. For advanced parkour tricks, you can see slow-motion renders and read descriptions of how to pull them off successfully. An introductory video shows you a series of parkour tricks, and there is a full version of the app that includes a full training mode instead of just the video how-tos. We'd like to see the app take more advantage of the iPhone screen, though, perhaps by allowing you to control an on-screen avatar and see how to perform the moves.

Ratings

Longevity	Fun factor	Practicality	Value
★★★☆☆	★★★★☆	★☆☆☆☆	★★★★☆

Overall Rating ★★★☆☆

■ Learn how to bounce off walls in style with this parkour tutorial.

■ Videos show just the basic move without any extras – or a voiceover.

Sportacular

Sports score app that features excellent alerts and reminders for all your sporting needs

■ Details for any game you select show you the real-time score.

■ Standings from around the league are updated in real-time.

Price: £1.19/$1.99   Developer: Intersect World

SportsRadio

Find just about any sports radio programme on your iPhone

Sports radio is one of the last vestiges of a transmission technology invented decades ago, but your iPhone is a capable radio streaming device. With SportsRadio, you can find those streams in a matter of seconds, click the one you want, and listen for free. The app offers the best sports radio shows such as ESPN and WFAN, and the quality is exceptionally good even over a 3G connection. The app lets you send status updates to Twitter and Facebook for the stream you're playing, or email your favourites to friends. One of the most useful features that might not be obvious: as new stations come online, they are added automatically to the list without having to update the app. Another perk: SportsRadio includes US, Canadian and international radio stations. It's one of the best ways to hear about both American football and European football from the same app.

Price: Free Developer: Citizen Sports

Any web page can show you sports scores and most of them will also do so in real-time. Sportacular from developer Citizen goes a major leap further, however, by alerting you to new sports games that have just started or recent score updates. Unlike the ESPN ScoreCenter app, which is more colourful and perhaps easier to use, Sportacular is deeper – it has sports scores for every major sporting event around the globe, including multiple soccer leagues and golf tournaments. The latest version of this app includes a cool swipe control feature for golf leaderboards, pre-game information for baseball, and a rumour mill alert system for ESPN and others that tells you about the world surrounding sports (including any arrests, snafus or blunders from major sporting celebrities). With the push notification alerts, you can even have your iPhone locked and still get sports score updates. The free app is heavily ad-supported but still delivers similar features to the paid app.

Ratings

Longevity	Fun factor	Practicality	Value
★★★★★	★★★★★	★★★☆☆	★★★★★

Overall Rating ★★★★★

■ The colourful interface is easy to read and helps you run through the stats.

Price: Free Developer: ESPN

ESPN ScoreCenter

Well-designed app with sports ticker and colourful 'card' interface

One thing you will see right away with the free ESPN ScoreCenter app is that the interface is incredibly bright and colourful – it is easy to swipe the cards (which almost look like playing cards) around on the screen to see additional scores, games, details and stats. The Sportacular app actually has a few extra features – such as push alerts that appear when your iPhone is locked – but ESPN has a corner on making scores simple to find, no matter which team or sport you follow. The app also has more sports than Sportacular, with leagues for cricket and rugby included. A sports ticker below the main screen shows you any major news in the sporting world – just like the American cable channel does. The app also has a slightly easier to use interface for finding box scores and game summaries than many other iPhone sport score apps, but does not have any extensive social-networking features.

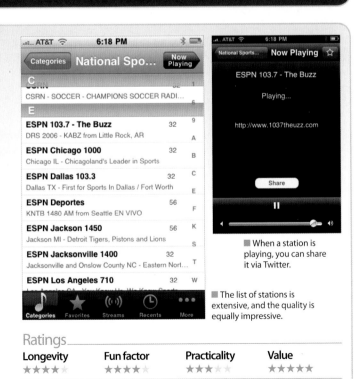

■ When a station is playing, you can share it via Twitter.

■ The list of stations is extensive, and the quality is equally impressive.

Ratings

Longevity	Fun factor	Practicality	Value
★★★★☆	★★★★☆	★★★☆☆	★★★★★

Overall Rating ★★★★★

Ratings

Longevity	Fun factor	Practicality	Value
★★★★☆	★★★★☆	★★★☆☆	★★★★☆

Overall Rating ★★★★☆

The path to iPhone enlightenment

iPHONE

HOME
iPHONE
REVIEWS
  iPhone Apps
  iPhone Acce...
  iPhone Hard...
VIDEO LES...
RINGTONES

Choose your path

safari **iPhone** iPod touch iPhone Kung Fu Tips Lessons 3G **Apple** iTunes **App Store**

Archives (By Month)

Select a month below ▾

Daily enlightenment

The latest iPhone news from across the web

 the iPhone blog

For those who dare to phone different

Quick App: Stickam Live Video for iPhone
October 1st 2009

Quick App Update: PCalc RPN for iPhone 1.8... With Censorship?!
October 1st 2009

iPhone Live! Tonight at 8pm ET/5pm PT
September 30th 2009

Akamai Network Ready to Stream HD to iPhone
September 30th 2009

Regarding Tweetie 2.0 Costing $3
September 30th 2009

iCreate

News and reviews from iCreate magazine

RingtoneFeeder
Weekly ringtones for the iPhone

MBUYER.CO.UK
...tal camera buyers' guide

Developer: Cobramobile
Category: Games
Price: £1.79

iBomber is yet another game that relies on sheer simplicity to create something that is effective and addictive. You are a World War II bomber, and you see the world from a bird's-eye view with cross hairs in the middle of the screen. You then use the accelerometer to direct your ...

>> Read More

Posted in Games, Reviews, iPhone Apps, iPhone Games
Comments added No Comments »

App Review – Let's Golf

Posted by KungFu Guru on September 25th, 2009

Developer: Gameloft
Category: Games
Price: £1.19

The best games are always the ones that come out of left field. You have a preconceived idea of how they will be and then they completely blow you away out of nowhere. That's what happened with Let's Golf. It looks like a teeny-bopper golf game with cutesy characters and slick ...

>> Read More

Posted in Games, Reviews, iPhone Apps
Comments added No Comments »

App Review – StockWatch

Posted by KungFu Guru on September 24th, 2009

Developer: Toughturtle
Category: Finance
Price: £1.79

As we're sure you've noticed, Apple provides its own stocks app. So what makes this title different from the free app? First up, it allows you to create a watchlist of unlimited stocks, mutual funds, indices, commodities and options. By tapping on each you can track its progress on a chart, ...

>> Read More

SEARCH

Video Lessons

Lesson 43 - Calculator
Lesson 42 - Send Video
Lesson 41 - Join WiFi
Lesson 40 - Voicemail
Lesson 39 - Mail Settings

View all lessons

iPHONE KUNG FU

THE GAME

AVAILABLE NOW!
Click the button above or search for iKungFu on the iTunes App Store to download the free game from iPhone Kung Fu.

♫ Free iPhone ringtones

Ringtone 28 - TappTrip
Ringtone 27 - PluckTastic
Ringtone 26 - CheapEazy
Ringtone 25 - BubbleBells
Ringtone 24 - SpaceBand

View all ringtones

Kung Fu Tweets

iphonekungfu: iPhone App Superbowl for all you NFL fans out there. 1st Quarter is live now, second coming soon: http://twurl.nl/bd4vip
September 25th 2009

iphonekungfu: RT @BenHarvell: Can anyone recommend NFL apps for our "Superbowl"? We've a good list but we want to hear from you: http://twurl.nl/bd4vip
September 24th 2009

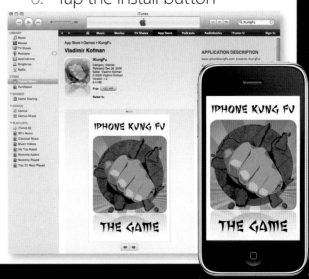

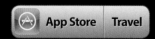
Travel

Travel with the iPhone has become even more rewarding, with a collection of apps that enhance your trip and keep you on time and on schedule. You never need to lug around hefty guide books again!

Price: £6.99/$9.99   Developer: Lonely Planet

Lonely Planet Audio Phrasebook

Don't just learn to speak a foreign language, have this app speak for you

The Lonely Planet Audio Phrasebook app, available for just about any language you can think of, including German, Mandarin, Spanish, and many others, allows you to select common phrases when you travel and have the app speak them for you. For example, you can select categories such as transportation and accommodations. Then, you select the phrase you want the app to speak for you, such as

"Where can I buy a ticket" and either learn how to say that yourself, or hold the phone out to someone who speaks the language. It's an ingenious approach, because it means you can quickly find a phrase and not get stuck in a bind when you are travelling. One example is that you can get directions to local hotspots in the area, report an emergency, or even link several phrases together –

■ Learn German – or any language – in the Lonely Planet series of audio phrasebooks.

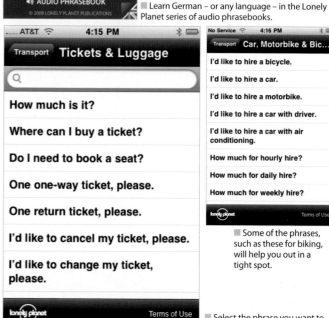

■ Some of the phrases, such as these for biking, will help you out in a tight spot.

■ Select the phrase you want to speak from the list.

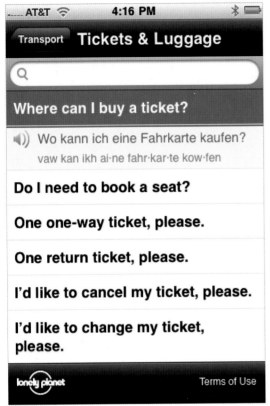

■ The phrasebook shows you the phonetic pronunciation for the phrase.

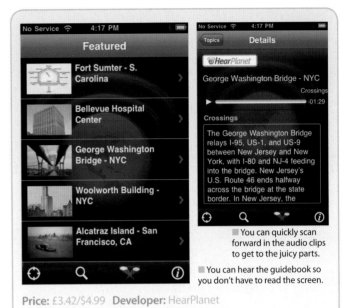

■ You can quickly scan forward in the audio clips to get to the juicy parts.

■ You can hear the guidebook so you don't have to read the screen.

for example, you can have the app speak the phrase "Where do I find tickets" and then "for bus" – which helps you find a bus station and tickets.

Another plus for using this app when travelling: not only do you hear the spoken phrase, but you can see a phonetic text string for how to say the phrase. It's easy to select the phrase you want, play it, and then speak the phrase yourself and learn it.

Audio phrasebook apps have improved significantly over the original versions. In tests, the phrases were spoken immediately after selecting a phrase, as opposed to the slight lag time from the previous versions. There are now over 600 phrases to pick from. The app is amazingly useful for travel because you never know what you will encounter, even if you know several key phrases (such as directions). For example, you might be in an airport and need to find a restroom, so you can have the app speak the phrase "Where is the restroom" for you. For world travellers, you can load up on several audio phrasebook versions for the countries you visit. Most importantly, compared to a desktop version of apps that teach you languages, the Lonely Planet Audio Phrasebooks are mobile and cost much less.

Ratings

Longevity	Fun factor	Practicality	Value
★★★★★	★★★★	★★★★★	★★★★★

Overall Rating ★★★★★

Price: £3.42/$4.99 Developer: HearPlanet

HearPlanet Premium

Listen to travel guidebook info for popular destinations

With 250,000 locations and thousands upon thousands of travel articles, HearPlanet is a powerful travel companion. The idea is that, instead of reading about places like London or San Francisco, you can just type in the location and listen to guidebook information – such as the best sights to see or the local sports attractions. This means you can spend more time viewing the scenery and less time staring at your smartphone screen. The app has plenty of extra features, such as the ability to find attractions near you in real-time and a map that shows the distance to the best locales. The map is especially useful, because you can press on icons for interesting hotspots near you. There is a featured content mode, and you can search for points of interest – such as a beach or camping site or just browse through the listings of audio guidebooks. HearPlanet Premium is a great travel companion.

Ratings

Longevity	Fun factor	Practicality	Value
★★★★	★★★★	★★★★★	★★★★★

Overall Rating ★★★★★

Price: £0.69/$0.99 Developer: Aaron Miller

Gate Maps

Consult the gate maps for the most popular airports

With 39 airports included (both in the United States and international), Gate Maps offers an extensive array of gate maps that help you find your bearings in an airport, or assist the person assigned to pick you up at the terminal. Most maps are highly detailed, showing parking lots, terminal wings, and gate assignments. The app is useful because it runs without needing a connection, which is handy in an airport where Wi-Fi and 3G are sketchy at best. And, even if you could connect to the web, many airline gate maps use Flash, which means you cannot view them on the iPhone. You can scroll around on gate maps and zoom in, but there are no interactive features – such as seeing which flights are at which gates or any real-time data (eg, delays) or your GPS location. Despite these drawbacks, this is an extremely handy little app that could well save you time and effort when getting to and from the airport.

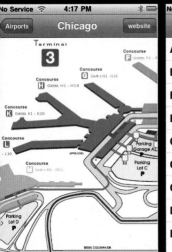
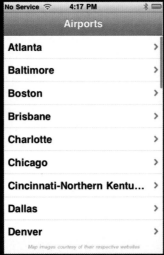

Maps for common airports show terminal wings and specific gates.

Ratings

Longevity	Fun factor	Practicality	Value
★★★☆☆	★★☆☆☆	★★★★☆	★★★☆☆

Overall Rating ★★★★☆

Price: Free Developer: Sumner Systems Management

Cheap Gas!

Find nearby gas stations and the current prices

GPS devices from Garmin and Magellan often include a feature to find nearby gas stations and report the price in real-time. Cheap Gas! accomplishes the same idea on your iPhone. You just start the app, and it finds nearby gas stations, showing you the cheapest price (you can view results by price or by distance from you). The app also lets you search for gas stations by zip code as well. Continuing the trend this year of augmented reality, Cheap Gas! has a Cyborg button that allows you to point the iPhone camera toward the direction you want to go to see pop-ups of gas stations with icons that show the price and distance. For finding gas when travelling, Cheap Gas! is a handy tool because you can quickly find nearby gas stations without having to use a GPS device or another app (such as Yelp) just to fill up your tank. It's a very useful iPhone app that could save you some of your hard-earned cash.

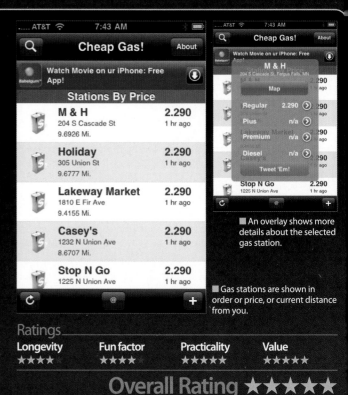

■ An overlay shows more details about the selected gas station.

■ Gas stations are shown in order or price, or current distance from you.

Ratings

Longevity	Fun factor	Practicality	Value
★★★★☆	★★★★☆	★★★★★	★★★★★

Overall Rating ★★★★★

West Ruislip
6494.89 km / 4035.7 miles

Nearest for
Central

Uxbridge
6494.13 km / 4035.3 miles

Nearest for   Also on
Piccadilly   Metropolitan

Chesham
6476.34 km / 4024.2 miles

Nearest for
Metropolitan

Nearest Tube

Price: £1.36/$1.99
Developer: Acrossair

Find the nearest London Underground tube

Some apps use Google Maps to show you directions. Nearest Tube uses augmented reality – a new concept where you use the built-in camera of the iPhone and see overlays that provides real-time information for the physical scene you are viewing. With Nearest Tube, the "augmented reality" is the location of London Underground trains.

There are three modes of operation. If you hold the iPhone flat you will see all 13 lines of the train system. When you move it at an angle, you will see the closest tube, along with information about how far away it is and the tube line. If you raise the phone up at a higher angle, you will see a list of all nearby tubes and their distance. As a first release, Nearest Tube works well, but does not have any extra info – such as costs or schedules – which is a real shame.

Ratings

Longevity	Fun factor	Practicality	Value
★★★☆☆	★★★★★	★★★☆☆	★★☆☆☆

■ This app shows an overlay on the iPhone camera for London Underground trains.

Overall Rating ★★★☆☆

IAmHere

Price: £0.69/$0.99   Developer: Exploding Orange

Send a quick note about your whereabouts, using the iPhone's GPS

IAmHere, like Loopt and Google Latitude, is a "location-awareness" app – an emerging concept where you report on where you are to those who need to know. For example, you might let family and friends know you are on a trip to Chicago, staying at a specific hotel. Whereas, you might let the general public know you are in the United States. With IAmHere, the options for location-awareness are more limited but put you in control of exactly who finds out about your current location.

The app is quite basic: you tap in an email address and a note, then press a button to send your location. Your recipient receives a Google Map for your location. There is no way to control the accuracy of the map – you can't just send your city location. However, IAmHere is a great tool for a quick update to a business associate or family member.

■ The app lets you tap in a note that accompanies a map of your location.

No Service 🗢   4:18 PM

Send I am here

Current location accuracy +/- 1566m.

Default email address:
johnmbrandon@gmail.com ❯

Default note:

Leaving for the day ❯

ℹ

No Service 🗢   4:18 PM

Cancel   Save

Leaving for the day

Q W E R T Y U I O P
A S D F G H J K L
⇧ Z X C V B N M ⌫
.?123   space   return

Ratings

Longevity	Fun factor	Practicality	Value
★★★☆☆	★★★☆☆	★★★★☆	★★★★☆

■ IAmHere lets you send a quick note about your current location.

Overall Rating ★★★★☆

Price: £0.69/$0.99   Developer: Hosn Entertainment

iLondon

A travel guidebook in your pocket, minus the coffee stains

The iLondon app is indispensable because you can quickly look up things to do and see in the city without the usual fuss of checking a guidebook, hiring a tour guide, or searching on the web. The app presents guidebook info – such as restaurant locations, bookshops, and hotels – in a "top ten" format as reported by reputable sources, such as local newspapers. You can drill down through the top ten lists, see a quick synopsis of the location, and click thumbnail photos to see the larger image, hours of operation, and a longer description. iLondon even shows you the closest tube to use for reaching the destination, and you can view where you want to go on Google Maps by clicking a button. You can even add a quick route by clicking on a train icon for where you are now and where you want to go and a larger map shows you the city highlights. This is a great app for tourists of the Big Smoke.

Ratings

Longevity	Fun factor	Practicality	Value
★★★	★★★	★★★★	★★★★

Overall Rating ★★★★★

■ The descriptions are succinct with the right amount of travel details.

Price: Free   Developer: Nodconcept

Room

You never have to be lost in your hotel again

Free, and highly useful, the Room app for iPhone is one of those travel aids that comes in handy at the most opportune times. It has a very simple utility: you tap in the room number for your hotel, and the apps saves it for you and places the number next to the icon so you don't even need to start the app to see the number.

You might wonder: why is that important? In modern hotels, your key card purposefully does not include a room number for security reasons, and the clerk usually writes the number on an over-sized card that is hard to carry around all day. Now, with Room on the iPhone, you can dispense with it and just jot the number down in this app, which serves as a reminder of the number and a reminder to track the number. Of course, the app could do a lot more – including a note about where the room is – but it's free and could prove useful if you have a dodgy memory like a lot of us.

Price: £0.69/$0.99   Developer: Alta Vida

Babelingo

Impressively deep language translator at a low price

You might have to check the price for the Babelingo a few times after you buy it – the app is outstanding value. Although it is not nearly as fun to use as the Lonely Planet Audio Phrasebooks, which speak the text you have chosen, Babelingo supports 11 languages and 300 phrases. The idea is that you can tap the phrase you want to say, and then show your iPhone to a hotel clerk, bus station manager, or bystander. Babelingo works both ways: you can view the English phrases and the translation, or view the foreign language and see the English translation. There are no phonetic pronunciations included here, but Babelingo does work well in a pinch on travel trips because there are so many phrases to pick from in categories such as conversations, the time, and medical issues.

While Babelingo may not include absolutely everything you may want from a translation package, it will still help you out in a travel-related bind, and for its measly price point, it really is quite an impressive package.

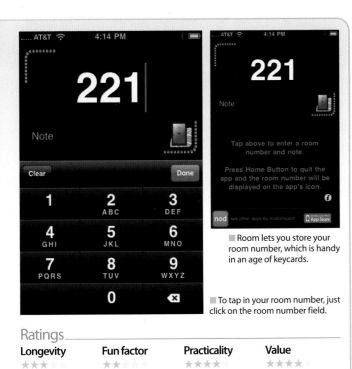

Ratings

Longevity	Fun factor	Practicality	Value
★★★	★★	★★★★	★★★★

Overall Rating ★★★★☆

¿A qué distancia se encuentra?

Categories such as Money help you travel with ease.

Each phrase shows on the screen in a readable font on a black background.

Ratings

Longevity	Fun factor	Practicality	Value
★★★★	★★★	★★★★★	★★★★★

Overall Rating ★★★★☆

Price: £3.14/$4.99 Developer: Mobiata

FlightTrack

Real-time flight info, gate delays, and other air travel details

Calling an airline to get info on flight delays is often an exercise in tedium. It takes too long, and details are somewhat hard to pry out of an automated calling system. FlightTrack is much more advanced, providing not just info about flight delays, but also a real-time map with weather info that is updated as the plane flies. The app also provides details about common aircraft. To add a flight, you just tap a new flight button and enter the airline and flight number, then choose a departure date. FlightTrack finds the flight quickly and reports the arrival time and gate number. With FlightTrack, you can not only choose an upcoming flight, but also track a flight for a business partner, friend or relative. You can save found flights and email updates on the flight, but there are no social networking features (yet) to send your flight status to Twitter, which is a slight defect. All in all, though, this is a great app for regular travellers.

Ratings

Longevity	Fun factor	Practicality	Value
★★★★★	★★★★	★★★★★	★★★★★

Overall Rating ★★★★★

FlightTrack just requires you to tap in the airline and flight number.

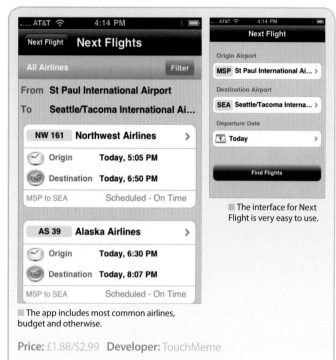

The interface for Next Flight is very easy to use.

The app includes most common airlines, budget and otherwise.

Price: £1.88/$2.99 **Developer:** TouchMeme

Next Flight

Making flying as simple as a tap of an iPhone

In some cases, when you travel, you want to find quick flight info fast. Next Flight has just one purpose: you can tap in your departure and arrival city and date, and then see exactly which flights are available and when. The advantage is speed; there are no extra features to get in the way, and you can quickly filter out airlines and view flight numbers. When you find a flight you want to investigate, you can view terminal information and which aircraft will be used. Next Flight allows you to send an email with the select flight info to yourself as a reminder or to other people in your travelling party. And there's a quick refresh button to make sure you are viewing up-to-date flights. The app's look and feel is a bit too textual – for instance, an icon for the aircraft model would make it easier to spot whether you will be flying in style or in cramped quarters – but overall this is a simple but useful app.

Ratings

Longevity	Fun factor	Practicality	Value
★★★★	★★★	★★★★	★★★★

Overall Rating ★★★★☆

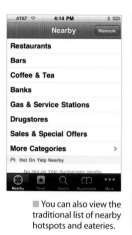

You can also view the traditional list of nearby hotspots and eateries.

Yelp now includes a Monocle mode that overlays real-time location info.

Price: Free **Developer:** Yelp

Yelp

Version 3.1 of this popular travel app adds augmented reality

Yelp is the well-known travel companion app that shows you nearby restaurants, bars, banks, gas stations, and coffee shops. The original claim to fame was the ability to filter the nearby options – based on the iPhone's GPS – on variables such as price, distance, and hours of operation, and Yelp offers a wealth of user reviews too. The latest 3.1 version adds an augmented reality feature called Monocle that only works with the iPhone 3GS. With it, you can point your phone in any direction to see pop-up overlays of what is nearby. True, the pop-ups have limited usefulness and it's easier to drill down the usual way through nearby businesses, but the overlay looks cool and is an impressive addition for those who are bored by simple text menus. Add in more traditional options of calling directly from the app and seeing the business on Google Maps and Yelp becomes a powerful tool.

Ratings

Longevity	Fun factor	Practicality	Value
★★★★	★★★★	★★★★	★★★★★

Overall Rating ★★★★★

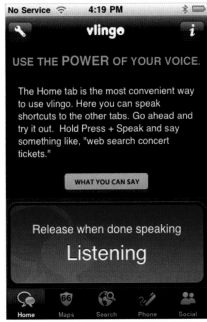

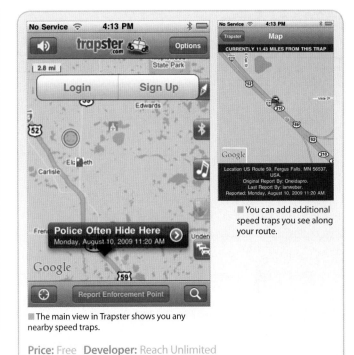

■ Searching for concert tickets is easy and the results are usually pretty helpful.

■ To search, just press and hold down the large button.

■ You can add additional speed traps you see along your route.

■ The main view in Trapster shows you any nearby speed traps.

Price: Free **Developer:** Vlingo

Price: Free **Developer:** Reach Unlimited

Vlingo
Speak your searches and make phone calls without typing

Trapster
Share speed trap info with other iPhone users – and much more

In the hectic pandemonium of travel, it's sometimes hard to punch in short messages or even dial a phone number – especially if you're carrying a guidebook or laptop bag. Vlingo solves this problem by providing a speech-to-text app that requires no typing. You can update your Twitter or Facebook status, search for a phrase, dial a contact, and even look up a business on a map. You press and hold down a button, speak a phrase, and Vlingo takes care of the rest. Tabs along the bottom of the app take you to the sections for maps, searches, and dialling or you can just use the home screen and have the app figure out what you want to do. Keywords are important – for instance, to update your Facebook status, you have to say "Facebook status… boarding a bus for Chicago". This is a great app that could make life a lot easier during the hustle and bustle of travelling.

A brilliant app that relies on the kindness of strangers, Trapster allows you to see speed traps on a map and adjust your speed accordingly. Yet, the app is also a social networking client that provides a way to share details about an entire trip, post photos, report on interesting locales, and even include information about the music you like. The latest version, which is vastly improved, shows a radar of your moving vehicle and works with the built-in mapping technology on the iPhone, including the GPS. You can share your trip and Trapster details (such as speed traps you see yourself while driving) on Facebook and Twitter automatically. The latest version also lets you control music playing on the iPhone, and the app fades music in and out when announcing a new speed trap alert. The app also lets you see and report police sightings for traffic spots and other traps.

Ratings

Longevity	Fun factor	Practicality	Value
★★★	★★★	★★★	★★★★

Overall Rating ★★★☆☆

Ratings

Longevity	Fun factor	Practicality	Value
★★★★★	★★★	★★★★	★★★★

Overall Rating ★★★★☆

Utilities

Turn your iPhone into a Swiss Army Knife with these handy utilities for just about any and every purpose: checking battery levels, testing network speed and converting measurements

Price: £1.19/$1.99   **Developer:** All About Apps

AppBox Pro

A wide assortment of utilities, all bundled into one easy-to-use app

A brilliant collection of utilities – all part of one app – AppBox Pro sets a high watermark for ease of use, practical functions and great design. Each utility is listed on two colourful screens. (You can just flip to the right for the second screen; the app hints at a day when there will be an even greater collection of apps with more utilities.)

Most of the utilities emphasise a practical function that takes advantage of the iPhone's accelerometer or touch screen in some unique way. There are 18 utilities in all, ranging from a simple ruler to a flashlight that emits a white glow for finding your way in the dark. You can re-arrange utilities on the two screens any way you want or

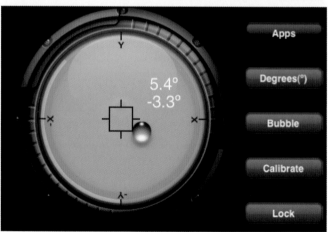

■ The Clinometer utility helps you find a level surface.

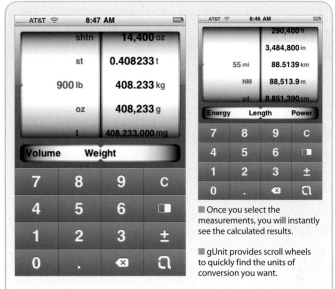

■ AppBox Pro shows you a list of handy utilities on multiple screens.

remove the one you will never use (such as a tip calculator). Some of the utilities are indispensable: there is one for seeing how much free storage you have on your iPhone, another for seeing battery life in various categories, such as time left for watching videos.

Interestingly, AppBox Pro duplicates several other apps – such as gUnit and Battery Go! – for about the same price as each single app. Those utilities still have value – providing direct access to functions, which is the only minor complaint about AppBox in that you have to first start the app, then click the utility you want to use. It can be difficult to figure out how to get back to the main AppBox Pro screen. With the Flashlight tool, for example, you have to click on the screen first, then press Apps.

That said, AppBox is still great value. The Clinometer helps you find a level on a flat surface, Dashboard shows you a quick peek at storage and battery usage (plus any interesting events for the day), Date Calc lets you determine how many days there are between calendar dates, and Loan helps you figure out the monthly payment required for a bank loan on a car or home (or any item you want to purchase). Overall, AppBox Pro is a handy program with a variety of utilities. Once you start using it, you can first delete a few extra apps on the iPhone and will find that it becomes indispensable.

■ Once you select the measurements, you will instantly see the calculated results.

■ gUnit provides scroll wheels to quickly find the units of conversion you want.

Price: £0.59/$0.99 **Developer:** Axonic Labs

gUnit

Converter app for units of measurement, such as volume, temp, length and energy

gUnit from developer Axonic Labs helps you find the conversion of length, volume, speed, temperature, weight and many other factors (but not currency, unfortunately) in one handy utility. The app uses two scroll wheels – one for the input measurement and one for the output. Once you tap in the number you want to convert, both scroll wheels change to show you the number. Using the large scroll wheels is handy because you might be in the middle of cooking supper or hammering on a beam in your garage. gUnit also has a small icon you use to remind yourself about what you are converting (the screen slides over to reveal miles and kilometres). The app supports multiple languages, including Chinese and Japanese, but the one minor gripe we have with it is that it does not do a good job of explaining measurements. For example, an overlay that shows the conversion ratio would help kids to figure out unit conversions on their own.

Ratings

Longevity	Fun factor	Practicality	Value
★★★★★	★★★★☆	★★★★★	★★★★★

Overall Rating ★★★★★

Ratings

Longevity	Fun factor	Practicality	Value
★★★☆☆	★★☆☆☆	★★★★☆	★★★★☆

Overall Rating ★★★★☆

Price: £2.39/$3.99   Developer: Software Ops

My Eyes Only Photo

Secure photo storage utility keeps your images private and safe

Securely protecting photos helps to keep them safe from being deleted, and also helps maintain some level of privacy. My Eyes Only (MEO) Photo is a smart app that adds 256-bit encryption to photos you add or snap with the iPhone's built-in camera. (256-bit encryption is the highest available for consumers and is probably overkill for an app on your iPhone. It is hacker proof.) When you do snap a photo, MEO Photo adds the encryption automatically. In tests, MEO Photo showed images fast even though they are encrypted, and the app lets you zoom in just as you do with the Camera app. You can also send photos by email to anyone – although you can't send an encrypted, compressed batch of images and the app doesn't support copy and paste. Software Ops has promised an update that lets you share images with other iPhone users over Bluetooth or Wi-Fi and keep them secure.

Ratings

Longevity	Fun factor	Practicality	Value
★★★☆☆	★★★☆☆	★★★★☆	★★★★☆

Overall Rating ★★★★☆

■ Here, MEO Photo is used to protect and encrypt a signed contract.

■ The interface for browsing encrypted photos is fast and easy to use.

Price: £0.59/$0.99   Developer: CollegeKidApp

Battery Go!

Quickly check the battery level remaining for specific tasks, such as movie watching

The battery indicator on the iPhone's home screen is great for a quick check on how much time you have to use the wonderful handset. However, it does not provide any details about how much juice is left for specific tasks, such as watching a movie or listening to Radiohead's latest album – even though those activities vary wildly in how much battery power they consume. Battery Go! from developer CollegeKidApp is a remarkably simple app that shows you how much usage you have left for talking on the phone, surfing the web over Wi-Fi, listening to music, or watching video. There is just one slider that shows you a theoretical usage model: if you have drained half of the battery, you can find out how much listening time you have left. You can see the difference between, say, talking on the phone over a 2G network versus connecting over a 3G network, but we'd like to see an indicator for music streaming.

Ratings

Longevity	Fun factor	Practicality	Value
★★★☆☆	★★☆☆☆	★★★★☆	★★★★☆

Overall Rating ★★★☆☆

■ You can see additional usage models for battery power on the second screen.

■ The main screen for Battery Go! is ultra-simple, showing battery usage left.

Price: £1.79/$2.99 **Developer:** Realmac Software

LittleSnapper

Snap photos, tag them with keywords and share them online

 Realmac Software's LittleSnapper provides a single purpose in life: it allows you to take photos and share them on a QuickSnapper.com account (which is now hosted at the Emberapp.com site). You need an account to upload images, but once you have one they will be added to a stream of uploaded photos. The advantage is that LittleSnapper provides a quick and easy way to upload images to a website without the usual hassles of storage allocations, settings for privacy, and so on. It is a quick utility for snapping photos and offloading them. The tool also lets you email photos and there is a built-in browser for snapping images of a website (although you can also accomplish this by using the iPhone browser and taking a screenshot). The interface for LittleSnapper uses a scroll dial. You can access your image roll and upload those images, configure account settings and access the web browser.

Ratings

Longevity	Fun factor	Practicality	Value
★★★☆☆	★★★☆☆	★★★☆☆	★★★☆☆

Overall Rating ★★★☆☆

■ The built-in browser is meant for snapping screenshots.

■ LittleSnapper uses a well-designed scroll wheel to access the main functions.

Price: Free **Developer:** Gogii

textPlus

Text messaging app has group chats and works with iPod touch

Text messaging rates do not apply to this excellent utility. textPlus – which is an ad-supported app – lets you send and receive text messages to other textPlus users, either on the iPhone or on the iPod touch. You can send out multiple texts and, when people respond, they are threaded into a chat window in a group chat. The app does not cost anything, since its developer Gogii has an arrangement with carriers to pay for the SMS text messages (and you get to look at ads). You can also use textPlus to send text messages and receive them back from anyone using standard text messaging on a mobile phone network (but they pay for the texts that they send on their phone). textPlus uses the new push features in iPhone OS 3.0 so you can receive an overlay text when a new text message comes in, even if the app is not running.

Ratings

Longevity	Fun factor	Practicality	Value
★★★★☆	★★★☆☆	★★★★★	★★★★★

Overall Rating ★★★★☆

■ To send a text, you tap in the phone number of any user.

■ Chats are threaded into one window, even for multiple texters.

Price: £0.59/$0.99 **Developer:** Yuyao Mobile Software

PDF Reader Pro

Read PDF docs on your iPhone – more importantly, it manages them for you

When you really need to read a PDF file on the iPhone, there are two methods available to you: you can either send one by email and the iPhone will use a built-in PDF reader. Or, alternatively, you can browse to a site on the internet and read them on the iPhone. PDF Reader Pro, perhaps an awkwardly named app, is actually adept at managing PDF files, but you can use it to read them as well. The best feature is that you can set up a simple Wi-Fi sync server – it's easy using a built-in option – and then upload PDF files to your iPhone over Wi-Fi on a home internet connection. (You just type an IP address that PDF Reader Pro provides on your Mac or PC browser.) It's also easy to view PDF files stored on the phone, change font size, view in landscape mode, jump to pages and read in either a fast/low quality and slow/high-quality mode.

Ratings

Longevity	Fun factor	Practicality	Value
★★★★★	★★★★★	★★★★★	★★★★☆

Overall Rating ★★★★★

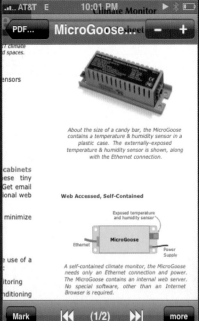

■ PDF Reader Pro shows you a list of stored PDF documents on your iPhone.

■ You can zoom in on docs, flip them around on the page and view them in landscape.

Price: £1.19/$1.99 **Developer:** Alessandro Levi Montalcini

Contact Tool

Search through your contact list using all kinds of criteria, from date of birth to nickname

Contact Tool from developer Alessandro Levi Montalcini might seem slightly superfluous for a smartphone that already has a great built-in Contacts app. Yet, Contact Tool lets you list contacts according to many useful variables – such as age, email, nickname, ringtone setting or where that person lives. For business use, the app provides a simple way to view all contacts by business name, department or title. There are grouping functions (say, by region or country) and a way to search for contacts. The app does not maintain any extra data beyond what is normally found on the iPhone, and in some ways Contact Tool lacks a few key features – such as the ability to link contacts together for a project you are working on or custom fields you want to use. However, the saving grace of this app is that it lets you do searches for contacts with no data -- such as those without a picture or a birthdate – and fill in missing contact info.

Ratings

Longevity	Fun factor	Practicality	Value
★★★★☆	★★★☆☆	★★★★☆	★★★★☆

Overall Rating ★★★★☆

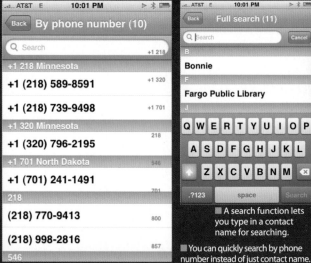

■ A search function lets you type in a contact name for searching.

■ You can quickly search by phone number instead of just contact name.

Price: Free (Requires Jott service)   **Developer:** Jott Networks

Jott

Note-taking app uses your voice, converts it to text

The Jott app lets you record notes to yourself, save them to the Jott website, and then receive them back in text form as an email or send the written notes (which you speak into the iPhone) to your business contacts or friends and family. You can also send notes to social networks – sending a status update to Twitter or Facebook, for example, and even send a calendar item to Google Calendar (but not to Microsoft Outlook, frustratingly). The primary strength of this app is that it actually works: speech-to-text conversion is amazingly accurate. Jott is constantly tweaking its service with a larger library of spoken words to convert accurately. The Jott service costs about $4 per month, which is not a bad price for unlimited speech conversions, although you need to upgrade to the next plan for longer speech notes. Jott is an excellent idea for business users who need to stay on task.

Ratings

Longevity	Fun factor	Practicality	Value
★★★★☆	★★★☆☆	★★★★☆	★★★★★

Overall Rating ★★★★☆

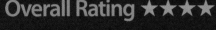

■ The app is free, but Jott service costs about $4 per month.

■ Jott is a well-designed app that lets you record notes and access them on the web.

Price: £17.99/$29.99   **Developer:** HP

HP 15C

A good, old-fashioned scientific calculator that will actually fit in your pocket

Ah yes, the HP 15C calculator. For those who remember the good old days of advanced scientific calculators before the computer came along and took away all the fun (or, depending on your perspective, made geekdom more respectable), the 15C was the classic, high-performance model from HP. This app, modelled faithfully on the actual physical version you could hold in your hand (and still available on eBay), provides all of the same functions including many scientific calcs and the SOLVE button used for programming complex functions – up to 448 lines. In landscape mode, you will see all the buttons arranged exactly as they are on the real calculator with light shading and the exact same font for the text on each key as the original. With the iPhone OS 3.0 release, which includes a scientific calculator, HP 15C is a bit less compelling, but still cool.

Ratings

Longevity	Fun factor	Practicality	Value
★★★★★	★★★★☆	★★★★★	★★☆☆☆

Overall Rating ★★★★☆

■ In landscape mode, HP 15C looks exactly like the original.

■ A stunning rendition of the original HP handheld calculator, if slightly overpriced.

Price: Free   Developer: Ookla

Speedtest.net Speed Test

Check the actual speed of your iPhone over 3G or Wi-Fi

■ A large speed dial shows you the test results in an easy-to-read format.

 You're sitting in an airport lounge or waiting in a library while using your iPhone and the speed over Wi-Fi seems unusually high. With Speed Test, you can find out exactly how fast (or slow) your internet connection is. The app doesn't really provide any extra features, and in some ways is an advertisement to use the Speedtest.net service on the web, but no matter: Speed Test offers a simple interface that shows a speed dial and the resulting speed amount. It works for both Wi-Fi and 3G access. The only minor glitch we found in testing is that, when you are testing 3G access with Wi-Fi turned off (the iPhone normally defaults to Wi-Fi if available), results can be a little sketchy. In several tests in a row, Speed Test gave slightly different results. The testing is based on the actual internet connection and congestion, but we wondered if the results would really vary that much sitting in the same place in a coffee shop.

Ratings

Longevity	Fun factor	Practicality	Value
★★★★☆	★★☆☆☆	★★★★☆	★★★☆☆

Overall Rating ★★★★☆

Price: Free   Developer: JiWire

Free Wi-Fi Finder

Looking for Wi-Fi nearby or far away? This app will help

 The iPhone does a wonderful job of showing any nearby Wi-Fi networks when you're out and about. The problem is, other than the name of the network, it's difficult to know exactly who owns the wireless feed and where it originates. And, of course – you can't find networks that are not located nearby. With the Free Wi-Fi Finder app, you can search in any location to see which free networks are offered, or use a nearby option – which scans for available networks. The app includes over 10,000 locations and you can filter out a few variables to narrow down your search – such as only searching in coffee shops or airports. The app also provides more info about the network owner, such as the location and their phone number. JiWire is a well-known service on the internet that reports on Wi-Fi networks reliably – it seems the app is updated almost daily. You can also bookmark commonly used networks to save the location details.

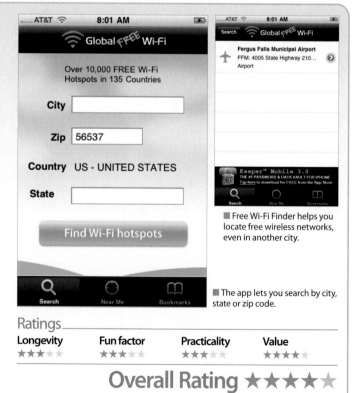

■ Free Wi-Fi Finder helps you locate free wireless networks, even in another city.

■ The app lets you search by city, state or zip code.

Ratings

Longevity	Fun factor	Practicality	Value
★★★☆☆	★★★☆☆	★★★☆☆	★★★★☆

Overall Rating ★★★★☆

Weather

If you rely on the weather, don't let the drab days spoil your fun. Here is a selection of apps that may well prove indispensable to those of you who regularly need accurate weather forecasts

Price: £0.59/$0.99   **Developer:** EquiQuery Inc

WindScale

Handy for sailors and weather watchers alike, the Beaufort scale makes its way onto the iPhone

Measuring the exact velocity of the wind without sophisticated equipment is not an easy task, even now, in the 21st Century. However, it was a lot more difficult around 200 years ago when the large sailing ships of the Royal Navy were at the mercy of strong winds and other inclement weather conditions.

The problem was that subjective views differed and one sailor's moderate wind may be another's gentle breeze. This led to indecision as to how to hoist sails. Admiral Sir Francis Beaufort (1774-1857) was well aware of the predicament and he realised that standardising wind speed observations could reap benefits. In 1805 he published a method of measuring the wind at sea based on what sails a ship could safely hoist. The Beaufort wind force scale (or the Beaufort scale as it later came to be known) was adopted by the Royal Navy in 1938 and the beauty of this

■ WindScale is useful for everybody from sailors to those worried about their hair.

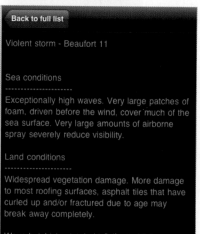

■ A Beaufort scale in your pocket – how handy is that?

■ Sea and land conditions enable you to objectively determine wind speed.

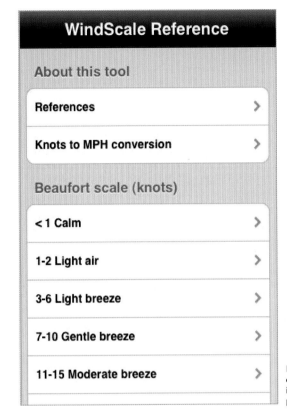

WindScale Reference

About this tool

References >

Knots to MPH conversion >

Beaufort scale (knots)

< 1 Calm >

1-2 Light air >

3-6 Light breeze >

7-10 Gentle breeze >

11-15 Moderate breeze >

■ Wind speeds can be displayed in knots or miles per hour.

simple tool lay in the way that it acted as an empirical measure for describing wind speed, with observations based on the conditions at sea. Many years later, the Beaufort scale was modified for use on land and the descriptions that go with it are still used today. The scale has 13 steps; force 0 indicates that there is no wind and force 12 is logged when the wind is a steady 63 knots.

If you need to know the wind speed at any time, EquiQuery's WindScale is well worth a look as it lets you view the Beaufort scale on your trusty iPhone or iPod touch. The app is designed for anyone who needs to know the strength of the wind and this includes not only sailors, fishermen, kayakers and windsurfers, but also golfers, hikers and virtually all other outdoor enthusiasts, as well as those who are simply worried about their hair or are trying to decide whether to take an umbrella with them or not when they go out. Descriptions of land and sea conditions are included in the reports and these enable the user to accurately and objectively measure the wind speed. The WindScale app is very good value for money at just 59p and for us the only remiss is the absence of a page that shows the Beaufort scale and wind speed together.

Ratings

Longevity	Fun factor	Practicality	Value
★★★★★	★★	★★★★	★★★★★

Overall Rating ★★★★★

Price: Free **Developer:** WeatherBug

WeatherBug
Free access to live local weather conditions and forecasts

If you are a frequent traveller who relies heavily on accurate weather forecasts, WeatherBug may well prove a killer app for you. Designed primarily as a service for providing live local weather updates, the app gives iPhone and iPod touch users instant access to a very large network of weather stations in the United States and literally thousands of other locations around the world. Features include the option to be able to display seven-day forecasts or hourly reports of actual weather conditions in up to ten saved locations. You also get National Weather Service (NWS) alerts, radar maps that show you the cloud base, cached weather forecast data that can be viewed offline and live weather cameras. The only niggle we have with WeatherBug is that the app is supported by adverts. However, this is a small price to pay for an accurate weather-forecasting tool that costs absolutely nothing.

Ratings

Longevity	Fun factor	Practicality	Value
★★★★★	★★	★★★★	★★★★

Overall Rating ★★★★

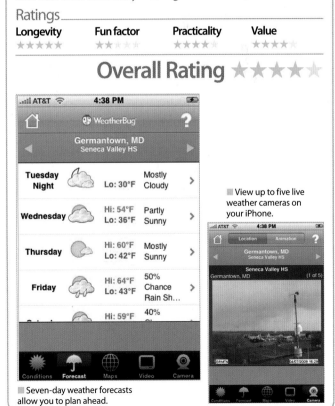

■ Seven-day weather forecasts allow you to plan ahead.

■ View up to five live weather cameras on your iPhone.

A mine of useful weather forecasting information

WeatherOnline

Price: £2.39/$3.99 **Developer:** WeatherOnline

■ The Radar function shows you the cloud base in the UK and most of Europe.

■ Need a weather overview for a specific country? This app is for you.

WeatherOnline (www.weatheronline.co.uk) is a wonderful resource for outdoor enthusiasts and indeed anyone else who relies on accurate, up-to-date weather forecasts for the UK, Europe and the rest of the world. The good news is that a mobile version of the service has now been made available to iPhone users. This brings quick and easy access to worldwide city forecasts and weather maps which show you an overview of the weather, as well as the maximum and minimum temperature ranges, precipitation and the option to view a neat three-day forecast. The majority of forecasts are updated every three to six hours and the Current Weather view every 30 minutes or so. WeatherOnline is a little overpriced and not quite as polished as apps such as Weather Pro and The Weather Channel (also available from the App Store). These niggles aside, it really is a mine of useful weather forecasting information.

Ratings

Longevity	Fun factor	Practicality	Value
★★★★☆	★★☆☆☆	★★★★☆	★★★☆☆

Overall Rating ★★★★☆

Sunrise Sunset Pro

Price: £1.19/$1.99 **Developer:** Kekoa Vincent

Accurately predict the times of dawn and dusk

Developed by Kekoa Vincent, Sunrise Sunset Pro is a simple but incredibly useful app as it lets you view the times of sunrise, sunset, civil twilight (dawn), sun transit (solar noon) and civil twilight end (dusk). Sunrise Sunset Pro is aimed squarely at anyone who needs to keep track of where the sun will be on any particular day and at any particular time. For example, if you are a dawn surfer or twilight jogger, Sunrise Sunset Pro will tell you the best time to set out. The app is easy to use, although the Position tab is initially a little difficult to understand. To explain, the compass face will show the sun and if it is near the outside of the ring, it is at a low inclination (typically sunrise or sunset). If it is in the centre of the compass, it is directly overhead (90 degrees). As mentioned it's an ideal app for those who need to know the whereabouts of the sun at any given time, but for others it's unlikely to be of much use or interest.

■ Accurate sunrise and sunset times are displayed for any given location.

■ View the position of the sun at various times during the day.

Ratings

Longevity	Fun factor	Practicality	Value
★★★★★	★★☆☆☆	★★★★★	★★★★☆

Overall Rating ★★★★☆

Price: £0.59/$0.99 Developer: MAAI

Bird's Eye View of Hurricanes

The power of nature as viewed from space

There are few weather phenomena as dramatic as a hurricane, cyclone or typhoon. A hurricane is a tropical cyclone, which is basically a low-pressure system that usually begins life in the tropics. The elements of a hurricane include a pre-existing weather disturbance, moisture, light winds and a warm tropical ocean. If the right conditions persist long enough, they will come together to produce the ferocious winds, torrential rain and huge waves that we associate with the phenomenon. The power of nature can at times be truly amazing and it is rare (nor advisable!) to actually witness a hurricane first hand. Bird's Eye View of Hurricanes does exactly what it says on the tin – it lets you browse photographs of hurricanes, cyclones and typhoons as they are viewed from space. If you really want to appreciate Mother Nature, check out the images of Hurricanes Andrew and Ingrid.

Floyd - 1999

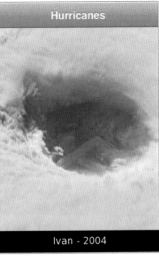

Ivan - 2004

■ Hurricane Floyd triggered the third largest evacuation in US history.

Ratings

Longevity	Fun factor	Practicality	Value
★★★☆☆	★★★☆☆	★★★☆☆	★★★★☆

Overall Rating ★★★★☆

Price: £1.19/$1.99 Developer: SIS Software

Wind Speed

Measure wind strength with this recreational anemometer

There are a growing number of apps making use of the iPhone's microphone to measure the velocity of the wind and Wind Speed is one of the latest. Essentially an anemometer (a wind speed meter), the app's developer, SIS Software, claims that Wind Speed will provide the user with a fairly accurate reading of the strength of any wind up to about 100mph. So how does it work? Simply point your microphone towards the wind and various algorithms will isolate wind from other sounds, such as noise and human voice. The app will then measure the volume of the wind and convert the reading into wind speed data. You can choose to display different units and these include miles per hour, knots, kilometres per hour and the Beaufort scale. If you are a watersports enthusiast, the Wind Speed app may well prove invaluable and it is certainly a whole lot less expensive than a dedicated anemometer.

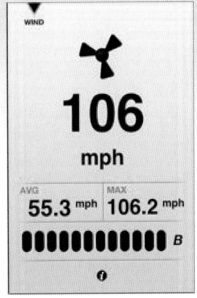

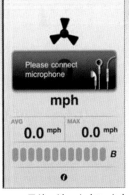

■ Algorithms isolate wind from other sounds.

■ Readings include average and maximum wind velocity.

Ratings

Longevity	Fun factor	Practicality	Value
★★★★☆	★★☆☆☆	★★★☆☆	★★★☆☆

Overall Rating ★★★☆☆

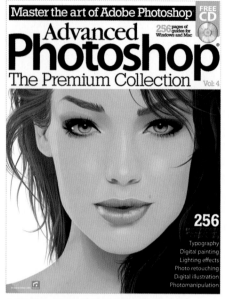

Master the art of Adobe Photoshop FREE CD
Advanced Photoshop The Premium Collection *Vol. 4*
256 pages of guides for Windows and Mac
256
Typography
Digital painting
Lighting effects
Photo retouching
Digital illustration
Photomanipulation

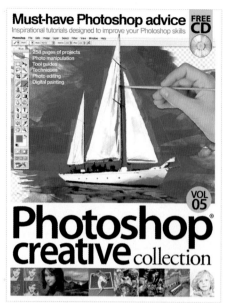

Must-have Photoshop advice FREE CD
Inspirational tutorials designed to improve your Photoshop skills
258 pages of projects
Photo manipulation
Tool guides
Techniques
Photo editing
Digital painting
VOL 05
Photoshop creative collection

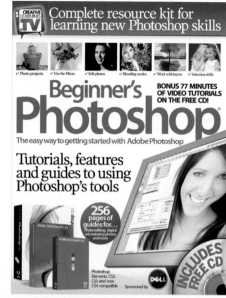

Complete resource kit for learning new Photoshop skills
BONUS 77 MINUTES OF VIDEO TUTORIALS ON THE FREE CD!
Beginner's Photoshop
The easy way to getting started with Adobe Photoshop
Tutorials, features and guides to using Photoshop's tools
256 pages of guides for...
INCLUDES FREE CD

Advanced Photoshop Premium Collection vol.4
256 pages of expert Photoshop tutorials, in-depth interviews and technical info on using Photoshop's tools.
Price: £12.99

Photoshop Creative Collection vol.5
This fantastic bookazine is packed full of inspiring tutorials designed to help improve your Photoshop skills.
Price: £12.99

Creative Learning.tv Beginner's Photoshop
Complete resource kit for learning new Photoshop skills with over 70 minutes of video tutorials on disc.
Price: £12.99

If you like this bookazine, why not try these?

From motoring to digital creativity, photography and Photoshop to science fiction and gaming

Retro Gamer Collection vol.3
It's here! The third anthology of classic **Retro Gamer**. Packed with the best articles to create an essential guide to retro gaming.
Price: £9.99

Pokémon World Ultimate Pokédex
493 Pokémon captured inside this expansive 212-page guide to Pokémon. Now updated with data from Pokémon Platinum.
Price: £9.99

Celebrity Twitter Directory
Your essential guide to the best real celebrity blogs on the world's hottest website, helping you decide which feeds to follow, and which to drop.
Price: £9.99

Your Digital SLR Camera vol.3
256 pages of DSLR advice. Master your SLR, learn shooting skills, fix your photos and expert advice on the best camera kit to buy.
Price: £12.99

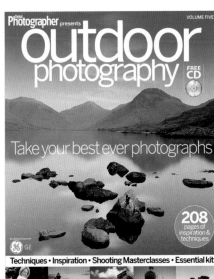

The complete A-Z of

The Chemical Touch: Lite Edition can be found on page 25.

Practice your piano skills, page 86.

rated iPhone Apps

Take great notes at page 124.

Find useful weather info at page 172.

Quick start:
How to install software on your iPhone or iPod touch

Found an app you want to try? Follow this quick guide to find and install it from the App Store built right into your iPhone or iPod touch...

01 Start your search
When the App Store loads, tap the search button at the bottom of the screen to be taken to the search screen, where you can easily look for the app.

02 Find the app
Start typing into the search field. As you do, the App Store will begin to bring up the results. Tap the application that you are looking for to see more details.

03 Tap the price
Tap the button at the top of the app description that tells you its price. The button will then turn green and say 'Install'. Tap it again to begin installation.

04 Sign in
You will be prompted to enter your iTunes account details. When done, click OK to confirm your purchase of the application and start the download process.

05 Watch the bar
You will now be taken to your final home screen, where the application will begin to download. When complete, the icon will become solid and you can tap it to launch.